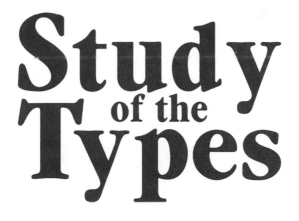

Study of the Types

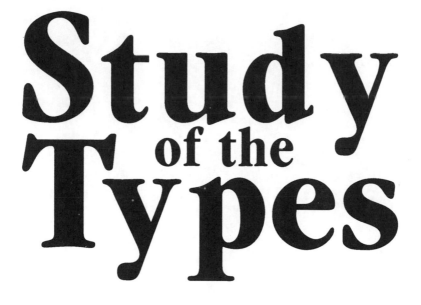

Study of the Types

Ada R. Habershon

kregel
PUBLICATIONS

Grand Rapids, MI 49501

The Study of the Types by Ada R. Habershon

Formerly published in two volumes as *The Priests and Levites* and *A Type of the Church* by Alfred Holness, London, n.d.

Published in 1957 and 1974 (enlarged edition) by Kregel Publications, a division of Kregel, Inc., P. O. Box 2607, Grand Rapids, MI 49501. Kregel Publications provides trusted, biblical publications for Christian growth and service. Your comments and suggestions are valued.

For more information about Kregel Publications, visit our web site at http://www.kregel.com.

Library of Congress Catalog Card No. 67-24340

ISBN 0-8254-2850-5 (paperback)

Printed in the United States of America

19 20 21 22 / 08 07 06 05 04 03

CONTENTS

PART I
THE STUDY OF THE TYPES

Contents

V. TYPES OF CALVARY, and their prominent lessons 35

(1) Where there was actual shedding of blood.

The coats of skins	A covering.
Abel's sacrifice	Acceptance.
Gen. xxii., "Jehovah Jireh".	Substitution provided.
The paschal lamb	Deliverance from wrath.
The burnt-offering	Acceptance.
The peace-offering	Peace and fellowship.
The sin and trespass offering	Forgiveness.
The day of atonement . .	Atonement.
The red heifer	Cleansing.
The bird in Lev. xiv. . . .	Cleansing and justification.
The sucking lamb	Christ crucified in weakness, our strength.
The one found slain . . .	His death required.

(2) Christ passing through the waters of death.

Jonah	The time in the grave.
The Ark	The only means of safety.
The Red Sea	Deliverance from our enemies.
The Jordan	Entrance into blessing.
Stones in the Jordan and the land.	Union in death and resurrection.
The tree cast into Marah .	Bitter turned into sweet.
The branch into Jordan . .	Uplifting that which is sunken.

(3) Other types.

The smitten rock	The gift of the Spirit.
The brazen serpent	The healing from the bite of sin.
Adam's sleep	The building-up of the Church.
The rent vail	Access to God.
The corn of wheat	The source of the harvest.

(4) A constantly-recurring type . . The Lord's Supper.

(5) A future reminder . . . . . The Lamb as it had been slain.

Contents

Contents

CONTENTS

PART II
PRIESTS AND LEVITES

Contents

Part I

THE STUDY OF THE TYPES

PREFACE

THE substance of these chapters has been given in various Bible Readings. Their object is not so much to attempt an explanation of the individual types, on which so many volumes have already been written, as to arouse interest in the study as a whole, and to emphasize the importance of comparing one with another. Not only does this method seem the surest way of arriving at the meaning of the separate types, but it is valuable as affording evidence of the presence of one Spirit inspiring the whole.

It has not been possible to do more than suggest some of the various methods in which the Bible types may be grouped together, and give samples of the great variety that exists amongst them.

These studies are but very imperfect outline sketches of bird's-eye views. To fill in too many details would have been in many cases to lose sight of the chief lines of the pictures; but if some are induced to explore for themselves, they will find out the endless beauties that surround them on all sides.

It would be impossible to acknowledge all the channels through which many precious things concerning the types have been received. We read a book or hear an address, and some thought strikes us; we make a note of it, and it becomes our own. Other thoughts are added on the same subject, and we soon forget through whom they came. If they are God-given this does not greatly matter; for in Bible study anything that is really original, anything that is simply our own, is not worth passing on to any one else. But if in the course of our study God opens our eyes to behold wondrous things, it is only that we may tell others of what we have seen. When they look for themselves and see the same things, they will soon forget who pointed them out. The man who finds the gold may be quite unknown, or is soon forgotten ; but the gold passes from hand to hand and others are enriched.

The one who is prefigured in the types is not a mere man, but is Jehovah-God—the great I AM ; and the chief scene which is foreshadowed is the most solemn event that has taken place on this earth. In considering the types therefore, and trying feebly to speak of them, the ground whereon we stand is holy ground.

May anything in these pages that is contrary to God's thoughts be forgiven for the sake of the great High Priest who bears the iniquity of our holy things ; and may He use what is of Himself to stimulate many to deeper and more reverent study of His Word, that His Name may be glorified.

I

Introduction

THE consideration of the Old Testament types is one of the most interesting and helpful subjects for Bible study, and at the same time is absolutely necessary if we are rightly to understand the Word of God.

The Old Testament is often viewed merely as a collection of historical tales, giving the origin of the Jewish people, and illustrating Oriental manners and customs; useful in supplying Sunday stories for the children, but of very little practical importance as to spiritual teaching.

The Bible may be compared to those beautifully illustrated volumes so often published, with a number of engravings of choice pictures at the beginning, followed by chapters of letterpress describing them, giving their history, or telling something of the life of the artist. We can scarcely conceive of any one trying to understand such descriptions without referring to the pictures themselves; yet this is how the Bible is often treated.

God has given to us a series of pictures in the early books of the Bible. The New Testament refers to and explains them ; yet many people are satisfied to read the New Testament without any reference to the types of the Old. They do not believe with St. Augustine that

> " The New is in the Old contained ;
> The Old is by the New explained."

" All Scripture is given by inspiration of God, and is profit-able, ... that the man of God may be perfect, throughly furnished unto all good works ; " and yet how many there are who are content to know little or nothing about parts of the Bible which have evidently been given to us by God for some purpose.

We are privileged to live in days of much Christian activity ; but while there is so much energy and zeal, it is possible to engage in "good works" without being "throughly furnished "— and thus the works themselves suffer.   Mary wrought a "good work " when she broke her alabaster box of ointment and anointed the Lord ; but it was the result of the "good part" she had chosen when she "sat at Jesus' feet, and heard His word."   It was there that she probably learnt His purpose concerning His resurrection, and knew that if she did not anoint Him for His burial "beforehand," she would have no other opportunity.   He would have His children still take that place, and in lowly dependence on Him learn what He would teach. He does not mean us to read the Old Testament as we should ancient Roman or Grecian history; but by careful study under His direction to find out His reasons for bringing the events to pass, or for allowing them to happen, and for giving us the record of these events.

The development and success of Christian enterprises is one of the bright features of the days in which we live ; but we cannot shut our eyes to the dark side of the picture.   There are other things which are also growing, and amongst them there is a marked advance in the spread of unsound doctrine. Many are giving up the simple truths of God's Word.   The Inspiration of the Scriptures is attacked on all sides ; the doctrine of Atonement by substitution is denied, or thought little of ; whilst other things are preached which are contrary to the Word.   This could not be so frequently the case if the Old Testament types were more carefully studied and more widely taught.   " The typology of the Old Testament is the very alphabet of the language in which the doctrine of the New Testament is written ; and as many of our great theologians are admittedly ignorant of the typology, we need not feel surprised if they are not always the safest exponents of the doctrines." *

Besides this, the personal loss is great to those who do not study for themselves this part of the Bible ; and yet we often meet those who have been Christians for years, and those who would be Bible teachers, who have never given their attention to it.

Many reasons are given for this neglect. Some think the types difficult ; others say the study is fanciful ; others that it is uninteresting ; and so from one cause or another they miss the rich treasure that they might otherwise obtain. The precious things of God's Word are not all upon the surface. We must dig in order to find them. Like the first sinking of the shaft, the work may be laborious at the outset, and therefore needs diligence ; but when we reach a rich vein of ore we are well rewarded, as we find that we have come upon a mine of inexhaustible wealth.

It is very important to understand what is meant by a type. In 1 Cor. x. we are told concerning the various wilderness experiences of the children of Israel, that "all these things happened unto them for types"; and Paul explains that the record of these events is given to us in the Bible for a special purpose, viz., to teach us certain lessons. This passage seems to cover all that befell God's redeemed people in their journey from the place of bondage to the land of promise ; and we may also conclude from it that other portions of their history are given to us with a similar purpose. But although teaching spiritual lessons, the incidents really took place. Some who are giving up their belief in the inspiration of the Bible would try and make us believe that though there is spiritual meaning in these old stories they are only traditions and fables ; not

* "The Literal Interpretation of Scripture." By Robert Anderson, C.B., LL.D.

records of real events, but merely allegorical, and no more to be taken literally than Bunyan's "Pilgrim's Progress." It is enough for us that the Lord Himself and the writers of the New Testament looked upon them as truthful records of actual events.

Certain Bible characters are clearly referred to in the New Testament as types. They were real living people, not mythical characters that never lived; and the record of their history is evidently given to teach us of Him whose coming they foreshadowed. The story of Joseph is a striking example of this; and when we see in his life a picture of "the sufferings of Christ and the glory that should follow," and the deliverance He has wrought, we understand how it is that so large a portion of the Book of Genesis is devoted to Joseph's history. He is perhaps the most complete type of our Lord that we can find; and unlike so many heroes of the Old Testament, there seems no blot on the page of his life to mar the picture.

But besides typical incidents and characters, there is another very important class of types, viz., all those things which were expressly commanded by God in connection with the Tabernacle and Temple service, and which in every detail were clearly given as types, "The Holy Ghost this signifying"— some lessons about our Lord and His work. Some would try to make us believe that the Hebrew religion, as described in the Books of Moses, was only borrowed from the heathen nations around; but the careful study of the types leaves no room for doubting that the whole Levitical economy was divinely instituted to foreshadow the work and person of the Lord Jesus Christ Himself.

We cannot state with certainty that anything is a type unless we have some warrant for doing so. If we can turn to no New Testament passage for our authority, or if there be no expression or analogy which indicates the antitype, it is safer and more correct to call it an illustration.

While visiting Northfield, some of us were looking at the beautiful model of Solomon's Temple, designed by Mr. Newberry, which is in the library of Mr. Moody's Seminary ; and a lady who had listened to our conversation, said she did not believe in any of the types as such—she thought it was all fanciful. We tried to explain to her that a true type was something designed by God to teach us a lesson ; and that if in the New Testament it was proved to be so, there was no fear of our being fanciful. We asked her if there were no types which she could believe.

" No," she said, " none."

" Do you not think that when John the Baptist said, ' Behold the Lamb of God,' he meant that all the lambs which had been offered in sacrifice before that time were types of the Lord Jesus ? "

" Yes," she said, " I see that."

" Do you not think that as Peter speaks of believers as lively stones built up a spiritual house, and of a royal priesthood, we may take the stones of the temple and the Levitical priesthood as types of believers ? "

" Yes, I can see that."

" Then, as we are told in Hebrews that the Lord Jesus Christ has consecrated for us a new and living way, ' through the vail, that is to say, His flesh,' may we not say fearlessly that the vail was a type of His incarnation, and the rending of the vail, of His death ? "

Yes, she could see that. And so after she had been obliged to acknowledge five or six very evident types, we recommended her thoroughly to work out these, and told her that we were sure she would want to go on with more. She was soon much interested in the study.

In these days of many conferences, why do we never hear of one for the Study of Types ? There are evangelistic services for the preaching of the Gospel ; there are conferences on Foundation Truths ; upon the Inspiration of the Word ; the

Coming of our Lord and other prophetic subjects; the unity and privileges of the Church, and conventions for "the deepening of spiritual life." All these subjects are included in the study of the types. Where can we find more beautiful *Gospel* subjects than in the Old Testament scenes, such as the lifting-up of the brazen serpent, the slaying of the paschal lamb, and many others? *Foundation truths* are clearly explained and illustrated; for such doctrines as the atonement, substitution, the value of the blood, are more plainly taught in the types than anywhere in Scripture—save in the accounts of Calvary itself, which they foreshadowed. Our belief in *the Inspiration of the Bible* cannot fail to be strengthened by the study. We shall find striking *prophetic pictures* in the Old Testament; for it is impossible to see the full beauty of many of the Levitical institutions apart from dispensational truth.

With regard to subjects relating to the privileges and the unity of *the Church*, these are again and again foreshadowed in the types. It is sometimes stated that the Church is not the subject of Old Testament prophecy; but even if this be so, it need not be excluded from the types. As early as the second chapter in the Bible we find the Church foreshadowed; for there we have the account of the formation of Eve and of her union with Adam, which Paul tells us in Eph. v. is a type of our relationship to Christ. Quoting from Genesis ii. 24, "They two shall be one flesh," he adds, "This is a great mystery; but I speak concerning Christ and the Church."

By far the largest number of conventions are those for "the deepening of spiritual life"; and beyond all others the subject of *holiness* seems to be emphasized in the types.

In the books of Moses we learn more clearly than anywhere else to have a right view of God's holiness and of our need. Eye-witnesses of the sufferings of Christ have given us accounts in the Gospels of that great antitype, the cross of Calvary; but we may fail to see all its varied aspects without the help of the types. The details which are brought before us in the minute directions respecting the offerings and the institutions of the Tabernacle, teach us many lessons and emphasize many truths which we might otherwise miss. How can we fail to learn more and more of God's abhorrence of sin, and our constant need of cleansing, as we see the wondrous provision that He has made for every kind of defilement ?

Thus we find prefigured in the types "all the counsel of God." Without the fuller revelations of truth in the Epistles they could not be wholly understood ; but with this teaching we can see meanings which must have been hidden from those who lived in Old Testament times.

It has been remarked that the types are only one little piece of the Bible, and this is probably a general opinion ; but is it correct ? Do they not run through the entire Book, involving in their study a growing familiarity with the whole of God's Word ? In the books of Moses and the historical books we have typical characters, events, and institutions ; in the poetical books we have typical utterances by typical characters ; in the prophecies we again have typical characters and events, and the fulfilment of the types is foretold ; whilst throughout the New Testament they are constantly referred to and explained, and the great Antitype is presented.

II

Reasons for Studying the Types

THERE are many reasons why in our study of God's Word we ought not to neglect the types which occupy so prominent a position.

(1) It is very clear that God Himself sets great value upon them. It was His Spirit who designed them; for we learn from the Epistle to the Hebrews that in the construction of the Tabernacle every detail was planned by Him. In speaking of the vail which divided the Holy Place from the Holiest of all, the writer says, "the Holy Ghost this signifying, that the way into the Holiest of all was not yet made manifest, while as the first Tabernacle was yet standing."

There was a meaning in that vail; it was not merely a hanging to divide between the two parts of the Tabernacle, but was meant to convey a great lesson. Other details of the Tabernacle and of all the types must be equally significant; and though all are not as clearly explained, we may, with the help of the Author, try to learn His meaning. Without such a Teacher, the difficulty of the study might indeed deter us; but we have the Lord's promise, "He shall teach you all things," "He will guide you into all truth," "He shall receive of mine, and shall show it unto you." When we read in the Gospels of the vail being rent, remembering the passage in Hebrews respecting the hanging up of that vail, we may write in the margins of our Bibles "the Holy Ghost this signifying, that the way into the Holiest of all" was *now* made manifest.

16

An invisible hand rent the vail " from the top to the bottom " ;
not from the bottom to the top, for then it might have seemed
as though man had something to do with it.   It was God
Himself who was completing the type, and adding the finishing
touches to the picture.

Does it not show the immense importance which He puts
upon the types, that at such a moment He did not forget to
mark the significance of that event to which so many of them
pointed, and by rending the vail declared that the closed way
was, by the death of His Son, now made open ?   " His decease
which He should accomplish at Jerusalem " had been the
subject of conversation when Moses and Elias talked with the
Lord Jesus Christ on the Mount of Transfiguration, and
afterwards all heaven must have been occupied with what was
taking place on Calvary ; but yet the types were not forgotten
by God.

So accurate are all their details, that each one must be
fulfilled by the great Antitype when He came.   Not only are
they pictures of long past events, which we may compare with
what happened afterwards, but they were the plans with which
the subsequent events must correspond.   Thus in John's
account of the crucifixion we read, " When they came to
Jesus, and saw that He was dead already, they brake not His
legs ;   .   .   .   for these things were done that the Scripture
should be fulfilled, A bone of Him shall not be broken."
Where is this Scripture, if not in the ordinance of the passover, when it was distinctly stated, " neither shall ye break a
bone thereof " ?

(2)   Our Lord thought much of the types.   Again and
again He referred to them and showed how they pointed to
Himself.   What a marvellous Bible-reading must He have
given to those two disciples on the road to Emmaus, when
" beginning at Moses and all the prophets, He expounded unto
them in all the Scriptures the things concerning Himself ; " and
from them answered His own question, "Ought not Christ to

have suffered these things, and to enter into His glory?" The
sufferings and the glory were predicted in the types as well as in
the direct prophecies; and it was no wonder that their heart
burned within them on that memorable walk, and later on in the
same evening, when "He opened their understanding that they
might understand the Scriptures." The events which had just
taken place were all foreshadowed there; but they had not understood the old familiar passages till He showed them how "all
things must be fulfilled which were written in the law of Moses,
and in the prophets, and in the psalms," concerning Himself.
Those who neglect the study of the types fail to see how much
there is of Christ in the law of Moses.

In the book of the Revelation it is as the Antitype of all the
sacrifices that He is chiefly seen. No less than twenty-eight
times is He spoken of as the Lamb. Even in chapter v.,
where the Apostle is expecting to see the Lion of the tribe of
Judah step forth in His strength, He appears as the "little
lamb"; and the beloved disciple sees Him again as he first
saw Him on that memorable day when John the Baptist
pointed out "the Lamb of God which taketh away the sin of
the world."

(3) Not only does Christ speak of the types, but they speak
of Him. If we would "grow in grace, and in the knowledge
of our Lord and Saviour Jesus Christ," we cannot do better
than study what they tell us of His person and of His work.
He said to the Jews, when He was on earth, "Had ye believed
Moses, ye would have believed Me, for he wrote of Me."
With the exception of a few such passages as Deut. xviii.
15–19, where the coming of the Messiah is clearly foretold, it
was in the types that Moses wrote of Christ. They all spoke
of Him: the tabernacle, the offerings, the feasts, told of
different aspects of His work for us; and as "in His temple
every whit of it uttereth His glory," so also in every one of
these earlier types.

(4) Another reason for valuing this part of God's Word is

the very high place that is accorded to the types by the writers of the New Testament. They are referred to as "the Scripture," and we know that "the Scripture cannot be broken." The types and shadows of the Old Testament must be fulfilled in the New. For instance, we read in 1 Cor. xv. 4, that Christ "rose again the third day, according to the Scriptures." Is not the resurrection of Christ prophesied in the types more plainly than anywhere else ? In the waving of the sheaf of the firstfruits "on the morrow after the Sabbath," immediately following the passover (Leviticus xxiii.), the very day is foretold ; and we know from another verse in 1 Cor. xv. that this refers to His resurrection, for Paul speaks of " Christ the firstfruits, afterward they that are Christ's at His coming."

(5) There are many passages in the New Testament which we cannot understand without having become in some measure familiar with the types. The Epistle to the Hebrews is almost entirely made up of references to the Old Testament : as the substance, Christ, is proved to be better than the shadows— better than Moses, than Joshua, than Abraham, than Aaron, than the first Tabernacle, than the Levitical sacrifices, than the whole cloud of witnesses in the picture gallery of faith ; and lastly, His blood is proved to be better than the blood of Abel.

We sometimes forget that the writers of the New Testament were students of the Old Testament ; that it was their Bible, and that they would naturally allude again and again to the types and shadows, expecting their readers also to be familiar with them. If we fail to see these allusions, we lose much of the beauty of the passage, and cannot rightly understand it. For instance, in Acts iii. Peter, when speaking of the Lord's return, says, " Whom the heaven must receive until the times of restitution of all things ; " and we shall quite miss the meaning if we fail to see the type to which he evidently refers. We read in Lev. xxv. that at the blowing of the jubilee trumpet, " ye shall return every man unto his possession and . . . unto his family." And " in the year of jubilee the field shall return . . . to him to whom the possession of the land did belong " (Lev. xxvii. 24). This is what will take place for Israel when their Messiah appears. The country will once more belong to them, and the Son of David will return to His family and to His land. This expression in Acts is an example of how the primary interpretation of a passage can be missed for want of seeing the Old Testament type to which allusion is made ; for it is often used as the ground on which to build all sorts of theories which are not in the Bible.

In the Gospel of John there are constant references to the types. In the first chapter our attention is drawn to the Lamb of God, and our thoughts go back at once to all the lambs that had before been sacrificed, from Abel's lamb in Gen. iii., to the last offered in the temple. In the closing verse of the chapter there is evident reference to Jacob's ladder. In verse 14 Christ is shown to be the Antitype of the Tabernacle, for it tells us how " the Word was made flesh and tabernacled among us " ; whilst in chapter ii. He compares Himself to the temple, for He says, " Destroy this temple, and in three days I will raise it up." In chapter iii. we see Him in the brazen serpent ; in chapter iv. He compares Himself to Jacob's well ; in chapter vi. He tells us that He was the true manna ; in chapter vii. we are reminded of the smitten rock, for He Himself was the rock out of which would flow the rivers of living water. In chapters viii. and ix. He is the light of the world ; in chapter x. the Antitype of all the shepherds of the Old Testament ; in chapter xii. He is the corn of wheat that brought forth the sheaf of the firstfruits ; in chapter xiii. we have the laver ; and in chapter xv. the true vine in contrast with the vine that He brought out of Egypt. Thus in almost every chapter an Old Testament type is brought before us.

If we compare John's Gospel merely to one type, the Tabernacle, it has been pointed out that it seems to divide itself into the three courts. In the first twelve chapters we have our Lord's ministry on earth, in the outer court to which all the people were admitted; and we have His last words to outsiders in the closing verses of chapter xii. As in the Tabernacle the first thing seen was the altar and the lamb, so we have in the opening chapter the Lamb of God that taketh away the sin of the world. In chapter xiii. Christ is preparing His disciples for service in the Holy place by use of the laver. In chapters xiv., xv, xvi., we see Him with them in the Tabernacle; and He teaches them much about the Holy Spirit, typified by the oil for the candlestick; and about prayer in His name, typified by the incense on the golden altar; while in the 17th chapter we have the High Priest alone in the Holiest of all.

(6) We have already seen that the types seem to cover the whole range of New Testament teaching. Not only are the Old Testament types unfolded in the New Testament, but the New Testament is enfolded in them.

(7) This study gives us a sure antidote for the poison of the so-called "higher criticism." If we acknowledge the Divine intention of every detail of the types, even though we may not understand all their teaching, and if we believe there is a lesson in every incident recorded, the attacks of modern criticism will not harm us. We may not be clever enough to understand what the critics say, or to answer their criticisms; but if our eyes have been opened to see the beauty of the types, the doubts which such writers suggest will not trouble us, and we shall have a more profitable occupation than reading their works. When so much of this destructive criticism is about, we cannot do better than urge all—even the youngest Christians—to take up the typical study of God's Word; for though He has hid these things from the wise and prudent, He reveals them unto babes.

The "higher criticism" and the study of the types cannot go together; for no one who has learnt the spiritual teaching of the Old Testament pictures would believe, or try to prove, that the Bible was not what it claimed to be.

III

Double Types

THE types are but a "shadow of good things to come, and not the very image of the things"; and therefore, like all shadows, they give but an imperfect representation, so that we often need to look at several together if we are to obtain a complete idea of the substance itself.

Most objects cast differently shaped shadows as the light falls upon them in various directions; and by comparing them, we may form a correct outline, even if the object itself be out of sight. If the shadows vary in some details, while they correspond in others, we may at once conclude that though the object is the same, the light is thrown upon it in different directions, and reveals shadows cast from opposite sides: so is it in the types.

Sometimes in the same type we may find different sides of truth represented by two similar things. Thus, in the cleansing of the leper there are *two birds*: one slain over the running water; the other let fly over the field—evidently typifying the death and resurrection of Christ.

On the Day of Atonement there were *two goats*: the one, God's lot which was killed, the blood being taken inside the vail; and the other, the scape-goat that bore away the iniquity of Israel to the land not inhabited—the first speaking to us of God's requirements, the second of man's need.

In other cases, in order to complete the picture, we have two types closely connected with one another, similar in many respects, but emphasizing different truths. For instance, on the journey from Egypt to Canaan the children of Israel had to pass through the *Red Sea* and the *Jordan*, and in both cases a way was made for them to cross on dry land. We are

told in Exod. xiii. 17 that they might have gone by the way
of the Philistines, when they would not have needed to pass
through either; but we are given the reason why God did not
lead them by this route: "For God said, Lest peradventure
the people repent when they see war, and they return to
Egypt." If the Red Sea had not rolled between them and
Egypt, they could easily have returned; and this is evidently
the key to the truth taught by the crossing of the Red Sea.
Both it and the passage of the Jordan speak to us of the death
and resurrection of Christ; but the former tells of deliverance
from Egypt, the latter of entrance *into* the land.

Twice over, when they crossed the Jordan, the children of
Israel were told to set up *twelve stones* for a memorial: a stone
for a tribe; twelve in the midst of the Jordan, and twelve on
the other side. The stones evidently typify the believer's
standing in its two-fold aspect. Those in the midst of the
river of death tell us that we are dead with Christ; and those
in the land that we are risen with Him.

In the same way we have the food of Israel, *the manna* and
the old corn. In John vi. the Lord explained that He Himself
was the bread sent down from heaven. The manna therefore
clearly represents Christ in the flesh, in His incarnation, the
provision for wilderness needs; while the old corn of the land
and the harvest which was ripe when they crossed the Jordan,
and of which they would eat three or four days later, when
they had waved the sheaf of the first-fruits, speak of Christ in
resurrection.

In studying these and other double types it is necessary to
put the two side by side if we would see the full meaning;
for mistakes are often made in interpretation from not following this plan. One type does not supersede the other, for
they are often both true at the same time. We may still feed
on the manna, though we have the old corn as well.

There are some teachers who only draw lessons from *the
wilderness* experience of Israel, and who do not see that our

position is also in *the land* as victors taking possession, step by
step, of what is ours in Christ. Others dwell entirely on the
position in the land, and say that we ought not to be in the
wilderness at all. Should we not rather take both? As one
has said, "We are, as to our bodies, in Egypt; as to our
experience, in the wilderness; and by faith, in the land." We
are represented by Peter as "strangers and pilgrims" passing
through a wilderness; and at the same time we are, according
to Ephesians i, in the land, in the heavenlies in Christ Jesus.
By-and-by, when faith has been changed to sight, we shall be,
as to our bodies and as to our experience, in the land.

In the two-fold sign that God gave to Moses to reassure
him when about to stand before Pharaoh, there was probably a
foreshadowing of God's power over sin and Satan. *The rod*
that was turned into a serpent, and when grasped by Moses
once more became a rod, tells of God's power over Satan; but
the hand that became leprous and was afterwards healed,
speaks of power over sin. God's redeemed people were to be
delivered from both these enemies.

The Tabernacle and *the Temple* give us different aspects of
God's dwelling-places; and in Gen. xxii. we have a double
type of our Lord Jesus—first in *Isaac* himself, and then in
the *ram* which God provided.

There is a striking typical scene in Deut. xxi. which, it has
been pointed out, is a picture of God's great inquest over His
Son. *One* is *found slain* in the field, and enquiry has to be
made as to who is guilty; when the city nearest to the
dead body has been condemned, the *heifer* is slain to remove
their guilt. Here, surely, we have another double type; for
the Lord's death is foreshadowed in the one found slain and in
the heifer: the first telling of the guilt of His murderers; the
other of how the guilt has been met.

If we are studying the characters in the Old Testament
which are types of our Lord Jesus Christ, in His different
offices, we shall find again and again that they seem linked

together in pairs. For instance, we have two high priests, two
kings, and two prophets, who separately and together were
types, and were closely associated with one another in their
lives. *Aaron* and *Eleazar* both typified Him as the High
Priest, and in some respects their offices were different.
Even while Aaron was still living, Eleazar had certain things
allotted to him in the service of the tabernacle. In Num. xx.
26 we have the account of the death of Aaron, and the robing
of Eleazar in his place ; prefiguring the great High Priest who
now lives after " the power of an endless life." Eleazar
therefore seems to be the type of the High Priest in resurrection life, in the power of the Holy Ghost ; for he was very
specially connected with the oil which typified the Holy
Spirit. To his office pertained " the oil for the light, and the
sweet incense, and the daily meal-offering, and the anointing
oil, and the oversight of all the Tabernacle " (Num. iv. 16).
He was " chief over the chief of the Levites " (Num. iii. 32),
reminding us of Him who in resurrection is the chief
Shepherd. The two orders of priesthood, that of *Aaron* and
Melchisedek, are brought before us in the Epistle to the
Hebrews as types of the priesthood of the Lord.

David and *Solomon* give us different aspects of His
kingly character. David, the shepherd-king, who had been
the slayer of Goliath, who was the fugitive and the wanderer,
and afterwards the conqueror of all his enemies, speaks to us
of the sufferings and rejection of God's Anointed, and finally
of His conquests ; Solomon, whom the Lord refers to in
Matt. xii. as a type of Himself, in his glory, his wisdom,
his riches, and reign of peace, typifies the millennial reign
of our Lord. Although the prince of peace, when Solomon
comes to the throne, he gathers out of his kingdom, in the
persons of Adonijah, Joab, and Shimei, " all things that
offend, and them which do iniquity," as the greater than
Solomon will do, when He comes in His glory (Matt. xiii. 41).
In their connection with the Temple also we need the double

type. David made preparation for its building, and purchased the site; while Solomon finished the work. If we only study them separately, the picture is incomplete.

Then we have two great prophets, *Elijah* and *Elisha*, who were closely connected with one another in their lives, and were both types of Christ, as He Himself shows in Luke iv. 25–27. Elijah fasted forty days. He raised the dead, and performed many other miracles. He ascended to heaven, and a double portion of his spirit came upon his follower. Elisha healed the leper, raised the dead, fed the multitude, and even in his grave caused the dead to live. Elijah's name is said to mean the strong Lord; and that of Elisha, God my Saviour. Their names therefore seem to indicate the general character of their testimony—the one that of judgment, and the other that of grace.

Thus, in the types of Christ as prophet, priest, and king, we find examples of how two characters are linked together to give us different sides of the picture. To these we might add many more, such as the two leaders, *Moses* and *Joshua*; but those which have been indicated will have been sufficient to show how important it is to study together, as well as singly, types which are evidently so closely associated with one another.

Besides there being many that thus go in pairs, we must remember in our study that a large number, if not all the types, probably have *a double meaning*. One interpretation will not exhaust all that may be learnt from them; for we find that, like so many other parts of God's Word, they can be taken in various ways.

For instance, amongst the characters just mentioned, where Elijah is the master and Elisha the disciple, Elijah represents Christ and Elisha the servant; and each of those who fore-shadowed Christ are also full of teaching as individual believers. We have another illustration of this double teaching in the Flood and the Ark. Salvation for all within the Ark is a favourite Gospel subject; and rightly so. Noah found grace in God's sight, and safety, not in himself, but in God's appointed place of refuge. The first "come" in the Bible is God's invitation to Noah, a "come" of salvation; and may well be compared to the Lord's loving word, "Come unto Me." But from His reference to the days of Noah in Matt. xxiv. we see that the judgment that came then may be taken in another sense—viz., as representing the judgments that will fall upon the earth at His coming in glory. "As the days of Noe were, so shall also the coming of the Son of Man be." The Flood was unexpected—so will His coming be: there was destruction on all that were not ready for it—so will it be when He returns to this earth. "For as in the days that were before the flood, they were eating and drinking, marrying and giving in marriage, until the day that Noe entered into the ark, and knew not until the flood came and took them all away; so shall also the coming of the Son of Man be." No great sins are mentioned; but they were not prepared.

Then comes that oft-quoted sentence, "One shall be taken and the other left"; and looking at it thus in its context we see that those who will be taken in that day will be taken away by the judgment as in the days of Noah, and those that are left will be left for blessing. In its primary meaning therefore this verse evidently does not refer to the Lord's coming for His Church to the air, but to the subsequent coming with His saints to the earth.

We may see yet a third meaning in the Flood and those who passed in safety through it; for the scene illustrates "the time of Jacob's trouble," and the preservation of the believing remnant. We are told in Rev. xii. that "the serpent cast out of his mouth water as a flood after the woman, that he might cause her to be carried away of the flood." The opening verse in the chapter reminds us of Joseph's dream: the woman is taken by many to represent Israel; and the time of persecution mentioned with such exactness in verses 6 and 14 to correspond with the great tribulation just before the Lord's return to the earth. A remnant of Israel will be preserved through the tribulation, as Noah and his sons were preserved through the Flood ; while the Church will have been taken away as Enoch was caught up before the Flood came upon the earth. Many believe this to be the teaching of Rev. iii. 10 ; and that to be kept from the hour must mean to be taken away before it strikes.

Other types will be found to have a dispensational interpretation as well as a general application. There is a Jewish aspect running through all the Levitical institutions ; and many of them become thus prophetic in teaching, while at the same time they are full of precious truths for us now. In the same way, in viewing Joseph as a type of Christ, we see that we may all come to draw our supplies from his store-houses ; but we can also see that his treatment of his brethren foreshadows the way in which the Lord's brethren after the flesh will at last acknowledge that they were "verily guilty" concerning their brother.

Stephen tells us that "at the second time Joseph was made known to his brethren." The first time they went down to Egypt for corn, they did not recognise the one who had opened the storehouses to them ; but when they were again driven by the seven years' famine into his presence, he made himself known to them. When He came, of whom Joseph was a type, His brethren did not recognise Him. "He came unto His own, and His own received Him not" ; but when He comes to them a second time, "the vail shall be taken away"; and He says, "they shall look upon Me whom they have pierced, and they shall mourn for Him."

Thus we have not only double types—those that need to be placed side by side to complete the picture—but we find that these very types have a double meaning. To see a Jewish or dispensational interpretation in them does not in any way rob them of their deep spiritual teaching, but only tends to show that the Bible is a divine Book.

IV

The Grouping of Types

THERE are many helpful ways of grouping the types together. For example, we often find that those which differ in many respects have one detail in common; and when this is the case, we may assume that the teaching conveyed by that one point is the same in each case, and by linking all together it is emphasized and impressed upon us.

Thus, in the Tabernacle and its service, and elsewhere, we again and again have the sufferings of the Lord Jesus Christ typified by the crushing or beating of different substances. In the tabernacle itself, the gold for the mercy-seat and for the candlestick was not only pure gold, but beaten gold. The spices for the holy ointment, for the incense and the frankincense, must be crushed, for they would not otherwise give forth their fragrance; and the perfume which was thus made was to be beaten very small (Exod. xxx. 36). The oil with which the ointment was compounded, and the oil for the meal-offering, was beaten oil; and for the candlestick "pure oil olive beaten for the light." The corn for the meal-offering was beaten out of full ears; and the flour for the same offering, which speaks to us of the Lord Jesus Christ offering to God a spotless life, was fine flour, as also the flour for the shewbread. There was no unevenness in Him. The Captain of our salvation was made "perfect through sufferings." In all His followers, even in those who are most like Him, there are many inequalities: they have some beautiful traits of character; but the very fact that these traits are so prominent

suggests that they are probably lacking in some other characteristic.   Our Lord was remarkable for no one attribute—He was
perfect in all.   He was like the fine flour, perfectly smooth
and even ; and the crushing and bruising served to prove this.
In Isa. xxviii. 28 we read that " bread corn is bruised," and
the manna needed to be ground in mills or beaten in a mortar.
All these different pictures speak to us of the sufferings of our
Lord throughout His lifetime.   We are told that Gethsemane
means " olive press " ; and it was not only on that last terrible
night that He visited it, for we read that He " ofttimes
resorted thither with His disciples."   His whole life was one
of suffering ; and as we have this again and again brought
before us in these types, we learn something of the meaning of
the words, " it pleased the Lord to bruise Him," and of Paul's
desire " that I may know Him . . . and the fellowship of His
sufferings."

It is also interesting to link together types which in
themselves closely resemble one another, especially those
which represent different aspects of Christ's life and work.
For instance, He is often foreshadowed by bread or corn in
various forms.   We have already looked at the manna and the
old corn, and the sheaf of the firstfruits, and have also mentioned the corn and the fine flour in the meal-offering.   He
was also typified by the unleavened bread that was eaten at the
feast of the passover.   There must be no leaven in anything
which typified Christ ; and for this reason it was forbidden
to be offered in the meal-offering, for throughout the Word it
always represents evil.   In John xii. our Lord compares
Himself to the corn of wheat, which, except it fall into the
ground and die, abideth alone ; but if it die it bringeth forth
much fruit.   In the memorial supper He brake the bread and
said, " This is My body which is broken for you."   In the
tabernacle we see Him in connection with Israel represented
by twelve loaves ; while it is said of the Church united to
Christ, " We being many are one bread [or one loaf]."   And

lastly, in Revelation, the hidden manna is promised to the overcomers. These types which are so similar seem to cover the whole of our Lord's life, and even look back into the past eternity. The manna that fell round about the camp of Israel represents the incarnation of the Lord Jesus Christ. He Himself says, " My Father giveth you the true bread from heaven; for the bread of God is He which cometh down from heaven and giveth life unto the world." But we also see from this passage that before He became manna for us He was the bread of God ; for these types not only speak of the Lord Jesus Christ as the food for man, but tell us of Him on whom the Father's heart delighted to feed. This thought is prominent in the meal-offering, where a handful was burnt upon the altar representing God's portion, and the remainder given to the priests ; telling us of the believer's fellowship with God concerning the person of their Lord.

In Psalm lxxviii. the description of the giving of the manna is very beautiful ; for it tells how God had " commanded the clouds from above, and opened the doors of heaven, and had rained down manna upon them to eat, and had given them of the corn of heaven. Man did eat angels' food," or as it is in the margin, " every one did eat the bread of the mighty." The manna before it fell to the earth was " the bread of God "—" the corn of heaven." The doors of heaven must be opened, and heaven must be emptied that earth might be filled. Thus we see that the manna speaks to us first of Christ from all eternity, and then of Christ in the flesh. The fine flour, as we have seen in the preceding group of types, tells us of His perfect life on earth, and of the suffering He underwent ; the corn of wheat which falls into the ground and dies, that it may bring forth much fruit, clearly typifies Calvary ; and so also does the broken bread, which reminds us of His body broken for us.

The old corn of the land, on which we are told the children of Israel fed when the manna ceased, seems to speak of

Christ in resurrection; or it may point back to Christ from all eternity laid up as the provision for His people. The sheaf of the firstfruits, which they waved on the first day of the week on the morrow after the Sabbath, plainly prophesied His resurrection. This waving of the firstfruits must have been one of the earliest acts of the children of Israel after they entered the land ; and they could only have eaten the old corn of the land by itself for two or three days. We are told that they crossed the Jordan in the time of harvest; they encamped at Gilgal on the tenth day of the month ; killed the passover on the fourteenth ; and waved the sheaf of the firstfruits on the morrow after the Sabbath immediately following the passover.

The sheaf of the firstfruits also speaks of His coming again, for it represents " Christ the firstfruits, afterward they that are Christ's at His coming"; and the " much fruit " brought forth by the dying of the corn of wheat also looks forward to that day when the Church will be complete, and " He shall see of the travail of His soul and shall be satisfied." The bread which we break at the supper of our Lord links together His death and His coming again ; for we remember His broken body and shed blood " till He come." Between His resurrection and coming again we have Christ the food of His people in the meal-offering, of which the priests partook, and in the feast of unleavened bread following the passover. " For even Christ our passover is sacrificed for us, therefore let us keep the feast."

The shew-bread, or bread of faces, and the hidden manna promised to the overcomers in Revelation, tell of Him who in His ascension glory is ever in the presence of God for us. Thus in this group of types we have brought before us the whole of His life and work.

Others might be added to this list, and especially the many scenes which picture God's provision in times of famine ; but perhaps the most beautiful picture is that of the corn in Joseph's storehouses.

Both Joseph and the corn which he stored are clearly fore-shadowings of Christ—another instance of the double types to which reference has been made ; and the familiar story is full of teaching as to the marvellous supply found in Him who is the Bread of Life. The corn which Joseph gathered " very much till he left numbering, for it was without number," reminds us of " the unsearchable riches of Christ." The opened storehouses, supplying to his needy brethren "as much as they can carry," give us in type the fulness of Him in Whom all fulness dwells. He will not only fill our sacks, but give us such a plentiful supply of the finest of the wheat, that our barns will be filled with plenty, and we shall have not only enough for our own needs, but also a supply for the needs of others.

The corn gathered in Joseph's wondrous storehouses provided food for the hungry, and also seed with which those who had themselves been fed could go forth and sow the fields. Joseph said to them " Lo, here is seed for you, and ye shall sow the land; . . . . seed of the field and for your food." We too find in the storehouses that God has provided for us, in the Incarnate Word and in the written Word, " seed to the sower and bread to the eater."

But before Joseph sent forth the Egyptians on this service they had to come to him in all their need. " We will not hide it from my lord how that our money is spent: . . . . there is not aught left in the sight of my lord but our bodies and our lands." They had come to the end of their own resources; and it is when we as poor sinners have come to the end of ourselves that there is room for Christ's fulness. It was when the prodigal " had spent all " that he said, " I will arise and go to my father," knowing that in his father's house there was bread enough and to spare. It was when the poor woman with the issue of blood had "spent all" that she came to Jesus and touched the hem of His garment. It was when the two debtors had " nothing to pay " that their creditor frankly forgave them both. We must bring empty sacks to Joseph's storehouses. Like these Egyptians, too, we cannot sow until we have first been fed; and we can only scatter what has supplied our own need. Joseph must supply the corn himself, both for our table and for our seed-basket. As Paul said to the saints at Corinth, " He that ministereth seed to the sower both minister bread for your food, and multiply your seed sown."

If we wished still to continue this study, we might add to these types some of the incidents which took place at Bethlehem—"the House of Bread." It was there that He was born who was the Bread of God sent down from heaven. "Thou Bethlehem Ephratah, though thou be little among the thousands of Judah, yet out of thee shall He come forth unto Me that is to be ruler in Israel, whose goings forth have been from of old, from everlasting." It was to Bethlehem that Naomi came from the far country, and found, not a famine, but a plentiful harvest; and a wealthy kinsman, who first allowed Ruth to glean in his fields, then took her to be his wife, and made her the joint possessor of all that he had. Bethlehem was the city of David where he to whom the Lord had said, "Thou shalt feed My people Israel," was anointed king. He had before fed and guarded his father's sheep in the fields of Bethlehem, the very fields where those other shepherds years afterwards were keeping their flocks when the angel first announced the birth of David's greater Son. There are many beautiful lessons to be learnt from the meanings of Bible names; and we may be sure that it was not by accident that these and other events took place at the city whose name signified "the House of Bread."

V

Types of Calvary

IN these days when the doctrine of Atonement by substitution is so often denied, the study of the types is of the utmost importance. It has frequently been noticed that the red line of the blood runs all through the Old Testament, and that thus we are constantly reminded of the shed blood, without which there is no remission. In the many foreshadowings of the work of Calvary we see a life laid down instead of the life of another, not merely as an example of self-sacrificing love, as men now try to teach. It must have been from these Old Testament types that the Lord answered His own question, "Ought not Christ to have suffered these things"; and as we study them we see the reasons for His sufferings.

If the disciples had understood that He was the great Antitype to which all had pointed, their faith would not have been so shaken; for they would have seen that it was only through death that He could redeem man. It is therefore of the utmost importance that we should be familiar with the Old Testament scenes and institutions which typified His death, even the death of the cross. Paul tells us in 1 Cor. xv. that "Christ died for our sins according to the Scriptures." The fact of His death needed not the testimony of the Scriptures; but the reason of that death could only be understood by the study of the prophecies and the types of the Old Testament.

To enumerate each of the latter would be impossible; but if only the best known are studied, it will be seen how all point to the great event which was the centre of the world's history: and yet how varied is the teaching, for each one seems to emphasize some particular truth.

The types which foreshadowed the death of our Lord may be divided into several groups.

I. First, we have those where there was the actual shedding of blood. Before the offerings were instituted in Leviticus many animals had been slain in sacrifice. We need only turn over a single page in our Bibles to see how God must have taught Adam and Eve to offer sacrifices. *The coats of skin* with which He clothed them evidently point to this, for to supply them there must have been death ; and so the garment which God provides can only be ours through the death of Christ. In the earlier part of this chapter we have Adam and Eve making for themselves aprons of fig-leaves, garments that were not fit for His presence ; but He Himself clothes them with that which speaks of Christ. In the following chapter, *the lamb* offered by Abel, in contrast to the fruits of the earth presented by Cain, teaches emphatically at the very beginning of God's Word that "without shedding of blood there is no remission"; and also shows that like Abel we can know even now that we are accepted of God because of the Lamb that was slain instead of us. In both the third and fourth chapters of Genesis we have man's way and God's way contrasted. The fig-leaves and the coats of skin, the fruit and the lamb, tell us that man's best is not enough, but that God has given His best. God must have taught Abel the need of the blood ; for we are told in Heb. xi. 4 that "by faith" he offered the lamb, and we know that "faith cometh by hearing." God testified of his gifts : but Cain's gift, though beautiful to look at and the fruit of much labour, was a false gift. We read in Prov. xxv. 14 that "whoso boasteth himself of a false gift is like clouds and wind without rain"; and the apostle Jude in speaking of the way of Cain and his followers says, "Clouds they are without water, carried about of winds." Religion without Christ and His death is a false gift.

The beautiful picture in Gen. xxii. emphasizes the thoughts of provision and substitution ; for *the ram* caught in the thicket was offered instead of Isaac. This is another instance of the double types ; for both Isaac and the ram are types of Christ on Calvary—Isaac the well-beloved son, whom the father spared not ; and the ram the substitute which God had Himself provided, and on account of which He gained the glorious title, " Jehovah Jireh, the Lord will provide." This is often quoted in connection with the supply of temporal needs ; but though these are included in the greater gift, the name, Jehovah Jireh, was first used at the time when Abraham said, " My son, God will provide Himself a lamb for a burnt offering." It is because He " spared not His own Son, but delivered Him up for us all," that He can " with Him also freely give us all things."

One of the most familiar types is that of *the Paschal Lamb.* The whole of the twelfth chapter of Exodus is full of teaching ; but the leading thought is evidently contained in the words, " When I see the blood I will pass over you." It tells of redemption by blood, the only means of deliverance from wrath ; and it speaks to us of the need of personal appropriation, for there is not only the shed blood, but the sprinkled blood. The lamb must not only be slain for all Israel, but the blood must be poured into a basin and sprinkled on the doorposts and the lintel, for the firstborn of each individual family.

There are many people who believe in the shedding of the blood; they believe that the Lord Jesus died, but they have not appropriated His work for themselves, and so are not resting under the sprinkled blood. To have rested only on the fact that the lamb had been killed would not have brought safety ; but having done what God had told them, the children of Israel were safe. Nothing but the blood could keep out the destroying angel ; the strongest buildings in the land are specially mentioned, but neither the throne nor the dungeon were secure—neither palace guards nor prison walls could ensure safety. We read that " there was not a house where there was not one dead " ; and though reference is made primarily to the houses of the Egyptians, it was true throughout the whole land, in the houses of the Israelites as well ; for in each home there must be death—either of the firstborn or of the lamb.

In the book of Leviticus we have the full account of the institution of the offerings, which were repeated all through the centuries that followed, till He came who was the Lamb of God, the Antitype of all.

The *burnt-offering*, like the sacrifice of Abel, tells us of acceptance ; the *peace-offering*, as its name implies, of peace through the death of another   Peace having been made, there is communion with God Himself over the death of the Lord Jesus ; for the priests were allowed to feed upon the sacrifice, a portion only being consumed on the altar as God's part, the remainder being for Aaron and his sons.

Time would fail to dwell on all the details of the work of Calvary which are so wonderfully brought before us in the offerings.   They themselves form a group of inexhaustible types which must be studied together.   In this chapter we have only space to mention the leading thought in each.   The key-word in Lev. i. concerning the burnt-offering seems to be in the 4th verse, where we read that the offering shall be "accepted" for the offerer ; in chapters iv. and v., where the subject is *the sin-offering*, the central word often repeated is, "it shall be forgiven him."   These two words, *accepted* and *forgiven*, clearly show the primary thought in the two offerings ; the one telling of Christ's perfect sacrifice to God the ground of our acceptance, the other of His bearing our sin.   In either case (chap. i. 4 and chap. iv. 4) the offerer was instructed to lay his hand on the head of the offering, and a wondrous transference took place, but in an opposite direction.   In the burnt-offering the acceptableness of the offering passed to the offerer and he was accepted ; in the sin-offering the sin of the offerer passed to the offering and he was forgiven.   There are many believers who know the Lord Jesus Christ as their sin-offering, but who do not seem to have the joy of knowing Him as their burnt-offering, and of seeing that they are indeed "accepted in the Beloved."

Each time the offerings were repeated they foreshadowed the death of Christ, and the teaching is the same ; but some of the scenes add touches of special beauty, as, for instance, the scene in 1 Sam. vii., when the children of Israel are led by Samuel to return to the Lord. They had sinned, the glory had departed, the ark had been taken ; but here they own their sin, and pour out water before the Lord in acknowledgment of their utter helplessness. Then we read that " Samuel took a sucking lamb and offered it for a burnt-offering wholly unto the Lord ; and Samuel cried unto the Lord for Israel, and the Lord heard him " : and the next verse tells us that the Lord thundered with a great thunder upon the Philistines. This was God's answer to the people, who, owning their own feebleness, linked themselves to the weakness of the little lamb. The incident has been beautifully compared with the passage in Rom. v. : "when we were yet without strength," typified by the pouring out of the water ; "while we were yet sinners," corresponding with their confession "we have sinned" ; and " Christ died for us," foreshadowed by the offering of the lamb.

The sin-offering and *trespass-offering*, the great *day of atonement*, the cleansing by *the red heifer*, and the provision for *the cleansing of the leper*, all speak of God's remedy for defilement ; and repeat again and again that the cross of Christ is the only ground for cleansing. With two or three other types they form a very important cluster which must be considered separately.

In the last mentioned of these, the cleansing of the leper, the prominent thought seems to be that of justification by the death and resurrection of Christ (see chapter ix.). It was no costly offering that was needed. The two birds—or sparrows, as we read in the margin—would be within reach of the poorest ; and we are reminded of our Lord's words, "Are not two sparrows sold for a farthing ? and one of them shall not fall to the ground without your Father." We may be sure that this was true of the little bird that was slain as a type of His Son. It was killed in an earthen vessel, and our Lord needed an earthen vessel in which to die. "Forasmuch then as the children are partakers of flesh and blood, He also Himself likewise took part of the same; that through death He might destroy him that had the power of death." The same word is used in the 22nd Psalm, where He says, "My strength is dried up like an earthen vessel."

Reference has already been made amongst the double types to the *one found slain* in the field in Deut. xxi., and the inquiry held over that death, teaching us that God will require the death of His Son. The people cried, "His blood be on us and on our children"; and we read in Num. xxxv. 33, "Blood, it defileth the land; and the land cannot be cleansed of the blood that is shed therein"; or, as it is in the margin, "there can be no expiation for the land, but by the blood of him that shed it." We see, however, that the heifer was here slain to meet such guilt.

II. There are many other foreshadowings of the death of Christ where there is no mention of the shedding of blood, and several of these are scenes which picture His passing *through the waters of judgment* and *death*. Like so many other typical substances in Scripture, water has several meanings, which may generally be easily discovered by the connection. When the thought is that of cleansing, the water evidently typifies the "washing of water by the Word," as in the Laver, and in John xiii. and elsewhere. Where there is refreshment and life-giving power, as in the water that flowed from the smitten rock, the well of John iv., and other wells, the rivers of John vii., the river of God, and the rain that refreshes the earth, we know that the Holy Spirit is prefigured.

Then again the instability, turmoil, and unrest of the sea is often symbolical of the unrest of the nations of the earth, as in Ezek. xxxi. 4, Psa. xviii. 4, Rev. xvii. 15; but when "the floods lift up their waves, the Lord on high is mightier than the noise of many waters." Water spilt or poured out on the ground indicates man's weakness, as in the type to which reference has just been made (1 Sam. vii.), and in 2 Sam. xiv. 14, and Psa. xxii. 14. But deep waters are an element of danger and destruction, and speak to us of sorrow and death; and thus typify the waters of judgment through which the Lord Jesus passed in death for us.

It is in this connection that they are so often spoken of in the Psalms, in many of which we have the utterances of our Lord Himself. " Thy wrath lieth hard upon me, and Thou hast afflicted me with all Thy waves " (Psa. lxxxviii. 7); " All Thy waves and Thy billows are gone over me " (Psa. xlii. 7); " Save me, O God; for the waters are come in unto my soul. . . . I am come into deep waters, where the floods overflow me. . . . Let me be delivered from them that hate me, and out of the deep waters. Let not the waterflood overflow me, neither let the deep swallow me up " (Psa. lxix. 1, 2, 14, 15). Another Psalm tells us that God's " judgments are a great deep " (Psa. xxxvi. 6); and thus several of the Old Testament pictures evidently typify the Lord Jesus Christ on Calvary passing through the waters of judgment and death for us.

We know from the Lord's own lips that *Jonah* is a type of Himself; for He said, " As Jonas was three days and three nights in the whale's belly, so shall the Son of Man be three days and three nights in the heart of the earth." The language of Jonah's prayer in the second chapter reminds us of many of the utterances in the Psalms as he cries, " Thou hadst cast me into the deep, in the midst of the seas, and the floods compassed me about; all Thy billows and Thy waves passed over me."

Noah was preserved in safety, and the waters of the flood touched him not, because he was safe in *the ark*; but the ark must pass through the waters, and the waves must beat upon it: and thus it tells of Christ, who having met the storm for us, is our place of safety.

In the *Red Sea* and the *Jordan*, through which God's redeemed people passed, we again have pictures of the death of Christ; the first, as we have noticed, teaching us of deliverance from Egypt, and the crossing of the Jordan, of entrance into the land of promise, the place of blessing. The crossing of the Red Sea points to that which is behind; the passage of the Jordan to that which is in front. The ark of the testimony, that went down first into the river and remained till all the people had passed over, foreshadowed Christ, the Alpha and Omega of our salvation, going down into death for us and meeting it to the full; for we are told that the Jordan was crossed at the time when the river overflowed its banks. The stones that were placed in the Jordan, as we have seen, speak of the believer's share in the death of Christ; and those in the land, of their having been raised with Him from the waters of death.

In the incident at *Marah*, where the bitter waters were made sweet by means of the tree that was cast into them, we probably have another foreshadowing of the same; as one has said, " Beauteous type of Him who was cast into the bitter waters of death in order that those waters might yield nought but sweetness to us for ever. We can truly say the bitterness of death is passed, and nothing remains for us but the eternal sweets of resurrection." The scene was very similar to that which took place in the time of Elisha on the banks of the Jordan, when *the axe-head* was made to float; and by analogy both seem more than mere illustrations of what the Lord has done by going down into the waters of death. In the former the bitter was made sweet: in 2 Kings vi. that which was lost and sunken was raised and restored. In each case it was by means of the tree or branch cast into the waters.

III. There are other types of our Lord's death which cannot be included in either of the former divisions, for they do not speak of the actual shedding of blood or of the waters of death. Amongst them there are two more wilderness pictures which must not be omitted.

The smitten rock was the source of the rivers of water; just as the death of Christ must precede the descent of the Holy Spirit. In promising the outflowing rivers of water in John vii., the Lord evidently referred to this type. We read, "This spake He of the Spirit, which they that believe on Him should receive: for the Holy Ghost was not yet given; because that Jesus was not yet glorified." The Apostle Paul tells us that "that rock was Christ"; but it needed only to be smitten once. Moses on the second occasion was told to speak to it; and for his disobedience to this command he was not allowed to enter the land. God thinks much of His pictures, and would not allow a hasty hand to thus add a stroke, which spoilt the whole by making it an incorrect representation of that which it was meant to typify.

When, long centuries afterward, Moses' prayer was answered, and he was allowed to "go over and see the good land that is beyond Jordan, and that goodly mountain," when he and Elias stood with the Lord on the Mount of Transfiguration, the subject of conversation was the decease "which He should accomplish at Jerusalem"—the Antitype of the smitten rock. Surely then Moses fully understood the meaning of the type which he had marred.

The scene in Numbers xxi., of the lifting up of *the brazen serpent*, is familiar to all from the reference in John iii., as a foreshadowing of the lifting up of Christ on Calvary; and here the truth emphasized is that the death of our Lord is the remedy for the bite of sin. "There is life in a look at the crucified One." He took upon Himself the form of that which had done the mischief; He was made "sin for us." The remedy was for all that were bitten. We read (vers. 8, 9) that it was for "every one" and "any man"; like God's work spoken of by Job, "which men behold, every man may see it; man may behold it afar off."

The earliest foreshadowing of the Lord's death seems to be given in *the deep sleep* that God caused to fall upon Adam when

He formed or builded Eve (see margin). We know from Eph. v. that this is a picture of Christ and the Church, and it was through the deep sleep of Christ that the Church could be builded up.

The rending of the vail of the temple at the moment that our Lord gave up the ghost was the conclusion of the Old Testament types. The vail which had hitherto hung between the Holy place and the Holiest of all had been to "divide" between the two (Exod. xxvi. 33), and teaches us that the Incarnation of our Lord, which is typified by the vail, could not of itself bring us to God. It was the rending of that vail that opened the way. Now we may by faith boldly enter into God's presence ; and by-and-by we shall actually go inside, "whither the Forerunner is for us entered." The rent vail would allow those who served in the temple to see into the Holiest of all ; and this is our privilege now. Our Lord said, "The world seeth Me no more, but ye see Me"; and we can by faith behold Him appearing as the great High Priest "in the presence of God for us."

We have in another group of types mentioned *the corn of wheat* which, falling into the ground, dies, and so brings forth much fruit. Here the Lord teaches that it was necessary for Him to die in order that He might have a glorious harvest.

Volumes have been and might still be written on these wonderful types ; but in this brief study we see that by grouping together those that speak to us of the cross of Christ, we have brought before us all the chief blessings that it has purchased for us.

We have a covering that fits us for God's presence in Gen. iii. ; acceptance in Abel's lamb and the burnt-offering ; substitution provided by God in Gen. xxii. and also in the offerings; deliverance from wrath in the Paschal Lamb ; peace and communion in the peace-offering ; forgiveness and cleansing in the sin and trespass-offerings, the great day of atonement, the red heifer ; and justification in the bird slain at the cleansing of the leper.

Then we see also deliverance from our enemies in the crossing of the Red Sea, and entrance into blessing in the passage of the Jordan ; the believer's union in His death and resurrection in the stones ; the bitter turned into sweet at Marah ; the sunken raised in 2 Kings vi. ; the gift of the Holy Spirit in the smitten rock ; the healing from the poison of sin in the uplifting of the brazen serpent ; the building up of the Church in Gen. ii. ; the only means of safety in the Ark ; access to God's presence in the rent vail ; and the ingathering of the harvest in the corn of wheat. In Jonah's history we have foreshadowed the exact time that would elapse between His death and resurrection ; and in the scene in Deut. xxi. we are taught that God will require the death of His Son.

These are but some of the most prominent thoughts brought before us in this rich cluster of types; but there are in each one many details which are full of beauty.

The Lord by instituting His supper has given us a constantly recurring type of His death—a shadow left behind as He returned into the light of His Father's house. The fact that He has commanded us to remember His dying love in the emblems of *the broken bread* and poured-out wine tells us that He values our thoughts. As the Psalmist says, " Let my meditation be sweet unto Him " (Psa. civ. 34, R.V.). His heart is gladdened by our study, as with grateful hearts we in the types " survey the wondrous cross on which the Prince of glory died."

We may well spend time therefore in studying the pictures which so wonderfully bring this before us ; and if they are precious to us here as we dimly see their meaning, we may surely look forward to the time when we shall understand them fully, where *the Lamb* that had been slain will be the centre of the glory, and His death the theme of our conversation.

VI

Types of the Resurrection

THE types of the resurrection of the Lord Jesus Christ are not so numerous as those of His death ; but it was clearly foreshadowed in the Old Testament. Paul tells us in 1 Cor. xv., as part of his gospel, that Christ " rose again the third day according to the Scriptures " ; and he evidently referred chiefly to the types in which it was foretold. Some of these have already been alluded to, but it may be well to group them all together. If, as we have seen, the ark passing through the waters of the flood was a type of Christ's death, the resting of *the ark on Mount Ararat,* and Noah stepping forth on to the new earth, would prefigure resurrection life. The types are all imperfect, and thus the ark fails ; for, unlike Noah, we never leave our safe retreat—it is "a shelter in the time of storm," and there is no safety except in abiding there.

It is remarkable that the date is given on which the ark rested upon the mountains of Ararat ; and that date probably coincides with the morning of the resurrection. Was this an accident—a mere coincidence—or was it not rather an indication that the day was known to God on which He would say, " Thou art My Son ; this day have I begotten Thee " ?

We are told that the ark rested on the seventh month on the seventeenth day of the month. The seventh month was the month Abib ; but from the time of the first passover it became the beginning of months, and " the first month of the year " (Exod. xii. 2). The lamb was killed on the fourteenth day of the same month ; and the third day after this was the seventeenth, the day on which the ark rested. Many therefore think that it was actually the day of the resurrection.

Another type—that of the waving of *the sheaf of the first-fruits*, to which reference has been made—clearly prophesied the day of the week on which the resurrection would take place. It was to be on the first day of the week ; for we read in Lev. xxiii. 11, " on the morrow after the sabbath the priest shall wave it." The corn of wheat had fallen to the ground and had died: it had been sown "in the field" (Exod. xxiii. 16), the field of the world ; and the sheaf of the firstfruits was the earnest of the glorious harvest that was to spring from that corn of wheat. " Christ the firstfruits ; afterward they that are Christ's at His coming." The resurrection of Christ is the guarantee of the resurrection of His people, when, at His coming to the air, " the dead in Christ shall rise first "; and when at His coming to the earth, all others included in the first resurrection will be raised.

But while the day of the week is clearly indicated in this type, we are not left in doubt as to which Sabbath was to precede the resurrection morning. It was the Sabbath after the passover ; and this we know was actually the case, " that the Scripture might be fulfilled."

In Numbers xvii. we have a beautiful type of the resurrection of the Lord Jesus Christ, in *the budding of Aaron's rod*. The twelve rods were laid up before the Lord. All were equally dead, and there was no sign of life in them; but when the morning came a wondrous miracle had taken place—one rod, that on which was inscribed the name of Aaron, had become full of life : buds and blossom and fruit had all appeared. No eye saw the change take place ; but when Moses came in the morning there was abundant evidence of life, reminding us of that morning when the women came to the sepulchre at the rising of the sun, and found that He whom they sought was not dead but was risen. The budding and blossoming rod was next shown to the people. The miracle was attested by many witnesses ; and so we read in Acts that our risen Lord " showed Himself alive after His passion, by many infallible proofs." "Him God raised up the third day, and showed Him openly—not to all the people, but unto witnesses chosen before of God."

The resurrection is one of the chief themes of the book of the Acts, for it was to this that the disciples gave witness. They did not need to testify of His death, for that was known to all Jerusalem; but to believe the fact of the resurrection was to believe in the Messiahship of Christ, and in His finished work. Aaron's rod was caused to bud, to prove that he was God's chosen one; and Jesus Christ our Lord was "declared to be the Son of God with power, according to the Spirit of holiness, by the resurrection from the dead" (Rom. i. 4). There could be no doubt that He was accepted by God, since He raised Him from the dead. After the rod had been shown to the people, it was laid up in the presence of the Lord; and so when God had raised Christ from the dead, "He was seen many days of them which came up with Him from Galilee to Jerusalem," and then "sat down on the right hand of the majesty on high." The rod of Aaron was "for the tribe of Levi"; and the resurrection of Christ, as we have seen in the previous type, was the guarantee that His people would be raised: for "if the Spirit of Him that raised up Jesus from the dead dwell in you, He that raised up Christ from the dead shall also quicken your mortal bodies by His Spirit that dwelleth in you."

The type fails in that the rod was to be kept as a token against the rebels. Christ's resurrection does not remind of sin, but of justification; for He was "delivered for our offences, and was raised again for our justification." The rod, although mentioned in Hebrews as among the contents of the Ark, was not found there in the time of Solomon; and the reason seems to be that in the temple, which prefigures Christ and His Church in resurrection glory, there was nothing to remind of wilderness failure.

There is probably a reference to Aaron's rod in Num. xx.,

when Moses was told to take the rod and to speak to the rock that it might give forth the water. The rock had been smitten previously, speaking to us of the death of Christ; and Moses was to hold in his hand the symbol of the resurrection, and the waters would flow—as we read in John vii. concerning the rivers of water: "This spake He of the Spirit, which they that believe on Him should receive; for the Holy Ghost was not yet given; because that Jesus was not yet glorified."

We read that Moses took the rod from before the Lord; and there is doubtless a connection between these types: the rock that had been smitten; the rod that had budded, and had then been in the presence of God; and the flowing waters. Peter tells us in Acts ii. 23 of the smiting of the rock: " Him, being delivered by the determinate counsel and foreknowledge of God, ye have taken, and by wicked hands have crucified and slain."   In verses 24, 31, 32 he speaks of the Antitype of the rod that budded and was laid up before the Lord, and of the rivers of water: "This Jesus hath God raised up; . . . therefore, being by the right hand of God exalted, and having received of the Father the promise of the Holy Ghost, He hath shed forth this, which ye now see and hear."

In the cleansing of the leper, as we have already mentioned, there is a foreshadowing of the resurrection.   Two birds alive and clean were to be presented for the man whose leprosy was healed.   One bird was killed in an earthen vessel over running water, and *the live bird* was to be dipped in its blood and let loose into the open field.   The shed blood of the first bird speaks to us of Christ's death; and the second bird of the resurrection of Jesus Christ, who is "gone into heaven and is on the right hand of God."   The bird flew away heavenward with blood on its wings; and the Lord " by His own blood . . . entered in once into the holy place, having obtained eternal redemption for us."

In grouping together the types of the resurrection there is one to which we have already referred, but which we cannot

omit here, viz., the entrance of the children of Israel into the
land after *passing through the river Jordan*. The Jordan speaks
to us of the death of Christ, and the passage through it of the
oneness of believers with Christ in death and resurrection.
Colossians iii. gives us the two truths : " Ye are dead,"
was typified by the twelve stones placed in the Jordan over
which the river flowed immediately after the people had
crossed. " They are there unto this day." Our union with
Christ involved a union with His death which can never be
changed ; but there is the other side of the truth : " If ye
then be risen with Christ, seek those things which are above,
where Christ sitteth on the right hand of God."

This was typified by *the stones* taken up out of the Jordan
and set up in the land ; as we read in Eph. ii., " God . . .
hath raised us up together, and made us sit together in
heavenly places in Christ Jesus." These stones represent the
standing of every believer—dead with Christ, and raised with
Him.

Our place in God's sight is in the land ; for He "hath blessed
us with all spiritual blessings in heavenly places in Christ."
While it is true that we must not be satisfied unless our
experience correspond with our standing, the teaching of the
Bible does not seem to warrant, as is sometimes taught, that
these things are necessarily a gradual experience, or take place
as a second blessing apart from conversion. If through want
of teaching we have failed to see our position, it does not alter
the fact that when we were united by faith to Christ we were
partakers of His death and resurrection, because in Christ.
Our standing from henceforth was in the land ; and the
fighting commenced that we might take possession step by
step of what God had given to us. We have not to put
ourselves to death or into the grave, as some teach ; but to
recognise that in Christ we have died, and have been raised
that we may walk in newness of life.

Three days and three nights are often typical of death and resurrection ; as for instance in the history of Jonah, whose "three days and three nights" are mentioned by the Lord as typical of the time which He Himself should spend in the heart of the earth.   Death and resurrection are probably signified in Moses' answer to Pharaoh, "We will go three days' journey into the wilderness, and sacrifice to the Lord our God."   Pharaoh wanted them to sacrifice in the land ; or, if they did leave it, not to go "very far away" : but God's purpose is that there shall be a complete break with the god of this world, which can only be made when we take our place on resurrection ground.   The ark of the covenant of the Lord, on one occasion, went before the children of Israel in a three days' journey to search out a resting-place for them.

In Heb. xi. we see that *Isaac* being received back by Abraham after he had willingly offered him up, was a figure of resurrection ; and as we know that Abraham is a type of the Father who spared not His Son, and Isaac of the Lamb provided by " Jehovah Jireh," we cannot be wrong in looking at the scene as foreshadowing both the death and resurrection of the Lord Jesus Christ.   Nor is it without significance that the account is followed in Genesis xxiv. by the beautiful picture of the faithful servant going forth to seek a bride for the son, who has thus in figure passed through death and resurrection.

There is a prophetic scene in the book of Kings in which there seems to be a reference at least to the resurrection. Jezebel's daughter, Athaliah, had attempted to destroy all the seed royal ; but though she thought she had succeeded, *one* "*from among the slain*" was taken and hidden in the temple of the Lord till the time for his proclamation as king.   He was the heir to the throne, but a usurper reigned ; just as now the heir to the same throne, the throne of David and the throne of Jehovah (1 Chron. xxix. 23), is hidden for a time in the presence of God, and will not be seen by the world till " the crowning day that's coming by-and-by."   The usurper thought to have destroyed Him on Calvary ; but He rose from the dead, and will soon take His power and reign. We see from Rev. ii. 20, 23, that Jezebel and her children are evidently types of Satan's power and the evil systems which he has introduced ; and Athaliah's reign is a striking picture of Christendom just now.

The position of the Levites, who are a type of the Church, on this occasion illustrates our attitude as waiting for the signal that shall call us to the side of the King's Son who "shall reign," that we may be "with the King when He cometh in and goeth out." The Levites of all the cities of Judah, and the chief of the fathers of Israel, were by the high priest let into the secret that changed their lives. He "showed them the king's son." They learnt that he was not dead, but that he was alive; and that when the right time had come he would be proclaimed king. Faith in the resurrection of the Lord Jesus has changed men's lives ever since that resurrection took place ; for we read, " If thou shalt confess with thy mouth the Lord Jesus, and shalt believe in thine heart that God hath raised Him from the dead, thou shalt be saved." No longer the servants of the usurper, but knowing that his dominion will soon cease, we wait for the Son from heaven, when we shall be caught up to meet the Lord in the air, and afterwards shall come with Him in His glory. " Surely I come quickly : Amen. Even so come, Lord Jesus ! "

VII

God's Dwelling Places

A VERY interesting study is that of comparing God's dwelling places throughout the Bible. The first is *the Tabernacle*, of which He said, "Let them make Me a sanctuary, that I may dwell among them." This was the first time that God had dwelt amongst men. He came down to visit Adam in Eden, when He walked in the garden in the cool of the day. Enoch and Noah walked with God, and He called Abraham His friend; but He had never before come down to dwell. In Gen. ix. 27, where it is prophesied, "He shall dwell in the tents of Shem," there may be an allusion to the Tabernacle. For more than five hundred years it was His dwelling place on earth. He went "from tent to tent, and from one tabernacle to another," until He gave directions for Solomon to build Him a house, and *the Temple* became His sanctuary, a "palace, . . . not for man, but for the Lord God" (1 Chron. xxix. 1).

These two, the Tabernacle and the Temple, were successively His dwelling place in Old Testament times. But after many years had elapsed *the Lord Jesus Christ* came; and in Him, on earth as now in heaven, "dwelleth all the fulness of the Godhead bodily." We read that "the Word was made flesh and tabernacled among us." He was Emmanuel, God with us, the Antitype of the Tabernacle and also of the Temple; for He was "greater than the temple" (Matt. xii. 6), and compares Himself to it more than once. "Destroy this temple," He said, "and in three days I will raise it up; . . . but He spake of the temple of His body." For thirty-three years He walked this earth, and when He ascended,

God came to dwell in another temple.   He now dwells in
the Church, not merely in the bodies of individual believers,
which are the temples of the Holy Ghost, but in "the
Church, which is His body."   As we read in Eph. ii. 20–22,
" Jesus Christ Himself being the chief corner-stone ; in whom
all the building fitly framed together groweth unto an holy
temple in the Lord : in whom ye also are builded together for
an habitation of God, through the Spirit."   It has been pointed
out that in this passage we have the Church as the antitype
both of the Temple and the Tabernacle.   In verse 22 there is
a building already completed in which God now dwells—a
building set up like the Tabernacle on desert sands.   In
verse 21 a Temple is spoken of which is still growing, and
which will only be completed when He presents to Himself "a
glorious Church, not having spot or wrinkle or any such thing."
The Tabernacle seems to be the type of Christ and His Church
now ; the Temple, of Christ and His Church in resurrection
glory, as we read in Peter, "Ye also as lively stones are built
up a spiritual house."   It is not yet finished.   As Solomon's
Temple "was built of stone made ready before it was brought
thither "—or "at the quarry," as we read in the Revised Version—so each stone in the Temple must be quarried, cut, and
shaped below.

Solomon himself adopted the plan which he recommends in
Prov. xxiv., "Prepare thy work without, and make it fit for
thyself in the field, and afterwards build thine house."   God is
doing this now.   The field is the world, and the stones are one
by one being made ready here.

We are told of the vessels of the Temple that "in the plain
of Jordan did the king cast them in the clay ground"; and so
must it be with "the vessels of mercy which He had afore prepared unto glory."   All the moulding and the cutting must be
done here ; and the building will not be completed till every
stone is finished, and "He shall bring forth the headstone
thereof with shoutings, crying, Grace, grace unto it ! "   The

corner stone in Eph. ii. is the foundation stone, and speaks of His first coming; but the head stone of the corner, in Psa. cxviii., and the headstone spoken of in Zech. iv., point to His second coming.

There is mention of *a future dwelling place* in Ezek. xxxvii. 26, 27, and other similar passages, where God promises that His sanctuary shall be in the midst of Israel. In Rev. xv. John sees "the temple of the tabernacle of the testimony in heaven"; and in chapter xxi. he hears a voice saying, "Behold, the tabernacle of God is with men, and He will dwell with them." We cannot tell how far these refer to the glorified Church; but we know that when He comes and the dead in Christ are raised, and we which are alive and remain are "caught up to meet the Lord in the air," we shall never again be separated from Him; for "so shall we ever be with the Lord." John tells us in the same chapter of Revelation that in the New Jerusalem he "saw no temple therein; for the Lord God Almighty and the Lamb are the temple of it"; and we know that the Lord Jesus Christ's prayer will then have been fulfilled, "that they all may be one: as Thou, Father, art in Me, and I in Thee, that they also may be one in us." It may be therefore that this future temple is Christ and His Church.

When Adam fell, the Lord said, "Behold, the man is become as one of us"; and so he was driven away from the tree of life. But Christ's prayer in John is "that they also may be one in us"; and in Revelation man is welcomed back to the tree of life, and Christ's prayer is answered.

In studying these dwelling places—the Tabernacle, the Temple, our Lord Himself, and the Church—we may trace many thoughts through each one, comparing them and contrasting them with one another.

First, there is *the pattern* for each. Moses is told to make the Tabernacle, and all its vessels, after the pattern which was shown him in the Mount (Exod. xxv. 9, 40). When David gave to Solomon the plan for every part of the Temple, he said, "All this . . . the Lord made me understand in writing by His hand upon me, even all the works of this pattern." We know that the Lord Jesus Christ is the express image of God's person, and every member of the Church is to be conformed to the image of His Son, "till we all come in the unity of the faith, and of the knowledge of the Son of God, unto a perfect man, unto the measure of the stature of the fulness of Christ." In God's dwelling place there is no place for man's designs or inventions. The pattern for all is Christ Himself.

There is *preparation* in each case. The Tabernacle must have been in God's mind when He told the people to ask of the Egyptians jewels of gold and jewels of silver; and when He put it into the hearts of their late oppressors to grant them all that they asked. He had told Abraham that they should "come out with great substance"; and thus when in Exodus xxv. He told them to bring an offering, they were well provided. So when God asks us to give Him something, He always gives it to us first. He makes preparation, and then allows us to say we will "prepare Him an habitation." When the materials had been given, He called out Bezaleel, whom He had filled "with the Spirit of God, in wisdom, and in understanding, and in knowledge, and in all manner of workmanship, to devise curious works," and put in his heart that he might teach others, and that the work might be done according to God's pattern.

David made great preparation for the Temple ; for he said, "The house that is to be builded for the Lord must be exceeding magnifical, of fame and of glory throughout all countries ; I will therefore now make preparation for it. So David prepared abundantly before his death " (1 Chron. xxii. 5). Six times over in 1 Chron. xxix. this preparation is mentioned ; for when David had prepared, the people also made preparation, and they could say, as their fathers in the wilderness might have done, " All this store that we have prepared to build Thee an house for Thine holy Name, cometh of Thine hand, and is all Thine own." This is the Bible meaning of consecration, filling our hand from God's hand, and then offering it to Him again (1 Chron. xxix. 5, 14, *margin*). Solomon also, as we have seen, made careful preparation before he began to build the house.

When the Lord Jesus came and tabernacled amongst men, He said, " A body hast Thou prepared Me." His going forth was "prepared as the morning"; and Simeon could say, " Lord, now lettest Thou Thy servant depart in peace, according to Thy word ; for mine eyes have seen Thy salvation, which Thou hast prepared before the face of all people." Now God dwells in " a people prepared for the Lord "—on earth in humiliation, as in the Tabernacle ; by-and-by in the glory, as in the Temple, when He will " make known the riches of His glory on the vessels of mercy which He had afore prepared unto glory." There is preparation also for God's future dwelling place. In Isa. ii. 2, we read, " It shall come to pass in the last days, that the mountain of the Lord's house shall be prepared (*margin*) in the top of the mountains, and shall be exalted above the hills, and all nations shall flow unto it " ; and in Rev. xxi. 2, 3, John sees "the holy city, New Jerusalem, coming down from God out of heaven, prepared as a bride adorned for her husband " ; and at the same time he hears " a great voice out of heaven, saying, Behold, the Tabernacle of God is with men."

Above the Tabernacle rested the Shekinah *cloud* that indicated God's presence. When Moses set up the Tabernacle, we read that " a cloud covered the tent of the congregation, and the glory of the Lord filled the Tabernacle ; and Moses was not able to enter into the tent of the congregation, because the cloud abode thereon, and the glory of the Lord filled the Tabernacle."

When all the work that Solomon made for the house of the Lord was finished, and everything was brought in and put in its place, and the Temple dedicated to God, " It came even to pass, as the trumpeters and singers were as one, to make one sound to be heard in praising and thanking the Lord; and when they lifted up their voice with the trumpets and cymbals and instruments of music, and praised the Lord, saying, For He is good; for His mercy endureth for ever : that then the house was filled with a cloud, even the house of the Lord ; so that the priests could not stand to minister by reason of the cloud : for the glory of the Lord had filled the house of God."

The bright cloud overshadowed the Lord Jesus on the mount of Transfiguration ; and as in the wilderness God spake to Israel out of the cloud, so He spake to the disciples : " And, behold, a voice out of the cloud, which said, This is My beloved Son, in whom I am well pleased : hear ye Him." The cloud was seen again when the Lord Jesus ascended ; for while the disciples were gathered around Him on the mount of Olives, "He was taken up, and a cloud received Him out of their sight."

We read in 1 Cor. x. 2 that all the children of Israel "were under the cloud, and all passed through the sea, and were all baptized unto Moses in the cloud and in the sea"; and this seems to indicate that the cloud was a type of the Holy Spirit, for " by one Spirit are we all baptized into one body." Lastly, in John's vision of the things which shall be hereafter, we read that "the temple was filled with smoke from the glory of God, and from His power : and no man was able to enter into the temple " (Revelation xv. 8).

Gold, which is taken to typify the divine, is found in each. The boards of the Tabernacle were overlaid with gold ; also the golden altar, the table of shewbread, and the ark, while the mercy-seat and the candle-stick were of pure gold. The latter alone must have been worth between £5,000 and £6,000 ; and the gold in the Temple more than £500,000,000— 108,000 talents (1 Chron. xxii. 14 ; xxix. 4, 7).

None of the wood, which is taken to represent the humanity, could be seen in either the Tabernacle or in the Temple ; and in the latter "there was no stone seen." All was overlaid with pure gold. Of our Lord Himself we read, " In the beginning was the Word, and the Word was with God, and the Word was God." He was the God-man; and the gold, the divine, though often hidden from view, was throughout His whole life seen in the miracles He wrought and the words He spake. On the mount of Transfiguration its full glory was seen; and even when " He humbled Himself and became obedient unto death, even the death of the cross," the centurion and they that were with Him said, " Truly this was the Son of God."

As God's dwelling place now, the Church too needs the gold; and every member of that Church must be born again, and be a partaker of the divine nature.

When in Rev. iii. Christ grieves over the lukewarmness of the Laodiccans, He says, " I counsel thee to buy of Me gold tried in the fire, that thou mayest be rich; and white raiment, that thou mayest be clothed; . . . and anoint thine eyes with eye-salve, that thou mayest see ": and we read in I Cor. iii. that at the Judgment-seat of Christ, when the works of believers will be tested, the gold, silver, and precious stones, will abide the fire.* In Solomon's temple " the floor of the house he overlaid with gold within and without "; and the priests' feet stood upon it, instead of as in the Tabernacle, on the sand of the desert: while in the New Jerusalem, in which the Lord God Himself and the Lamb are the temple, we read that the street of the city was pure gold.

The *exterior* of these dwelling places may well be compared and contrasted. The Tabernacle was covered with the badger skins, and the beauties within were hidden. There could have been nothing attractive in its appearance; and it was very

---

* It may be that the gold, white raiment, and eye-salve, represent God Himself—Father, Son, and Holy Ghost: for we read in Job xxii. 25 (*marg.*), " The Almighty shall be thy gold "; in Rom. xiii. 14, " Put ye on the Lord Jesus Christ "; and in 1 John ii. 20, " Ye have an unction from the Holy One, and ye know all things." It was God Himself that the Church at Laodicea wanted; and He was willing to come and dwell with any who heard His voice and would open the door to Him.

different from the glory of the temple of Solomon, which was
" garnished with precious stones for beauty."

Our Lord when He was on earth was like the Tabernacle, so
that the prophet could say, " When we shall see Him, there is
no beauty that we should desire Him.   He is despised and
rejected of men. . . . He hid, as it were, His face from us
(*marg.*); He was despised, and we esteemed Him not "—so is it
with the Church now.   " The disciple is not above his Master,
nor the servant above his Lord " ; and in her pilgrim character
the Church too is despised and rejected of men.   The little
company at Ephesus was not thought to be of much importance.
As the Apostle wrote his letter to them, and compared them
to the Temple and the Tabernacle, probably he was thinking
of that other temple at Ephesus, one of the seven wonders of
the world, of which we read in Acts xix., Demetrius feared
" that the temple of the great goddess Diana should be
despised, and her magnificence should be destroyed, whom all
Asia and the world worshippeth."   That temple has long since
been destroyed, and we can see its remains in the British
Museum ; but the believers at Ephesus formed part of a
temple which, like Solomon's, will be " exceeding magnifical,
of fame and of glory throughout all countries."   When in
resurrection-glory Christ comes with His Church, to be
admired in all them that believe, the beauty of that Temple
will be seen by the whole universe.

Many other thoughts may be traced through God's dwelling
places in the various dispensations.

VIII

The Ark of the Testimony

ALTHOUGH it is helpful to compare the types one with another, it is also necessary to study each one separately. For example, in the Tabernacle it is well to examine each piece of furniture, and to trace through the Word the various references that are made to it. We shall thus notice several allusions to the Candlestick, from the time it was constructed in the wilderness to the time when it was used at Belshazzar's feast, and the handwriting of judgment was seen "over against the candlestick." This was a solemn warning against that which had been dedicated to the service of the Lord being used for other purposes. In the same way we shall see the Brazen Altar in the time of Solomon, Ahaz, and Hezekiah—used by Solomon when offering a thousand burnt offerings; set aside by Ahaz, and an altar copied from a heathen king substituted for it; then restored and cleansed by Hezekiah amidst songs of rejoicing.

The condition of the people might be judged from the value that was set upon God's altar; and it is the same now; for if the substitutionary work of our Lord Jesus Christ is thought little of, spiritual life must be feeble in the Church or in the individual.

The Ark of the Covenant is however the object which is most frequently alluded to, and is very full of spiritual teaching in the various incidents in its history, as we follow it through the wilderness and the Jordan to Gilgal, round the walls of Jericho, to Shiloh; then to the land of the Philistines, and back again through Bethshemesh, Kirjath-jearim, and the house of Obed-edom, till it finally rested in its place in the tent in Jerusalem and in the temple of Solomon. The history of the nation was intimately connected with the history of the Ark. If it were in

61

captivity, they were in trouble and distress; but when it occupied its right place, they were prosperous and happy.

While in the Tabernacle and Temple every whit uttered His glory, the Ark more than any other object there, seems to foreshadow the Lord Jesus. There is no doubt as to its being a type of Himself. The purpose for which it was made proves this; for God said to Moses, "There I will meet with thee, and I will commune with thee from above the mercy-seat." We read in Rom. iii. of Him "whom God hath set forth to be a propitiation—or mercy-seat—through faith in His blood." He Himself is the throne of grace, where God meets with the sinner; He is God's meeting place with man.

It is noticeable that the apostle speaks of Him here under the title of " Christ Jesus." The order of His name is not without meaning; and this speaks of the anointed and exalted One, who once was the suffering Man on earth. The name Jesus is not here used alone—for that would speak to us of His life of humiliation on earth; nor is it put first, still emphasizing His character as the suffering One; but it is " the Man in the glory " that is now the mercy-seat where we may obtain mercy for the past, and grace for the present and future.

The Ark was made of shittim wood, or acacia (R.V.), overlaid with gold; and this is generally taken to represent the twofold nature of our Lord, the human and the Divine. It has been said that the materials of which it was composed represented His person; the purposes for which it was used, His work.

The Ark was the place where the tables of stone were safely deposited when God gave them a second time to Moses. On the first occasion when he came down from the Mount and heard the sound of shouting in the camp, he dashed the tables of stone in pieces—emblematic of the way in which the people were breaking God's law, as man has always done. The second time provision had been made. The tables were put straight into the Ark, and Moses adds, " There they be "; reminding us of Him of whom it is said, " Thy law is within My heart "—-the only place where it has been kept unbroken. But the tables of stone were also the covenant ; and it was under this aspect that Solomon spoke of them when he said, " I have built the house for the name of the Lord God of Israel, and in it have I put the ark wherein is the covenant of the Lord that He made with the children of Israel." The tables of the covenant were safe within the ark, reminding him that God was a God that kept His covenants (2 Chron. vi. 10, 11, 14). Israel might fail, but God would never fail.

We are not under a covenant as they were, for it has long since been proved that man could never keep his part ; but Christ has become for us " the surety of a better covenant," which is between Himself and His Father. A promise, on the one hand, of eternal life, which God that cannot lie promised to His Son before the age began—a gift which was given to Him for the Church then (Titus i. 2 ; 2 Tim. i. 9) ; and, on the other hand, the guarantee from the Son that He would keep that which the Father had given Him. The covenant with Israel was safe in the Ark. The promises of God to the Church " in Him are Yea, and in Him Amen."

Other things were in the Ark in Tabernacle days—-the pot of manna, and Aaron's rod that budded ; proofs of God's wilderness provision and His choice of the Anointed One. But in the Temple we find they were no longer there ; probably because these two things had been laid up before God as a token against the rebels, and there will be nothing to remind of this in the glory.

The Cherubim were of one piece with the solid gold of the mercy-seat. Several different interpretations are given of the Cherubim. Some look upon them as the attributes of God ; others as His executive upon earth ; and others as emblems of redeemed man. The fact of their oneness with the mercy-seat and their being represented on the vail, and therefore being rent with it, rather points to the last interpretation ; and the figures of the living creatures in Ezekiel and Revelation v.

also seem to justify this conclusion, as they picture perfect ministry on earth or in the glory.

The three persons of the Trinity in type are all linked together in connection with the Ark; for while it foreshadows the work and person of the Lord Jesus, the cloud that rests above it seems to typify the Holy Spirit: and God spoke to the people from above the mercy-seat.

The type would not be complete if there were nothing in it to speak of the death of our Lord Jesus Christ; but we have this also, for it was a "blood-stained mercy-seat." The blood of the sacrifices—first of the bullock, then of the goat—was sprinkled upon it on the day of atonement. The Cherubim bent their gaze upon that blood, and God's eye rested upon it; and because of the blood He could accept the people. It was an atonement, or covering; for God Himself cannot see through the precious blood. It is an all-sufficient covering for our sin; so that we read, "On that day shall the priest make an atonement for you, to cleanse you, that ye may be clean from all your sins before the Lord." It might be said in this type as at the passover, "When I see the blood, I will pass over you." In each the blood was for the eye of God alone; for none might enter the Holiest of All save the high priest, and he only on this one occasion.

The Ark was never exposed to the gaze of the people; for even when carried from place to place it was covered with the vail, the badger skins, and the cloth of blue. When the Tabernacle was to be removed, the vail would be lowered upon the Ark, that none might look upon it; and so the vail of His Incarnation covered our Lord when here on His journeyings. The Ark was also protected by badger skins, like the Tabernacle itself. A twofold meaning is given to these skins: first, that their unattractive exterior represented our Lord's humiliation, which hid the glory so that He was despised and rejected of men; second, that they were that which protected from all contamination with evil—and probably there is truth in both interpretations. Above the badger skin was the cloth of blue ; and as it was carried on the shoulders of the priests, that one spot of blue would be conspicuous in the midst of the congregation, for it was the only piece of furniture so covered. The blue is always taken to represent the heavenly ; and we know that when the Lord Jesus was on earth this was indeed His character (John iii. 13). As we carry Him about now, our testimony is to be pre-eminently a heavenly one.

The Ark was to be the centre of the encampment—"Jesus in the midst" ; and when the camp journeyed, "as they encamp so shall they set forward, every man in his place." If every one takes his right position in relationship to the Lord Himself, they will also be in the right place with reference to their fellow-Christians.

Once in the wilderness journey we hear of the Ark leaving its central position and going in front of the people ; and then it was as a rebuke to Moses for having suggested that they needed any one but God Himself to be to them "instead of eyes," and to search out a resting-place for them (Num. x. 33). God did not approve of any one else choosing their way, and so changed the order of their encampment. "And the Ark of the covenant of the Lord went before them in the three days' journey, to search out a resting-place for them."

But there may be also here a picture of what our Lord Himself has done in going before His people in that wondrous three days' journey of His death and resurrection. Truly by it He has found for them a resting place, and has gone on before to prepare a place for them.

We next have the account of the Ark in Jordan. The words in Josh. iii. remind us of Heb. xii. 1, 2, " When ye see the Ark . . . go after it." We are to "run, . . . looking unto Jesus." Here again the Ark went first, and remained until " all the people were passed clean over." Christ is "the Author and Finisher of faith"—the Beginner and Completer ; He is " Alpha and Omega, the beginning and the end, the first and

the last." The children of Israel were told to sanctify themselves ; we are to " lay aside every weight." The Ark went
into the Jordan and remained there, that every one of the
people might pass over on dry land ; He "for the joy that
was set before Him," of bringing "many sons unto glory,"
" endured the cross."

It is in connection with this scene that we for the first time
have mention of " the Lord of all the earth." It is a title only
used in connection with the children of Israel in their land.
For the first time as a nation their feet stood there ; and for the
first time God took this name. In connection with the return
of Israel to the land, when they will become the centre of
blessing for the whole earth, the title is again made use of in
Isa. liv. 5 ; Micah iv. 13 ; Zech. iv. 14 ; vi. 5. During the
captivity He is repeatedly called "the God of heaven."

Immediately after the passage of the Jordan we read of the
Ark being carried round the walls of Jericho. Day after day it
was carried in solemn procession round the city, once each day,
till on the seventh day the priests bare it round seven times,
and the walls fell to the ground. Jericho, we are told, means
" fragrant with spices," and may represent the allurements of
the world which are so often spread before the believer when
he has crossed over Jordan and stands in the land.

We are not commanded to fight against the world, but to
carry Christ with us against the temptations, and we shall gain
the victory. John says, " Whatsoever is born of God overcometh the world ; and this is the victory that overcometh the
world, even our faith. Who is he that overcometh the world
but he that believeth that Jesus is the Son of God ? " In this
last sentence we have His twofold nature ; and this, as we
have seen, was represented in the shittim wood and the gold
of which the Ark was composed.

Shortly after Jericho was taken, we read of the disaster at Ai
through the over-confidence of the people, and their under-
estimating the enemy ; and when Joshua is overwhelmed with

their failure and defeat, he falls on his face before the Ark in confession. We know that the throne of grace is the place where we may come to obtain mercy for past defeat and grace for future victory.

In Joshua viii. 33, 34, we find that the Ark is in the midst when the blessings and cursings are read to the people, "according to all that is written in the book of the law." He whom the Ark symbolized will be in the midst as the Judge, in the day that God hath appointed, "in the which He will judge the world in righteousness, by that Man whom He hath ordained"; and He is now in the midst of the Church, as John saw Him walking in the midst of the candlesticks, judging their works, and pronouncing blessings and warnings.

In 1 Sam. iv. we have a description of the Ark falling into the hands of the Philistines. "The Ark of God was taken"; or, as the Psalmist describes it, God "forsook the Tabernacle of Shiloh, the tent which He placed among men, and delivered his strength into captivity, and His glory into the enemy's hand." So we read that the Lord Jesus was taken. It was true of the Philistines as of the enemies of the Lord, "Thou couldest have no power at all against Me, except it were given thee from above." Both of the Ark and of Him whom it foreshadowed it might have been said, "Him, being delivered by the determinate counsel and foreknowledge of God, ye have taken." The Israelites "fled every man into his tent"; and "they all forsook Him and fled."

But though in the fourth chapter we read that the Philistines proved stronger than Israel, in the following chapter we read that Jehovah was stronger than Dagon. The idol fell when God's Ark was placed in the temple; and so when Christ comes into the heart the idols fall. This is very different from what the hymn says:

"..... I have all my idols torn
From my heart, and now He keeps me by His power."

It is His presence alone that can do it. The strong man

armed may keep his palace, but when the Stronger than he comes in, He overcomes him. We are not able to turn out the strong man, or to tear down the idols. Even if we were able to empty the house, unless His presence fill it, the evil spirit would return once more. Reformation is not sufficient ; there must be Christ in the heart.

When in the garden the chief priests and Pharisees came to take Him, He had only to proclaim His name, " I AM," and " they went backward and fell to the ground ; " showing that the same Divine power dwelt in Him as in the Ark of old.

Its history at this time furnishes us with a wonderful illustration of the truth of 2 Cor. ii. 15, 16. " We are unto God a sweet savour of Christ, in them that are saved, and in them that perish. To the one we are the savour of death unto death ; and to the other the savour of life unto life." During the seven months that it dwelt in the land of the Philistines the Ark brought nothing but death and destruction. It was carried from place to place ; but the judgments grew worse. What a contrast to the history of its sojourn in the house of Obed-edom, where it brought nothing but blessing ! To the Philistines it was " the savour of death unto death " ; and to Obed-edom, " the savour of life unto life." " All that pertained to him " came in for a share of the blessing ; and it became noised abroad, so that the king heard of it. So will it be with the one in whose heart the Lord has made His abode —others will hear of it, and will want to have the same blessing. Here the type fails ; for Obed-edom had to lose the Ark from his house when David took it to Jerusalem, though we do not hear that he lost the blessing. " We will come unto him and will make our abode with him," is the promise to each one who loves Him and keeps His words ; and if others gain the blessing through us, we shall not be the losers.

The judgments that fell in connection with the Ark are very suggestive. The men of Bethshemesh were smitten for looking into it ; showing that it was too holy to be gazed at with curious eyes. "No man knoweth the Son but the Father"; and the mystery of His Incarnation and Godhead is one into which we must not try to examine too closely. How many have gone astray by endeavouring to intrude into these things! If Moses was not allowed to approach the burning bush to "see why" it was not consumed—for God said, "Draw not nigh hither; put off thy shoes from off thy feet, for the place whereon thou standest is holy ground"—surely this far greater mystery should be treated with still deeper reverence by us.

The judgment that fell upon Uzzah would never have come if God's directions had been followed. In sending home the Ark the lords of the Philistines had set it upon a new cart drawn by two milch kine; and "the kine took the straight way . . . along the highway, . . . and turned not aside to the right hand nor to the left." In fetching the Ark from Kirjath-jearim David forsook the old-fashioned way which God had commanded. He had said that it was to be carried on the shoulders of the priests; but David used the new cart in imitation of the Philistines. When the kine stumbled, the Ark shook, and Uzzah put out his hand to take hold of it, and was smitten before the Ark. What may be allowed in His enemies will not do for His people who have His law. As one has said, "The nearer a man is to God, the more solemnly and speedily will he be judged for any evil: judgment must begin at the house of God." To try and improve what God has instituted, by copying the religion of the world, is sure to bring judgment: yet how many are doing this at the present day!

David was greatly afraid at this manifestation of power, and was like Peter when he cried, "Depart from me, for I am a sinful man, O Lord"; but he learnt the lesson which God intended: for in 1 Chron. xv. we find him telling the people that the judgment fell because they "sought Him not after the due order." And he tells them that "none ought to carry the Ark of God but the Levites, for them hath God chosen to carry the Ark of God"; so "the children of the Levites bare the Ark of God upon their shoulders with the staves thereon, as Moses commanded, according to the word of the Lord." There was no difficulty this time; for "God helped the Levites that bare the Ark," as He always helps those who follow His directions.

Reference is made in the 132nd Psalm to the bringing up of the Ark from the house of Abinadab, "Lo, we heard of it at Ephratah (Bethlehem); we found it in the fields of the wood" (Kirjath-jearim). David was full of joy at the prospect of having it in his possession. There is always rejoicing when we can say with Philip, "We have found Him."

The subject of ministry before the Ark is too large a subject to be touched here.

When the man after God's own heart was rejected by Jerusalem, and the usurper was received in his stead, the Ark of God was carried out of Jerusalem, and with the rejected king crossed over the brook Kidron; reminding us of Him who in the darkest hour of His rejection crossed over the brook Kidron with His disciples (John xviii. 1).

When the temple was finished and dedicated to the Lord, we find that the Ark was brought into its place, and set in the centre of the scene which so wonderfully foreshadowed the day when God's Temple will be finished, and the redeemed will be gathered round Himself in the glory. In John's vision he caught a glimpse of the Ark; for "the Temple of God was opened in heaven, and there was seen in His Temple the Ark of His testament."

When that day comes there will be "no more need to carry the Tabernacle, nor any vessels of it for the service thereof"; for the Lord God will have "given rest unto His people." As He chose the Levites of old, He has chosen us to bear His name now; but the time for our testimony will then be over.

IX

God's Sevenfold Provision for Cleansing

IN studying the types connected with the Tabernacle and
its service it is well not only to group together those that
resemble one another as to outward form—such as the
offerings, etc.—but to consider at the same time those which
seem to have been instituted for similar purposes, though in
themselves very different.

A most important series of types is brought before us in
those which represent the provision that was made for meeting
defilement. It is impossible to obtain a clear view of their
spiritual meaning if they are only considered singly ; but by
looking at this wonderful sevenfold foreshadowing of God's
provision, we see how perfectly He has met His own requirements, and our need, by the death of His Son. The following
is the list of these seven types, and the special kind of defilement for which each one was ordained.

(1) The great *Day of Atonement* was the day on which the
guilt of Aaron and his house, and of the whole congregation,
was put away.

(2) The *sin offering* met sins of ignorance "against any of
the commandments of the Lord."

(3) The *trespass offering* was provision (*a*) for hearing false
swearing, and not witnessing against it (the sin of the nation in
Matt. xxvi. 60, 61) ; (*b*) for touching certain unclean things in
ignorance ; (*c*) for uttering a rash oath ; (*d*) for sins of ignorance in the holy things of the Lord ; (*e*) for certain sins
against the eighth, ninth, and tenth commandments.

(4) The *ashes of the red heifer* were for defilement from contact with death.

(5) The *cleansing of the leper* was for uncleanness left by leprosy.

(6) The *laver* was for the washing of the hands and feet, in order to remove defilement from contact with the earth, etc.

(7) The *golden plate* on the mitre of the high priest with its inscription, "Holiness to the Lord," was to be worn upon his forehead, that he might "bear the iniquity of the holy things, which the children of Israel shall hallow in all their holy gifts."

The first four give us different aspects of the work on Calvary; the fifth, as we have seen already, adds to this the thought of the resurrection; the sixth represents the washing of water by the Word; and the seventh represents the work of the High Priest.

Though all these types speak of Christ, the defilement which is to be removed and the methods of cleansing vary much. One, therefore, cannot be said to supersede the other; for they must each give some distinct teaching. None must be left out, if we are to have a complete picture of God's provision for our need; and the more we study them, the truer will be our view of His holiness, of His estimate of sin, and of our constant need of cleansing.

(1) The first of this series, the great *Day of Atonement*, had a collective and national aspect, and the guilt of a whole year's iniquities, transgressions, and sin, was put away. The service of the day is divided into two parts—the offering of the bullock for Aaron and his house, and the offering of the two goats for the congregation : and it is probable that there is dispensational teaching in this. Aaron and his house seem to have special reference to the Church; while the congregation of Israel would represent the nation itself, for whom the Day of Atonement will have its true fulfilment on the great day of their national humbling, when they look upon Him whom they have

pierced, and mourn because of Him. This is clearly seen in Lev.
xxiii., when this feast-day is shown to come between the feast
of trumpets—the calling together of the nation—and the feast
of Tabernacles, the millennial reign of Christ. But besides this
dispensational interpretation there is an application now for us.
Reference is evidently made to this type in Heb. ix., where
the writer speaks of the three appearances of the Lord. First,
in the *past*, " He appeared to put away sin by the sacrifice of
Himself "—represented by the slaying of the bullock and the
goat ; now, in the *present*, He appears "in the presence of God
for us "—as the high priest when He entered with the blood
into the Holiest of all ; and lastly, in the *future*, "unto them
that look for Him shall He appear the second time without sin
unto salvation "—coming out in blessing, like Aaron of old,
the question of sin having been settled for every one for whom
he carried in the blood—every one of the redeemed host of
Israel.

(2 and 3) The *sin offering* and the *trespass offering* are often
considered together ; but though closely resembling one
another, they differ in some respects. The sin offering, as so
often noticed, deals with sin, the root, as well as sins and
transgressions, the fruit ; but it is important to notice that each
included sins of ignorance.

For an Israelite to plead that he did not know God's law
would not relieve him of responsibility. " Though he wist it
not, yet is he guilty." Nor are we free from guilt in His sight,
even though through ignorance we fail to do His will. These
offerings prove that it is not enough for us to content ourselves
with thinking that we are walking " up to our light "; we
should rather seek to be "filled with the knowledge of His
will," knowing that anything short of this is sure to lead us
into sin. Paul called himself "the chief of sinners," although
his sin had been done ignorantly and in unbelief.

The word translated " sin " means *to come short*, or *to
miss the mark*. According to " The Englishman's Hebrew

Concordance," the word used in Judges xx. 16, "Every one could sling stones at an hairbreadth and not miss," might be as correctly rendered "not sin." There are two ways of missing a mark—we may aim in a wrong direction, or we may not have strength to shoot far enough. Many lose sight of this latter way of missing the mark, and think that if they aim correctly there is no sin. We are warned against coming short of the *glory* of God (Rom. iii. 23), the *grace* of God (Heb. xii. 15), and the *rest* of God (Heb. iv. 1). "He that sinneth against Me wrongeth his own soul" (Prov. viii. 36), is rendered in the R.V. margin, "He that misseth Me," in contrast to the preceding verse, which says, "Whoso findeth Me, findeth life."

The following are some of the Bible definitions of sin: "sin is the transgression of the law" (1 John iii. 4); "all unrighteousness is sin" (1 John v. 17); "whatsoever is not of faith is sin" (Rom. xiv. 23); "sin, because they believe not on Me" (John xvi. 9); "to him that knoweth to do good, and doeth it not, to him it is sin" (James iv. 17); and we read that "an high look and a proud heart, and the plowing of the wicked is sin" (Prov. xxi. 4); "the thought of foolishness is sin" (Prov. xxiv. 9); it is also sin to wrong a poor brother (Deut. xv. 9; xxiv. 15); and to defraud God (Deut. xxiii. 21).

(4) The cleansing by means of *the red heifer*, at the first glance seems to resemble in some respects the trespass offering, as both were provided for touching something unclean; and therefore for want of closely studying the two together, the cleansing of the red heifer is generally made to supersede the trespass offering. Again and again we read in commentaries that the former was for wilderness defilement; and no distinction is made between it and the sin and trespass offerings. It was evidently provided to meet a different sort of defilement; and although it emphasizes the thought of the offering of the sacrifice once for all, other truths are prominent in the other types. Thus the cleansing of the leper seems the only

one of the seven that speaks of the resurrection of Christ as well as of His death; and the trespass offering adds the thought of reparation to God and man. In fact, each one of the seven adds some truth which is omitted in the others.

In the ordinance of the red heifer, in Num. xix., there is nothing to indicate that the defilement was contracted through ignorance or carelessness, as in the case of the trespass offering. It might have been necessary and lawful; for some one would of necessity be in the tent when a man died (ver. 14); it would be necessary for some one to touch the body (vers. 11, 13); it would be necessary for it to be buried; but although the contact might be necessary, defilement was contracted, and God provided a sin offering (Num. xix. 9, R.V.) to meet this defilement.

The one historical record of the use of the ashes of the heifer seems to bear out this thought. In Num. xxxi., the children of Israel are commanded to arm themselves and go against the Midianites to "avenge the Lord of Midian"; and having done this, "whosoever hath killed any person, and whosoever hath touched any slain," are commanded to purify themselves according to the law in Num. xix. This seems to indicate that the defilement met by the cleansing of the red heifer might be necessary and lawful; and yet it was defilement, and could only be removed by the application of the remedy provided.

In our daily life, and in our work for the Lord, we are constantly obliged to come into contact with spiritual death; so that we cannot fail to contract defilement, which will hinder communion, unless we are living in the power of the finished work of Christ; for there is an affinity between the sin that dwelleth in us and the sin which is abroad in the world. The ashes speak of the finished work; for they show that the sacrifice has been accepted. Reference is evidently made to this type in Heb. ix. 13, and possibly in Heb. x. 22.

The suggestion that the red heifer was God's provision for

inevitable defilement, would not imply that it afforded an excuse for sin, or that it was necessary to yield to temptation ; but would rather teach that such is God's holiness, that in the unavoidable contact with the spiritual death that is all around us, our hearts become defiled, and that Christ's death is God's remedy for this, as well as for all other sin. This is a very different sort of defilement from that for which provision was made in the other types of this group.

The *red heifer* probably has a special Jewish application in connection with the bloodguiltiness of the people on account of the death of their Messiah.

In Num. xix. it was to be used for individual cleansing, and was not instituted as a national ordinance, like the great Day of Atonement ; but the two prophetic passages which probably refer to this type seem to speak of it as a national cleansing, in connection with the future of Israel.

In Ezek. xxxvi. 24, 25, we read : "I will take you from among the heathen, and gather you out of all countries, and will bring you into your own land. Then will I sprinkle clean water upon you, and ye shall be clean"; and in Zech. xiii. 1, "In that day there shall be a fountain opened to the house of David, and to the inhabitants of Jerusalem, for sin and for uncleanness."

We have seen that the water of purification, which was used with the ashes of the red heifer, was for cleansing from defilement caused by contact with death. We are told by Haggai that Israel as a nation has thus become defiled before God. "Then said Haggai : If one that is unclean by a dead body touch any of these, shall it be unclean ? And the priests answered and said, It shall be unclean. Then answered Haggai, and said, So is this people, and so is this nation before Me, saith the Lord ; and so is every work of their hands ; and that which they offer there is unclean."

The people of Israel have become defiled because of the blood that they have shed. The same chapter of Ezekiel which tells of their being sprinkled with clean water, gives this as a reason for the pouring out of God's wrath upon them (Ezek. xxxvi. 18). The promise of the fountain opened " for separation for uncleanness," in Zech. xiii. 1, *marg.* (the very word used concerning the red heifer in Num. xix. 13), immediately follows the mention of the nation's guilt in having slain their Messiah ; for the closing verses of the twelfth chapter tell us of their looking upon Him whom they have pierced, and mourning for Him. Then we read, " In that day there shall be a fountain opened for the house of David, and to the inhabitants of Jerusalem." They had said, " His blood be on us and on our children " ; but He prayed, " Father, forgive them, for they know not what they do "—and here God makes provision for their cleansing from defilement.

If an individual had slain a man in battle, he needed the cleansing of the red heifer ; if he had but touched the dead body of any man that was dead and were not purified, we read " that soul shall be cut off from Israel, because the water of separation was not sprinkled upon him—he shall be unclean ; his uncleanness is yet upon him." Thus Israel as a nation has been cut off. " Unclean by reason of a dead body " (Num. ix. 10), they are unable to keep the passover feast ; but here is a fountain opened for separation for uncleanness. They were indeed the murderers of their Messiah ; they had themselves " pierced " Him, and no sacrifice in the Levitical offerings was provided for the sin of murder ; but He prayed, " Father, forgive them ; for they know not what they do." In the day when they look upon Him whom they have pierced, and mourn for Him, will He not, like Joseph, reassure His guilty brethren, and say to them, " So now it was not you that sent me hither, but God " ; telling them that it was God who smote Him, that it was He who had said, " Awake, O sword, against My Shepherd, and against the Man that is My Fellow " ?

In answer to the prayer of Moses, Miriam was healed from

her leprosy ; and though she was treated as unclean, her defilement was regarded as far less than that which she had really
contracted.   It may be, therefore, that in answer to the prayer
of the great Intercessor, of whom Moses was a type, Israel as
a nation, though cut off for a time, will be judged as unclean,
not as though they were murderers, but as though they had
merely been present at the death of their Messiah.

The inhabitants of Jerusalem are specially mentioned in
Zech. xiii. ; and we are reminded of the ceremonial enjoined in
Deut. xxi., where a dead body being found in the field, the
distances of the neighbouring cities were to be measured, and
the elders of the city next to the slain man were to take a
heifer and kill it in an uncultivated valley.   The heifer, like
that mentioned in Num. xix., was to be one which had not
been wrought with, and which had not drawn in the yoke.
Then " all the elders of that city, that are next unto the slain
man, shall wash their hands over the heifer that is beheaded in
the valley ; and they shall answer and say, Our hands have
not shed this blood, neither have our eyes seen it.   Be merciful,
O Lord, unto Thy people Israel, whom Thou hast redeemed,
and lay not innocent blood unto Thy people of Israel's charge.
And the blood shall be forgiven them.   So shalt thou put away
the guilt of innocent blood from among you, when thou shalt
do that which is right in the sight of the Lord " (vers. 6–9).   In
that day, the inhabitants of Jerusalem, the city next unto the
slain Man, will not be able to offer this plea, for their hands
have shed His blood ; but yet the fountain will be opened for
them, and they will be sprinkled with clean water.

It is very evident that in Israel's case, as in our own, the red
heifer aspect of the work of Christ will not supersede the sin
offering and trespass offering.   After the return of the people
to the land we have many references to the sacrifices ; and
mention is made of the passover, burnt-offerings, meal-offerings,
peace-offerings, sin-offerings, trespass-offerings, drink-offerings,
and firstfruits.   These are again to be offered ; and in

Ezek. xliv. 26 we have a suggestion of an individual use of the water of purification.

(5) *The cleansing of the leper.* Leprosy is always taken as a type of sin, and represents it under a terrible form ; for it was and is an incurable disease. It could only be removed by miraculous power ; so that the king of Israel when desired to heal Naaman exclaimed, "Am I God, to kill and to make alive?"

The various miracles of healing which our Lord performed during His public ministry bring before us the different aspects of the ruin wrought by sin and Satan, and show how Christ is able to overcome their power, undo their work, and restore that which He took not away. Three times He raised the dead, as a sign that His voice could reach those who were dead in trespasses and sins—natural death was but a picture of spiritual death. Palsy might be taken to represent the enfeeblement of sin ; fever, the restlessness and contagion of sin ; blindness, the ignorance of sin ; demoniacal possession, the enmity of sin ; deafness, inability to hear ; and dumbness, inability to testify. In the man with a withered hand we see inability to work ; in the impotent man inability to walk ; in the woman bowed down with the spirit of infirmity the degrading and depressing tendency of sin.

Many of these diseases are negative in character; but leprosy represents the corruption of sin, and speaks to us of its activity and progress. The two chapters in Leviticus (chapters xiii. and xiv.) are full of typical teaching ; but there is a great difference between the two. In the thirteenth chapter, the man who had something " like the plague of leprosy " must be brought to the priest, that he might pronounce whether it were leprosy or not. Various directions are given by which he could recognise the plague from that which was merely like it, the one great test being whether it spread or not. If after careful watching for some days it proved to be real leprosy, the man was pronounced unclean, and must dwell "without the camp." If the disease did not spread, or if it covered the whole body without there being any raw flesh (as in vers. 12, 13), the priest knew that it was not true leprosy; the man was clean, and needed only to wash his clothes. The ceremonial enjoined in Lev. xiv. was neither for the leper who is described in chapter xiii. 45, 46, nor for the man who was pronounced clean by the priest because not suffering from leprosy. These rites could not take away the plague, but were for one who had had leprosy and had been cured. They were for "the day of his cleansing," and implied his confession that he had been a leper, and that God had healed him (vers. 2, 3). A miracle must have taken place to change the man described in verses 45, 46 of the preceding chapter into the cleansed offerer of Lev. xiv. In the one he was smitten with a loathsome disease and dwelt alone—"without the camp"; in the latter, the leprosy having been healed, the priest comes to him "out of the camp," and after following the directions laid down for his cleansing, pronounces him clean, and presents him "before the Lord"—an expression which is used eight times in chapter xiv.

This chapter does not therefore seem to teach, as generally stated, that the application of Christ's death and resurrection can remove the leprosy of sin. This is brought before us elsewhere. The thought here is justification rather than forgiveness. The various sin offerings to which we have already alluded speak to us of the removal of the guilt of sin; this chapter tells us that the vilest sinner who is cleansed by Christ is made fit for the presence of the righteous God who "justifieth the ungodly." It is not enough for the sinner to be forgiven, he is also accounted righteous.

In the bird that was let fly over the field we have a beautiful picture of the resurrection and ascension of the Lord; and it is the only one of these seven types which seem to touch upon the resurrection. This is very significant if the leading thought of the chapter is justification—for He "was raised again for our justification."

It is remarkable that we have no record of the use of these rites till our Lord Himself came, and having cured the lepers, commanded them to go and show themselves to the priest, and offer for their cleansing "those things which Moses commanded, for a testimony unto them." Our Lord says, "Many lepers were in Israel in the time of Eliseus the prophet ; and none of them was cleansed, saving Naaman the Syrian "; and he would not heed the ceremonial cleansing required by the law of Moses. Other prophets may have had the God-given power, but we are not told of it ; and the very silence as to other cases of healed lepers emphasizes the fact that a miracle was needed to remove this terrible disease.

The laws commanded by Moses were at all times a testimony to God's hatred of corruption and defilement, and to the coming of the One by whose power alone the leper could be healed.

David, in Psalm li., probably alludes to this type, though it is often taken as referring to the "red heifer." He prays, " Purge me with hyssop, and I shall be clean ; wash me, and I shall be whiter than snow."

In both ceremonies the hyssop was used, and the water and the blood ; and in Lev. xiv. the blood was actually sprinkled on the unclean person. Leprosy made a man "white as snow" (2 Kings v. 27). David prayed that he might be cleansed, and thus figuratively become "whiter than snow." In the earlier verses of the Psalm he owns his corruption, and longs for the removal of his leprosy. In his confession he adds, " that Thou mightest be justified "; and we see here, as from the story of the publican in Luke xviii. 14, that when the sinner justifies God, God justifies the sinner.

The man that was a leper was to "dwell alone," as we have noticed; while the one to be cleansed was to be presented " before the Lord "; and thus David prays, " Cast me not away from Thy presence " (Psa. li. 11).

The oil touching the members and poured upon the head seems to be beautifully suggested in his prayer, " Make me to hear joy and gladness ; take not Thy Holy Spirit from me. Restore unto me the joy of Thy salvation ; and uphold me with Thy free Spirit." The oil of gladness and of the Holy Spirit rests upon those who have been " justified freely by His grace "; and by the mercies of God they are called upon to present their bodies " a living sacrifice."

In the case of the cleansed leper, the ear, the hand, and the foot, were to be touched ; but David felt that he needed the heart to be set right (ver. 10).

The cleansing of the leper had to be accompanied with sacrifices, " such as he is able to get " (Lev. xiv. 31) ; to which David seems to allude in Psa. li. 16, 17, 19. He would need the cleansing of the red heifer for slaying Goliath, and for all the other conquests which had been accompanied with bloodshed (1 Chron. xxviii. 3) ; but it would not meet the case of the murder of Uriah, nor bloodguiltiness—there was no provision for such guilt (Num. xxxv. 31) ; but David felt that his sin had made him unclean as a leper in God's sight.

(6) *The Laver.* The interpretation of the scene in the thirteenth of John is evidently the explanation of the laver ; and from our Lord's comment on His own act of washing the disciples' feet, we see that both were types of His provision for maintaining the communion of His people. The laver spoke of preparation for service and worship in the holy place. The priests had been washed already, and needed not save to wash their hands and feet. The disciples were clean, for they had been bathed, but could have no part in fellowship with their Lord unless their feet were washed. Is there not in these two a suggestion of a different dispensation ?—for the hands were not washed in John xiii. There is much of doing under the law ; whereas under grace all has been done for us ; and if the walk is right, the work will be acceptable.

There were very few directions for the construction of the laver. Its size is not given, nor the amount of water it contained. That which it typified was an unlimited provision. Eph. v. 25 is foreshadowed by the brazen altar, where " Christ

also loved the Church and gave Himself for it." The following verse gives the antitype of the laver, "That He might
sanctify and cleanse it with the washing of water by the Word";
while the twenty-seventh represents the Church by-and-by,
"that He might present it to Himself a glorious Church, not
having spot, or wrinkle, or any such thing": no longer in the
outer court, where the brazen altar and the laver stood, but in
the Holiest of all, "within the vail, whither the Forerunner is
for us entered."

The laver was made of mirrors (Exod. xxxviii. 8) and represented a mirror. There are two whom we see in the mirror of
God's Word: first ourselves, and then Himself. "As in water
the face is reflected (Prov. xxvii. 19), so in the living stream of
revealed truth a man sees his own image."

The apostle James tells us that "if any be a hearer of the
Word and not a doer, he is like unto a man beholding his
natural face in a mirror; for he beholdeth himself, and goeth
his way, and straightway forgetteth what manner of man he
was." Paul tells us in 1 Cor. xiii. 12 of another Face that we
may see in the same mirror; dimly it may be as yet, but as we
gaze we exclaim with the disciples of old, "What manner of
Man is this?" "Now we see in a mirror darkly, but then face
to face." In 2 Cor. iii. 18 he tells us the result of thus gazing.
"We all with open face beholding as in a glass [or reflecting as
in a mirror] the glory of the Lord [in the face of Jesus Christ,
ch. iv. 6] are changed into the same image from glory to glory."
We ourselves become mirrors to reflect His image.

Reference has already been made to the various meanings
of water; and we have seen that when its cleansing properties
are referred to, the Word is symbolized. "Now ye are clean
through the Word which I have spoken unto you." "Sanctify
them through Thy truth: Thy Word is truth." "Wherewithal
shall a young man cleanse his way? By taking heed thereto
according to Thy Word."

(7) The last on our list is the mitre of the high priest, with

its *plate of gold*, on which was inscribed, " Holiness to the Lord." In wearing this upon his forehead we read, he shall " bear the iniquity of the holy things which the children of Israel shall hallow in all their holy gifts ; and it shall be always upon his forehead, that they may be accepted before the Lord." In all our worship and all our service there is sin ; and we need our great High Priest to appear in the presence of God for us.

" Wherefore He is able also to save them to the uttermost that come unto God by Him, seeing He ever liveth to make intercession for them." The coming unto God here referred to is evidently the drawing near in worship, so often mentioned in Hebrews. We may come boldly ; but as the word " therefore," in Heb. iv. 16 teaches us, it is because *He* is without sin, not because *we* are.

As Dr. Bonar beautifully expresses it : " There is forgiveness, not only for our omissions of duty, but for our duties themselves ; not only for our prayerlessness, but for our prayers ; not only for our long rejection of Christ, but for our sins in coming to Him ; not only for our unbelief, but for our faith ; not only for our past enmity, but for our present cold-hearted love ; not only for the sins we bring to Christ, but for our way of bringing them ; not only for the sins we carried to the altar of burnt-offering and laid upon the bleeding sacrifice, but for our imperfect way of taking them, the impure motives that defiled our service, and also for the sins mingling with our worship when standing within the vail, in the sanctuary where the majesty of the Holy One has made its abode."

If there were more study of these seven types, we should not so often hear Christians saying that they were without sin ; for by means of these pictures we see how many forms of defilement there are, how abhorrent they are to God, and yet how He has wonderfully provided for all in the Lord Jesus Christ. We shall never get beyond the need of this provision till we awake in His likeness.

X

The Offerings

THE method of placing several types side by side is a Scriptural one, as we see from the opening chapters of Leviticus. The Holy Spirit has Himself adopted this plan here, and has given us a wondrous group representing the work and person of our Lord in various aspects.

Many have written on the Offerings; and those who have studied them most would probably agree that they are only just beginning to see their beauty. " Jesus Christ and Him crucified " is the subject that they bring before us; and it seems strange that any Bible-loving Christian should be content to leave these pages of the Book unexplored.

The study of the Offerings is a great safeguard against confused views on holiness, sanctification, sin, etc. It is impossible to have a low estimate of what sin really is, as we study God's requirements, and the provision He has made.

No survey of the types would be complete without a glance, at least, into this inexhaustible store of treasures; and therefore a few thoughts are here given, which have been gathered from many sources, and which have proved helpful in the study. Several points have already been alluded to in preceding chapters.

The order of the Offerings in Leviticus is from the Godward aspect. First there is the Burnt-offering; then the Meat or Meal-offering; the Peace-offering; the Sin-offering; and the Trespass-offering. When as sinners we come to God, it is in the opposite order that we catch glimpses of the various aspects of the work of Christ. We first learn that we need forgiveness for definite acts of sin which we have committed, and our need is met by the Trespass-offering; then we learn not only that we have sinned again and again, but that we have an evil nature; yet that God has made provision for this in the Sin-offering. Next we are taught to enter into the meaning of the Peace-

85

A Study of the Levitical Offerings

THE OFFERING	CONSISTED OF	GOD'S PART ON THE BRAZEN ALTAR	PRIESTS' PORTION	TYPICAL OF THE LORD JESUS	REFERENCES
Burnt-Offering	Bullocks, goats, sheep, rams, lambs, turtle-doves, young pigeons	All burned	Skin	In His life and death, perfectly accomplishing the will of God.	Leviticus i. ; Leviticus vi. 8-13; Ephesians ii. 1-6; Hebrews x. 7
Meal-Offering	Fine flour, green ears, frankincense, oil, salt	A handful, part of oil, all frankincense, all priests' offering	All remainder	As Man, presenting to God an un-blemished life	Leviticus ii. ; Leviticus vi. 14-23; Hebrews vii. 26
Peace-Offering	Male and female of herd and flock, bullocks, lambs, goats	All the fat	Heave-shoulder, and wave-breast	By His death becom-ing our peace and the ground of com-munion	Leviticus iii. ; Leviticus vii. 11-13; Romans v. 1 ; Colossians i. 20
Sin-Offering	Male and female of herd and flock, or turtle-doves, young pigeons, $\frac{1}{10}$ ephah of flour	All the fat, blood at the bottom of altar (and on horns of incense altar).	Offering where blood was not taken into Taber-nacle	On the Cross made sin for us	Leviticus iv. ; Leviticus vi. 24-30 ; 2 Corinthians v. 21
Trespass-Offering				By His sacrifice be-coming answerable for sins and trans-gressions against God and man.	Leviticus v. ; Leviticus vi. 1-7; Leviticus vii. 1-7; Colossians ii. 13, 14; 1 Peter ii. 24

offering and Meal-offering, and to feast upon them. And, lastly, we see the Burnt-offering aspect of Christ and His work, and are taught something of what He is to God ; and our standing in Christ, " accepted in the Beloved."

The work of Christ is one ; and although the Offerings fore shadow its different aspects, they are closely allied to one another. Thus in the case of the Burnt-offering and Sin-offering, both sacrifices were slain in the same place, viz., by the brazen altar (Lev. vi. 25) ; the fat of the Sin-offering was burned upon the Burnt-offering (iv. 19) ; and the remainder of the Sin-offering was burned on the spot where the ashes of the Burnt-offering had been poured out (iv. 12 ; vi. 11) ; while the offerer in both instances laid his hand on the head of the animal at the door of the Tabernacle of the congregation, or rather, the Tent of meeting.

There is no mention of sin in the Burnt-offering, for it speaks of justification rather than forgiveness ; and thus is a fore-shadowing of the truth of Acts xiii. 39, " By Him, all that believe are justified from all things " ; while the Sin-offering aspect of the work of Christ is the preceding verse, " Be it known unto you therefore, men and brethren, that through this Man is preached unto you the forgiveness of sins." In the Burnt-offering God views the sinner, in Christ, as justified, or as though he had not sinned ; and in the Sin-offering He makes provision for his guilt.

While the thought of sin is not brought before us in the Burnt-offering, it is implied indirectly in the fact of our need of acceptance. We read, " it shall be accepted for him, to make atonement for him." *Atonement* means " covering," and the need of this covering implies sin ; but being covered by Christ, " Who of God is made unto us . . . righteousness," we are viewed as righteous. " The Lord our Righteousness " means much more than the mere so-called imputed righteousness of Christ. It is not merely that His devotedness, His law-keeping, His obedience, is put down to our account, but that God sees us in Him in all His perfectness.

The animals offered for Burnt-offerings might be taken from the herd or the flock. The people might offer bullocks, sheep, goats, turtle doves, or young pigeons ; the variety is generally taken to denote the different measure of spiritual appreciation with which we view Christ as our Burnt-offering. Though our want of appreciation may interfere with our enjoyment, we are blessed according to God's estimate of His excellency, not according to our own ; and for each one a whole Christ is needed. Strength characterizes the bullock (Prov. xiv. 4) ; submission the lamb (Isa. liii. 7) ; and mourning innocence the dove (Isa. lix. 11 ; xxxviii. 14 ; Matt. x. 16).

When the Burnt-offering was from the herd or the flock, the priests had to cut it up and lay it in order upon the altar. Each part was examined by them. Mr. Spurgeon, speaking of Heb. xii. 2, said that "Looking unto Jesus" might be read "Looking into Jesus"; and he compares it with the duty of the priests in connection with the Burnt-offering : as we gaze we see more and more how entirely Christ was well-pleasing to the Father. The head is generally taken to represent the intelligence, the thoughts ; the fat, the general health and vigour, or excellency ; the inwards, the motives and affections; and the legs, the walk.

Lev. i. 9 speaks of washing in water : this would seem to refer to testing by the Word. In whatever way Christ is tested or examined His excellencies are revealed.

The ashes of the Burnt-offering were first placed at the east end of the altar (Lev. i. 16) ; and the ashes spoke of accepted sacrifice. In the twentieth Psalm David prays, " The Lord hear thee in the day of trouble. . . . Remember all thy offerings, and accept [or, as we read in the margin, "turn to ashes"] thy burnt sacrifice." God showed His acceptance of the offering by sending the fire ; and the ashes proved that the fire had said, " It is enough" (Prov. xxx. 16). The fire did its work on Calvary. God is satisfied ; and we take our stand now and throughout eternity, like the priests in 2 Chron. v. 12, at the place of the ashes, the place of accepted sacrifice.

The Tabernacle faced east and west; and the place of the ashes, the point nearest the entrance, was toward the east, while the mercy-seat was toward the west.

Is there not a tabernacle interpretation to that familiar passage in Psa. ciii. 12 ? Primarily, it speaks of the measureless distance between the east and the west, in the infinitude of space, as it tells us that, " As far as the east is from the west, so far hath He removed our transgressions from us"; but is there not also an infinite distance between our position as sinners, coming to the tabernacle for the first time, and standing by the brazen altar at the place of the ashes, and the position we occupy when with boldness we enter through the vail into the Holiest of all, and approach the throne of grace ? As far as the place of the ashes is from the mercy-seat, so far hath He removed our transgressions from us.

There is a beautiful description of a scene in the time of Hezekiah when the Burnt-offering was offered amidst a rejoicing and worshipping multitude. " When the Burnt-offering began, the song of the Lord began, . . and all the congregation worshipped, and the singers sang, and the trumpeters sounded; and all this continued until the Burnt-offering was finished."

To see the Lord Jesus Christ as the Burnt-offering is sure to bring joy to our hearts; and when He came down to do the will of God a chorus of praise began in heaven, which was heard even upon earth. It is described in the Gospel of Luke, where we read that a multitude of the heavenly host were heard " praising God and saying, Glory to God in the highest, and on earth peace, good-will toward men"; or, as in the Revised Version, " peace among men in whom He is well pleased."

The Burnt-offering was perfectly acceptable to God, and in Him men could find favour. The heavenly host could not sing as redeemed ones, or praise because they were thus accepted; but there was joy in the presence of the angels when the good Shepherd voluntarily went forth. "All this continued until the Burnt-offering was finished"; and we can catch an echo of the shouts of triumph that rang through heaven when He returned, as we read the exultant words in Psa. xxiv., "Lift up your heads, O ye gates, and be ye lift up, ye everlasting doors, and the King of glory shall come in. Who is this King of glory? The Lord, strong and mighty, the Lord mighty in battle." The battle was over; the Burnt-offering had been accepted. By-and-by the everlasting doors will open a second time, as in the Psalm, and the King of glory will enter—not alone, but accompanied by all those who had seen Him as the Lamb of God. "Who is this King of glory? The Lord of hosts—He is the King of glory."

In the Meat-offering, or the Meal-offering, there is no mention of death as such, for it speaks rather of the spotless life of Christ as presented to God. We have seen that His sufferings are expressed in the bruising, beating, and crushing, needed to prepare the various substances that were offered.

One of the chief lessons taught by the Meal and Peace-offerings is, that while a portion was burned upon the altar, the priests were permitted to feed upon the remainder. They fed on that in which God delighted—"the bread of God," as it is termed (Lev. xxi. 6, 8, 17, 21, 22; xxii. 25). In the Peace-offering two portions are specially mentioned as the food of the priests—the heave shoulder, and the wave breast (Lev. vii. 31–34). The shoulder indicates the place of strength, and the breast the place of affection; and these two are particularly the food of the believer. The two thoughts are often linked together. The high priest bore the names of the children of Israel upon his shoulders, and in the breast-plate upon his heart (Exod. xxviii. 12, 29), reminding us of how we too repose on the shoulders of His strength and the breast of His never-dying love. "He shall gather the lambs with His arm, and carry them in His bosom" (Isa. xl. 11). "The beloved of the Lord . . shall dwell between His shoulders" (Deut. xxxiii. 12). He says, "I have strength" and "I love" (Prov. viii. 14, 17); and "He is mighty in strength and heart" (*marg.*, Job xxxvi. 5); while the Apostle Paul's two prayers for the Ephesians are characterized by these thoughts. The prayer in the first chapter is that they may know the *power* ; in the third chapter that they may know the *love*.

The subject of feeding upon Christ as typified by the offerings is a very full one.

In Lev. xxii. 4 we read that a leper, or one with a blemish, might not eat of them. If there be known sin, there can be no fellowship and no feeding. The prodigal in the far country remembered the food in his father's house, and said, " How many hired servants of my father's have bread enough and to spare, and I perish with hunger ! "

One who was unclean must wait till the evening sacrifice had been offered. " When the sun is down he shall be clean, and shall afterward eat of the holy things " (Lev. xxii. 7) ; but it would thus be in the twilight, not in sunshine—the brightness would be gone. Is it not often so with us ? When having lost communion we have been restored, and may feed once more, the brightness is dimmed for a time, and we seem to be feeding in the twilight instead of in the full sunshine.

It was the privilege of all the priests to eat of the offerings, " one as much as another " (Lev. vii. 10) ; " Of His fulness have all we received." There was to be a daily portion " due for every day " ; and when in the time of Hezekiah the temple worship was purified and revived, the priests and the Levites confessed, " We have had enough to eat, and have left plenty " (2 Chron. xxxi. 10). This, too, is our experience in our Father's house. There is " bread enough and to spare " ; and like Paul, we can say, we " have all and abound."

Lev. xxii. 10 tells us of some in the household of the priest who might not eat—no stranger (compare Eph. ii. 12, 19), or sojourner (see 1 John ii. 19), or a hired servant (John xv. 15). The prodigal knew that there was a great difference between the position of a hired servant and a son ; but when his father received him as a son, and said, " This my son," he could not, as he had intended, ask to be made as one of the hired servants.

The next verse tells us of two classes who might have their

portion. " If the priest buy any soul with his money, he shall eat of it " (compare 1 Cor. vi. 20 ; 1 Pet. i. 18, 19 ; and Acts xx. 28) ; " and he that is born in his house : they shall eat of his meat " (compare 1 Pet. i. 23 and 1 Pet. ii. 2).

The Sin-offering and Trespass-offering differed from the others in that the body of the animal was burned, not on the brazen altar, but outside the camp. Everything burned upon the altar of Burnt-offering was a sweet savour to God ; but He hid His face from the Lord Jesus as the Sin-offering, and it was then that He cried, " My God, My God, why hast Thou forsaken Me ? " Even as the Sin-offering He was still well-pleasing to God ; and this is expressed by the fat of the Sin-offering being consumed upon the altar of Burnt-offering.

In Lev. iv. there are Sin-offerings mentioned for four classes of people : for the priest, the whole congregation, a ruler, and one of the common people ; and they probably speak to us of the provision that has been made by God to meet sin in our various relationships. Thus " the Sin-offering for the priest would meet sin in our position as priests before God ; that for the whole congregation would represent our collective position as the assembly of God ; that for the ruler, our position relative to those whom we may influence ; and that for one of the common people, our individual position."

In the first two, the Sin-offering for the priest and that for the congregation, the blood was taken into the holy place, sprinkled seven times in front of the vail, then put upon the horns of the golden altar, and the remainder poured out at the bottom of the brazen altar. " The blood sprinkled before the vail re-established God's relationship with His people, the vail covering the place where God met with them ; the blood on the golden altar re-established the worship of the assembly ; and the blood at the brazen altar re-established the individual communion—all of which had been interrupted by sin."

In the Trespass-offering, where the trespass was against the Lord, the sacrifice preceded reparation (Lev. v. 15, 16) ; where the trespass was against man, reparation preceded sacrifice (vi. 5, 6).

A very interesting study is to classify the passages referring to the work of Christ according to their different aspects and the offerings appropriate to them.

Thus in Isa. liii. we have all the Offerings; the Burnt-offering in verse 11, "By His knowledge shall My righteous servant justify many"; the Peace-offering in verse 5, "The chastisement of our peace was upon Him"; the Sin-offering in verses 6, 10, 12, "The Lord hath laid on Him the iniquity of us all," "When Thou shalt make His soul an offering for sin," and, "He hath poured out His soul unto death"—for in the Sin-offering the blood was poured out at the bottom of the altar. The Sin-offering on the great Day of Atonement, when the scapegoat bore away the guilt of the people, is suggested in verses 11 and 12: "He shall bear their iniquities," and, "He bare the sin of many." The Trespass-offering is in verse 5, "He was wounded for our transgressions, He was bruised for our iniquities"; and there is the bruising of the fine flour for the Meal-offering in verses 3 and 10, "He is despised and rejected of men, a Man of sorrows and acquainted with grief," and, "It pleased the Lord to bruise Him."

In the first chapter of John's Epistle we seem to have set before us the five-fold view of the work of Christ in the same order as in the Offerings, beginning, as in Leviticus i., with the Godward side, and ending with the provision for our sinfulness. In verses 1 to 3 we have the Burnt-offering aspect, the offering that was all upon God's altar, of which the priests might not partake, but which they could only look upon and their hands handle. In verses 3 to 7 there is the thought of fellowship and joy: as in the Meal-offering and Peace-offering, the priest partook of "the food of the offering," "the bread of his God," so we can say, "Truly our fellowship is with the Father, and with His Son Jesus Christ." And in verses 7 to 10 we have God's provision for sin and sins, as typified by the Sin-offering and the Trespass-offering.

The following passages, amongst others, would give us also the Burnt-offering aspect of the Lord's life and work—those that speak of His perfectly doing the will of His Father, Matt. xxvi. 39 ; John iv. 34 ; and Heb. x. 7 ; of His voluntary offering, John x. 11, 15, 17 ; xv. 13 ; Heb. ix. 14 ; x. 10 ; Isa. l. 5, 6 ; of His obedience, Rom. v. 19 ; Phil. ii. 5–8 ; and of our acceptance, Eph. i. 6 ; and 1 Pet. ii. 5.

Many verses tell of Him as the Meal-offering—such as those that speak of His perfect and suffering life, of His preciousness to God, of His being anointed with the Holy Spirit, and being entirely under His guidance, etc.

Christ as the Peace-offering is brought before us in Col. i. 20 ; Eph. ii. 13–17 ; feeding in communion on the Peace-offering in John vi. 51–57 ; and in 1 Cor. x. 16 ; and offering the Peace-offering in 2 Cor. ix. 15 ; Heb. xiii. 15 ; for it was the thanksgiving sacrifice.

The Sin-offering aspect is constantly referred to, where the Lord Jesus is spoken of as " being made a curse for us " (Gal. iii. 13) ; afflicted by God (Lam. i. 12 ; iii. 1–19 ; Psa. xxii.) ; and a sacrifice for sin (John i. 29 ; Rom. v. 8 ; viii. 3 ; 2 Cor. v. 21 ; 1 Tim. i. 15 ; Heb. x. 18 ; 1 John i. 7).

We see Him as the Trespass-offering where we read of trespasses put away (Col. ii. 13, 14 ; 2 Cor. v. 19) ; sins forgiven (Matt. xxvi. 28 ; Eph. i. 7 ; Col. i. 14) ; and an offering for sins (1 Cor. xv. 3 ; Gal. i. 4 ; Heb. x. 12 ; 1 Pet. ii. 24 ; iii. 18 ; Matt. i. 21 ; Psa. xl. 12).

The Burnt-offering and Peace-offering may both be represented in Eph. v. 2. " An offering and a sacrifice to God for a sweet-smelling savour," for both were a sweet-smelling savour to God. The word *sacrifice* in Leviticus usually refers to the Peace-offering.

The four offerings are indicated in Heb. x. and Psa. xl. " Sacrifice and offering Thou didst not desire ; . . . Burnt-offering and Sin-offering hast Thou not required."

XI

Typical Colors and Substances

THOSE who have made any study of the types will not doubt that there was a meaning in the colours which Moses and the children of Israel were commanded to use in the construction of the Tabernacle. Where God told them to use blue, and purple, and scarlet, there was some significance in those shades ; and green and yellow would not have answered the same purpose.

The embroidered curtains really formed the Tabernacle itself. Beneath were the "boards of the tabernacle," above were the goats' hair curtains forming "the tent," which was "spread abroad over the Tabernacle"; and they evidently speak of the glories of the Lord Jesus Christ under different aspects.

The meanings of the colours are not clearly stated ; so that with regard to some of them there is a slight difference of opinion. All however seem to agree that _the blue_ speaks of heaven, and here refers to the heavenly character of our Lord— the One who came from heaven, has gone back into heaven, but who was, even when here on earth, the heavenly One.

Some think that _the scarlet_ refers to suffering ; others that this is represented by _the red_ in the "rams' skins dyed red," and that the scarlet in the embroidered curtains refers to earthly glory, the glory of a worm ; for it was obtained from the worm, and the Hebrew word is the same (Psa. xxii. 6 ; Job xxv. 6). Others again think it speaks of earthly glory in connection with Israel, scarlet representing the national colour. Those who hold this view, take _the purple_ to represent His Kingly glory, especially as Son of Man, over the whole world. Several passages bear out this interpretation. Purple is often mentioned in connection with the trade and wealth of Gentile powers : Lydia was a seller of purple ; and the robes in which Daniel and Mordecai were arrayed were purple robes.

The scarlet line from Rahab's window may have represented the national colour of Israel ; and we are told that the scape-goat, when it bare away into the wilderness the guilt of the nation, had a piece of scarlet tied to one of its horns.   Only one piece of Tabernacle furniture had a covering of scarlet when carried from place to place, viz., the table of shewbread ; the one which had so clearly a reference to Israel in the twelve loaves that were laid upon it.   Only one had a purple covering, and that is equally suggestive.   The brazen altar was not for Israel only, for the death of the Lord Jesus was for all the world.   We do not read in John iii. 16, " God so loved *Israel* that He gave His only begotten Son " ; but, " God so loved *the world.*"   The purple covering linked with the altar of Burnt-offering speaks to us of " the sufferings of Christ and . . . the glory that shall be revealed."   The world last saw Him as the suffering Man on the cross of Calvary ; they will next see Him as the Son of Man coming in His glory.

The *fine twined linen*, of which the curtains were made, is interpreted for us in Revelation, where we are told that the fine linen, clean and white, in which the Lamb's wife is arrayed, is the righteousness of the saints.   Here it would refer to the righteousness of the Lamb Himself.

If the above meanings are correct, we have a four-fold view of our Lord corresponding with the aspects which characterize the four Gospels.

Matthew tells us of the Son of David, symbolized by the scarlet.*

Mark, the perfect Servant—by the fine linen.

Luke, the Son of Man—represented by the purple.

John, the Son of God—by the blue.

---

* It is remarkable that in this Gospel the robe in which our Lord was arrayed is described as a scarlet robe.

Though we cannot be certain of the significance of these colours, we may be sure that there was some teaching in them; and that it is well for us to search, with the help of other Scriptures and the guidance of the Holy Spirit, into His object in thus making use of them.

The same applies to many substances which evidently have a typical meaning, not a few of them being interpreted for us either directly or indirectly. The minute instructions in connection with the Offerings, and the Tabernacle and Temple, indicate their importance. In the latter, the *gold*, *silver*, and *brass* had each its place. We have seen that *gold* represents the Divine. The *silver* used was the redemption money; and therefore we may conclude that silver speaks of redemption; and that thus the Tabernacle, on its sockets of silver, stood on "redemption ground." The *brass*, or copper, is generally taken to represent judgment; for brass is that which can stand the fire. " His feet were like unto fine brass, as if they burned in a furnace" (Rev. i. 15). In the Tabernacle it surrounded everything, and was the basis for the whole; for all the outer court stood upon brazen sockets. The altar of burnt-offering and the laver were made of brass, and each of these is connected with the thought of judgment.

There were five substances mentioned in connection with the meal-offering. Three were commanded, and two were forbidden. Oil, frankincense, and salt, accompanied the sacrifice; but leaven and honey were not to be presented. *Oil* had to be poured on all the meal-offerings, telling of the presence and power of the Holy Spirit, so constantly spoken of in connection with the life of our Lord (see Matt. i. 20; Isa. xi. 2; Luke i. 35; iii. 22; iv. 1, 14; Acts x. 38; Psa. xlv. 7; lxxxix. 19, 20; Isa. lxi. 1). We, too, need the oil in every part of our lives. We need it on our head as the anointing oil; on our ears, hands, and feet, consecrating us to His service; in our hands in worship, as we bring the meal-offering to God; on our feet, the feet dipped in oil (Deut. xxxiii. 24), that our walk may show that we are indeed guided by the Holy Spirit (Rom. viii. 14 ; Gal. v. 16, 25) ; and we need the oil for our wounds, to comfort and to heal. " There is treasure to be desired, and oil in the dwelling of the wise," we read in Prov. xxi. 20 ; and in many other places in the Word we may learn lessons from the oil as a type of the Holy Spirit, as to the conditions for the filling of the Spirit, "empty vessels," etc. (2 Kings iv. 3), and the result, beauty (Hos. xiv. 6), and honour (Judges ix. 9).

The *frankincense* in the meal-offering was all burned upon the altar ; it all belonged to God, and speaks to us of " the preciousness of Him whose "Name is as ointment poured forth," and of whom it is written, " All Thy garments smell of myrrh, and aloes, and cassia."

Salt was to be present in the meal-offering ; for while leaven and honey cause corruption, salt is that which prevents it, and may therefore be looked upon as typifying judgment upon and testimony against sin. " Let your speech be alway with grace, seasoned with salt," would thus mean that though we are to be gracious and kind, it is not to be at the expense of faithfulness. We are not to wink at sin, but to reprove it. It is often easier to take no notice of what is said in our presence ; but there is to be salt as well as grace, and this was always noticeable in our Lord's life and conversation. In the Revised Version we read that the incense described in Exod. xxx. 34–38 was " seasoned with salt." " Have salt in yourselves, and have peace one with another," was the Lord's command ; and if, as one has said, we judge ourselves, we shall be less likely to see faults in others.

Leaven evidently denotes evil, and so could not be present in that which represented Him who was " in all points tempted like as we are, yet without sin." There was to be no leaven in the house of the Israelite at the passover (Exod. xii. 15 ; Deut. xvi. 4) ; and probably this is the reason that in John xviii. 28, we read that the priests and the Pharisees would not go into the judgment hall lest they should be defiled, for the house of a Gentile would contain leaven. Christ speaks again and again of the leaven of the Pharisees, Sadducees, and Herodians (Matt. xvi. 6, 11, 12 ; Mark viii. 15 ; Luke xii. 1) ; and in Matt. xiii. 33 He compares the kingdom of heaven to three measures of meal, into which leaven has been cast till the whole has been leavened. This is often taken to represent the power of the Gospel working in the world till the whole is converted ; but by comparing the passage with the other mentions of leaven it is very evident that it refers to the working of an evil principle, such as we read of in 2 Thess. ii. 7, which has so permeated the whole of Christendom that it is impossible to divide between the good and the evil : " The mystery of iniquity doth already work." The Apostle Paul adopts the same simile, and twice says, " A little leaven leaveneth the whole lump " ; referring in 1 Cor. v. 6, to evil walk, and in Gal. v. 9, to evil doctrine.

Lev. ii. 12 tells us that the oblation of the firstfruits was not to be burned on the altar ; and this is explained by Lev. xxiii. 17, which states that leaven was present. Two offerings of firstfruits were to be brought and waved before the Lord : the one mentioned in verses 10, 11 ; the second, after fifty days, in verse 17 ; and these two were evidently typical of " Christ the firstfruits ; afterward they that are Christ's, at His coming "— the sheaf referring to the Lord's resurrection, and the two wave-loaves, baken with leaven, to " them that are Christ's at His coming " (1 Cor. xv. 23). Hence the presence of the leaven, which is met by the sin-offering in verse 19. The sheaf of the firstfruits required no sin-offering, because there was no leaven.

There is one mention of leaven in connection with the peace-offering (Lev. vii. 13, 14), in the thanksgiving sacrifice, teaching that even our holiest things are mixed with sin ; and here again the leaven is met by blood.

There was to be no *honey* in the offerings. Honey seems generally to typify the sweetness of human nature, and could not be acceptable to God. Prov. xxv. 27 says, " It is not good to eat much honey ; so for men to search their own glory is not glory"; and Prov. xxvii. 7 tells us that "the full soul loatheth an honeycomb" (*marg.*, treadeth under foot); and it well describes the attitude of the heart that is satisfied with Christ, towards worldly amusements, pleasures, glory, etc. We are often asked if this or that is wrong; but the question is rather, Are we satisfied with Christ? If so, the other is distasteful to us; we do not want it. There are two things lying all around us in our pathway—the manna and the honey—and we must stoop to pick up the one, and trample under foot the other. The manna was just as sweet as the honey, for "the taste of it was like wafers made with honey" (Exod. xvi. 31): and so the Word is said to be "sweeter also than honey and the honeycomb"; and again the Psalmist says, "How sweet are Thy words unto my taste! yea, sweeter than honey to my mouth."

There are some things which have *various meanings*; and care must be taken to notice the connection in order to ascertain what the meaning is. This has already been referred to in the case of water, which, we have seen, sometimes symbolizes the Word, sometimes the Holy Spirit; or again may tell of death and judgment, the weakness of man, or the unrest and turmoil of the nations—according to the different qualities to which reference is made.

In the same way *fire* has many applications. It represents *God's presence*, as on Mount Horeb, in the burning bush, and at the giving of the law, and as in the pillar of fire which guided Israel through the wilderness. When fire fell upon a sacrifice it denoted *acceptance*. It was probably by fire that God testified to Abel's gift, and it fell on the altar of burnt-offering, in Lev. ix. 24, and also on the offerings of Gideon, David, Solomon, and Elijah. The fire that consumed what was placed on the altar of burnt-offering, as well as the fire which was taken from it to the golden altar, did not speak of judgment, but of favour; for the sacrifices on both rose to God as a sweet smelling savour.

The thought of *judgment* is in the fire that consumed the sin-offering outside the camp. The words used for burning are different ; for while the one referring to the altar of burnt-offering means burning as incense, the other denotes consuming in wrath—see Lev. iv. 19, 21.

(1) Here therefore we have the fire of judgment on the substitute, as also probably in the paschal lamb that was roast with fire.

(2) Fire fell in judgment on the wicked—on Sodom ; on Egypt in Exod. ix. 23, 24; on Nadab and Abihu; on the camp of Israel in Num. xi. 1, and at Korah's rebellion ; and upon Ahaziah's messengers to Elijah. The difference between these two kinds of fire is clearly shown in Lev. ix. 24, and x. 2. In both cases we read, "there came" or "went a fire out from before the Lord"; but in the one it was as a mark of favour and acceptance of the burnt-offering, in the other it was a terrible visitation of judgment.

(3) Israel will have to pass through the fire of judgment (Zech. xiii. 6–9 ; Isa. iv. 4 ; and Matt. iii. 11, 12). We read in the last passage, "He shall baptize you with the Holy Ghost, and with fire : whose fan is in His hand, and He will throughly purge His floor, and gather His wheat into the garner ; but He will burn up the chaff with unquenchable fire." The baptism of fire in the one verse is probably explained in the following. He will purge His floor by the wind, and consume the chaff with the fire. To baptize with the Holy Ghost and with fire, cannot mean one and the same thing ; and in the beginning of Acts i. the fire is omitted. "Ye shall be baptized with the Holy Ghost not many days hence." The baptism of fire is still future for Israel.

(4) The fire of judgment will fall on His enemies at the Lord's coming to the earth (2 Thess. i. 8 ; Isa. x. 16, 17 ; and Isa. lxvi. 15, 16).

(5) It will destroy those who are incited to rebellion by Satan after the Millennium.

(6) We read of the fire of eternal judgment.

There are, however, still several things which are symbolized by fire. " God's *Word* is as a fire," as we are told three times in Jeremiah, v. 14 ; xx. 9 ; xxiii. 29 ; then there is the refining *fire of trial*, Mal. iii. 2 ; 1 Pet. i. 7, by means of which God can "take away the dross from the silver, and there shall come forth a vessel for the finer " ; and, lastly, there is the fire which shall *test believers' works* at the judgment-seat of Christ, when everything shall be tried by fire, and when only that which " may abide the fire " will be preserved.

" *The cloven tongues* like as of fire " may have symbolized the Holy Spirit ; but there do not seem to be other passages which distinctly state that fire is typical of the Spirit, though it is through His indwelling that God's presence is a reality, and through His influence that God's Word becomes as fire, and trial does its refining work.   It is not, however, safe to take all the above mentions of fire and refer them indiscriminately to the work of the Holy Spirit.   This is sometimes done, and thus passages are made to teach something quite different from their primary meaning.

XII

The Garments of the Believer

MANY typical incidents which have one feature in common may be linked together into helpful Bible studies. For instance, the Word is full of instructions to believers as to the garments which they are to put off, and those which they are to put on; and these are beautifully illustrated by many Scripture scenes.

They divide themselves into three classes: those that speak to us of man-made garments, God-given garments, and Spirit-wrought garments. The first we are to put off; the second God puts upon us; and the third the Spirit works through us.

Satan, in the garden of Eden, stripped man of his robe of innocency, and left him naked and unfit for God's presence. We have this in the tenth of Luke, in the parable of the man who went down from Jerusalem to Jericho and "fell among thieves, which stripped him of his raiment, and wounded him, and departed, leaving him half dead." He was on his downward road, with his back on the place of blessing, going towards the place of the curse, and he lay thus by the roadside—a picture of man's helpless condition, after Satan had done his work, stripped him, wounded him, and left him to die. In the story of the demoniac we have another illustration of this. When the Lord met him he "ware no clothes, neither abode in any house, but in the tombs," the place of death; but when the devils had been cast out, he was found "at the feet of Jesus, clothed, and in his right mind."

When Adam and Eve found out their condition, they at once tried to remedy it—"The eyes of them both were opened, and they knew that they were naked; and they sewed fig-leaves together, and made themselves aprons." They probably thought, as so many of their descendants have since done, that they were doing "their best." The *margin* reads, "Things to gird about "—how different from the girdle of truth which God provides ! Those fig-leaves were but a picture of themselves ; for, plucked from the parent stem, death had set in, and though for a time they might remain glossy and beautiful, they would soon be withered and dead. The fig-leaf aprons were not sufficient to make them fit for God's presence ; and when they heard God's voice and hid themselves from Him, they still felt that they were naked. So it is always with the garments that man makes for himself, though Satan would persuade him that he is well clad. "Ye clothe you," says Haggai, "but there is none warm " ; and we read in Isa. lix. 6, "Their webs shall not become garments, neither shall they cover themselves with their works," for "All our righteousnesses are as filthy rags."

Though we have this sad picture of man's condition in Gen. iii., the chapter does not close without the Holy Spirit telling us of God's remedy. "Unto Adam also, and to his wife, did the Lord God make coats of skins, and clothed them." With the first dress, the fig-leaf aprons, God had nothing to do ; and with these coats of skins man had nothing to do. They were entirely provided by God, and spoke of Christ Himself, "the Lord our righteousness," who becomes indeed our robe of righteousness as we obey the command, "Put ye on the Lord Jesus Christ."

These coats of skins remind us of one of the laws of the burnt-offering in Leviticus, which ordained that "the priest that offereth any man's burnt-offering, even the priest shall have to himself the skin of the burnt-offering which he hath offered." The burnt-offering represented, as we have seen, the Godward aspect of Christ's work in all its perfect accep-tance ; an offering and a sacrifice to God for a sweet-smelling savour. The priests might not partake—it was all for God, all consumed on the altar ; but Aaron's sons presented it, and to them belonged the skin, in which they might clothe themselves —a beautiful figure of the standing of the believer as "accepted in the Beloved."

The change of raiment that is needed by each of us is illustrated by several Bible incidents. We do not read that Adam and Eve put the coats of skins over their fig-leaf aprons. They had surely done with the latter for ever. When the prodigal returned to his father's home and the father said to the servants, " Bring forth the best robe, and put it on him ; and put a ring on his hand, and shoes on his feet," the best robe was not put over the rags in which he returned ; they were no longer needed.

We read in the story of Bartimæus that when he had heard the glad message, " Be of good comfort, rise, He calleth thee, he, casting away his garment, rose, and came to Jesus." His beggar's cloak would have hindered him from quickly answering that call—just as man's fancied righteousness often keeps him from Christ. Elisha, when Elijah had been carried up to heaven, "took hold of his own clothes and rent them in two pieces," and then "took up also the mantle of Elijah that fell from him "—-the token of the prophetic office, and the symbol of its power. Casting away his own garment, the last relic of the old life, he took up Elijah's mantle, and went forth in his power.

Man is often inclined to try and patch up the old rags, and put on "some of self and some of Thee" ; but Christ's parable tells us how useless this is. "No man putteth a piece of a new garment upon an old ; if otherwise, then both the new maketh a rent, and the piece that was taken out of the new agreeth not with the old." The garment which God gives " agreeth " not with the " filthy rags."

Man-made garments, as one has said, are thus described in Scripture : "original, but not sufficient (Gen. iii. 7) ; natural, but not clean (Zech. iii.) ; smart, but useless (Isa. lxiv. 6) ; and mended, but made worse (Mark ii. 21)."

Joshua, the high priest, when he stood before the angel of the Lord, needed a change of raiment. " Now Joshua was clothed with filthy garments and stood before the angel. And He answered and spake unto those that stood before Him, saying, Take away the filthy garments from him. And unto him he said, Behold, I have caused thine iniquity to pass from thee, and I will clothe thee with change of raiment. And I said, Let them set a fair mitre upon his head. So they set a fair mitre upon his head, and clothed him with garments."

Released captives do not continue to wear their prison garments. Joseph, when called to stand before Pharaoh and brought hastily out of the dungeon, changed his raiment; and when the king of Babylon released Jehoiachin from prison, he " changed his prison garments, and he did eat bread continually before him all the days of his life." The Lord Jesus Christ proclaims " liberty to the captives, and the opening of the prison to them that are bound " (Isa. lxi.) ; and He too gives a change of raiment. The same passage tells us that He gives the "garment of praise for the spirit of heaviness." The spirit of heaviness was the old dress which we wore when we were the captives of Satan ; and "the garment of praise" is the change of raiment which He gives when He sets us free.

We need to be suitably dressed to appear before the King ; for His household cannot be clothed in rags, or even in a dress of their own providing. In Matt. xi. 8 we are told that "They that wear soft clothing are in kings' houses"; or in Luke vii. 25, "They which are gorgeously apparelled . . . are in kings' courts"; and if we can say with the bride, "the King hath brought me into His chambers," we know that it is only after He has made us fit for His presence.

At the marriage feast of the king's son, the man who had not on a wedding garment was cast out because he trusted in his own dress, and not in that provided by the king. The apparel of the guests and servants reflects honour or dishonour on the king himself. We see in the story of the visit of the

Queen of Sheba to Solomon's court, that "the attendance of his ministers, and their apparel, his cup-bearers also and their apparel," were amongst the things that moved her to say, "It was a true report which I heard in mine own land of thine acts and of thy wisdom." Their appearance brought honour to Solomon; and the dress which God gives to us will bring honour to Himself, and not to us, when the Lord Jesus Christ appears in His glory and is "admired in all them that believe."

In the book of Esther we read of one whom the king delighted to honour, being arrayed in the royal apparel which the king himself used to wear. This was a very unusual and special mark of favour, shown on one occasion; but it is just what the Lord has done for us. In clothing us in His own robe, He has treated us as He did Israel of old, when He found her with none to pity, and arrayed her in beautiful garments (Ezek. xvi.); so that it could be said, "Thy renown went forth among the heathen for thy beauty: for it was perfect through My comeliness, which I had put upon thee, saith the Lord God." He has shown His love to us in providing us with Christ Himself, the Lord our righteousness, "Who of God is made unto us wisdom and righteousness." It is still one of His attributes, as of old, that He "loveth the stranger, in giving him food and raiment" (Deut. x. 18).

We may learn many lessons from the garments of the priests and Levites. Before they could draw near to do the service of the Tabernacle they were to wash their clothes; even as we too must wash our robes, and make them white in the blood of the Lamb. The Preacher says, "Let thy garments be always white" (Eccles. ix. 8); and the Apostle James tells us to keep ourselves "unspotted from the world."

The priests and Levites were robed in white linen, like the bride in Rev. xix.; and each of their different garments has special typical meaning for us.

Another aspect of God's provision is pictured in the garments of the pilgrim. All through Israel's wilderness journey, God sustained them, that "they lacked nothing, their clothes waxed not old, and their feet swelled not." On that night in Egypt when they first ate of the paschal lamb, they were directed to do so with their loins girded and their shoes on their feet ready for the journey; and those shoes lasted all through their wanderings. A long journey generally causes the traveller's garments to wear out. When the Gibeonites wanted to make it appear that they had come from a far country, they put on "old shoes and clouted upon their feet, and old garments upon them," and said, "These, our garments and our shoes, are become old by reason of the very long journey"; but the garments of the children of Israel had lasted for forty years. Our pilgrim dress will also last throughout the pilgrimage. Besides this, it will stand the fire, like the garments of Shadrach, Meshach, and Abednego. When they were cast into the fiery furnace the fire had no power upon them, "neither were their coats changed, nor the smell of fire had passed on them." We may be called to go through the fire; but the garments He provides will not be singed.

The warrior's dress is well described in Eph. vi.; and the overcomer's in Rev. iii. 4, 5, where it is said, "They shall walk with Me in white"; and, "He that overcometh shall be clothed in white raiment." The victor in his triumph is expected to appear in appropriate dress. Sisera's mother looked for her son to return from his victory with "a prey of divers colours of needlework, of divers colours of needlework on both sides, meet for the necks of them that take the spoil" (Judges v. 30). The soldier's armour is ours now; and if we make use of it we shall be clothed as overcomers by-and-by.

There is a beautiful little parable in Rom. xiii. when the apostle, picturing the close of the night season and the near approach of the daybreak, urges all to awake out of sleep, to cast off the works of darkness, the apparel belonging to the night, and to clothe themselves for the day in the armour of light—which he explains in a later verse is to put on the Lord

Jesus Christ.   If we are expecting the coming of the Lord, we shall not want to be found sleeping and unprepared for His presence ; like the bride in the Song who heard the voice of the Beloved at her door, but was not ready, for she had put off her coat (Song of Solomon v. 3) ; but shall want to be like the Bride in Rev. xix., where we read, "Let us be glad and rejoice, and give honour to Him ; for the marriage of the Lamb is come, and His wife hath made herself ready.   And to her was granted that she should be arrayed in fine linen, clean and white ; for the fine linen is the righteousness of saints."

There is evidently a difference between the garments of fine linen and the garments that typify the Lord Himself.   We are told that the fine linen represents the righteousness of saints ; and by the Revised Version we see it is in the plural, and means righteous acts—the works which as believers, through the power of the Holy Ghost, we are enabled to do to His glory, not to our own ; for we are told to "give honour to Him," because "His wife hath made herself ready."

These garments may be called "Spirit-wrought garments" ; but they must as much come from God as those which we have called the God-given garments.   The acts spoken of must be done in the power of the Holy Spirit, and must not be merely the result of carnal energy.   Having been saved and fitted for God's presence, our life is to be one which will bring glory to God.   "Righteousnesses" wrought in our own strength, both before and after believing, are but as filthy rags ; but righteousnesses worked out in dependence on the power of the Holy Spirit are as fine linen.

The God-given and Spirit-wrought garments strikingly illustrate the two-fold sanctification of the believer.

In Heb. x. 10 we read that "we are sanctified through the offering of the body of Jesus Christ once for all."   The words "are sanctified" might, it is said, here be translated "have been sanctified" ; and they refer to our standing in Christ, the perfected sanctification, which is ours directly we are united to

Him, "who of God is made unto us wisdom, righteousness, sanctification, and redemption." We can add nothing to it—it is finished, perfect; but in verse 14 we are told that "by one offering He hath perfected for ever them that are sanctified"—or, are being sanctified, referring to a progressive sanctification. Our experience is to be in keeping with our standing, and we are daily to become more like Christ. We are sanctified by the power of the Holy Ghost; and this is a growing sanctification. The God-given garments seem to represent present sanctification, perfect in Christ; the Spirit-wrought garments progressive sanctification.

The bride in Psa. xlv. 14 is to be brought to the King in raiment of needlework; not a machine-made garment, but one which is wrought stitch by stitch in the life. For this, industry and God-given skill are needed. "Drowsiness shall clothe a man with rags" (Prov. xxiii. 21); but the wise woman of Prov. xxxi. 22 is represented as making herself "coverings of tapestry; her clothing is silk and purple." We are therefore to be diligent in the service of the Lord, that we may be like the people mentioned in 1 Chron. iv. 21, the families of them that wrought fine linen, of the house of Ashbea. *Ashbea* means "earnest entreaty"; and thus they represented a little group that belonged to the house of prayer, whose life was spent in weaving fine linen.

The Spirit-wrought garments cannot be commenced till the filthy rags—the man-made garments—have been put aside, and we have accepted the God-given dress, the Lord our righteousness.

Many other passages might be added; but those to which reference has been made will have been sufficient to show how we may group together typical scenes, from the beginning of the Bible right down to its closing chapters.

It has been impossible in this chapter to do more than enumerate the pictures; but each one needs careful study, that its beauties may be seen.

XIII

Typical Places

THERE are many typical places in the Bible, and they may be divided, generally speaking, into two classes.

First, there are those whose names are full of meaning, so that the events which happened there seem to have an additional significance ; and second, there are certain spots where two or more typical scenes have taken place.

A lecturer in connection with the Palestine Exploration Fund, referring to his experience as secretary for twenty-five years, stated that the discoveries not only proved that the Bible events might have taken place as described, but that in many cases they could have happened nowhere else. This was testimony resulting from exploration in the actual soil of Palestine. Those who dig into the typology of the Word would say the same from a spiritual instead of a merely geographical point of view. Many Scripture incidents with deep spiritual meaning could have happened nowhere else ; for they foreshadowed greater events which took place on the same spot.

Amongst the first class we have such places as *Bethlehem*, the "house of bread," to which reference has already been made ; and *Hebron*, "fellowship," at which so many incidents happened suggestive of what characterizes the place of fellowship. In Hebrews the meaning of the name *Salem* is given as well as that of Melchisedek, as a proof that he was a type of the Lord Jesus—"First being by interpretation King of righteousness, and after that also King of Salem, which is, King of peace"—clearly showing that this is a Scriptural and not a fanciful method of looking for types.

Gilgal, the place of the rolling away of reproach, is very suggestive. At this, the first encampment after the crossing of the Jordan, the people were circumcised; and typically, Gilgal is taken to signify judgment of the flesh, for it is often associated with power over evil.

We have seen that the stones taken from the Jordan speak of the believer as "risen with Christ"; and that those which were left in the river illustrate another truth in Col. iii., "Ye died" (R.V.). Gilgal speaks of what is taught in the fifth verse: "Mortify, therefore, your members which are upon the earth." In the day of victory the children of Israel were again and again led back by Joshua to the camp at Gilgal (Joshua x. 43); for it is at such times that there is danger of the flesh being puffed up. Samuel also made them return hither; for we read in 1 Sam. xi. 13, "To-day the Lord hath wrought salvation in Israel. . . Come, and let us go to Gilgal, and renew the kingdom there." It is very suggestive that in chap. xv. 33, we are told that "Samuel hewed Agag in pieces before the Lord in Gilgal." This is one of the events which we can see could not have happened so appropriately anywhere else. The Amalekites, who came upon Israel in the wilderness, immediately after the rivers of water from the smitten rock had quenched the thirst of the people, are taken to typify the flesh. They were descended from Esau, and therefore were allied to the children of Israel. The scene in Exod. xvii. seems to represent the opposition of the flesh immediately after the Spirit has been given; and when Joshua has been victorious, the chapter closes with the declaration of eternal enmity between God and Amalek. At that time a new title was given to the Lord by Moses, "Jehovah Nissi; for he said, Because the hand of Amalek is against the throne of the Lord, therefore the Lord will have war with Amalek from generation to generation"; or, as we read in Rom. viii., "Because the carnal mind is enmity against God; for it is not subject to the law of God, neither indeed can be." To make peace with the foe is to cease to recognise this; and it was in direct disobedience to God that Saul spared Agag, the king of the Amalekites. His death at the hand of Samuel was in itself a type of the judgment of the flesh; and that it occurred at the place which seemed to typify this judgment makes the scene doubly significant.

Many other places with names full of meaning might be mentioned; but our object here is merely to suggest this method of study to those who have not yet tried it for themselves.

The second class affords an even more interesting field for research; for it proves again and again the wonderful appropriateness of the places chosen by God, and emphasizes what we have noticed before, that every detail in scenes which foreshadowed the work and person of His Son were of intense importance to Him.

There is in *Mount Moriah* a striking example of this. When God would test Abraham's faith, and at the same time give a picture of His own great love in not withholding His Son, His only Son, He directs him to a certain mountain, "the place of which God had told him," as it is twice called (Gen. xxii. 3, 9). The altar on which Isaac was to be bound, and the ram offered, must be erected on one particular spot which God alone could point out. No other hill in all Palestine would have been so appropriate, for the scene is thus linked with two other altars.

The Lord appeared to David at the threshing floor of Araunah the Jebusite on Mount Moriah (2 Chron. iii. 1); and thus the angel was commanded to sheathe his sword, and God said, "It is enough," where He had before told Abraham to stay his uplifted hand. There is in many respects a wonderful resemblance between the two scenes, both telling of the sacrifice which God had provided. David gratefully erected his altar; God sent down the fire: and we read that "David saw that the Lord had answered him." The words in Gen. xxii. were still true, "As it is said to this day, in the mount of the Lord it shall be seen." Was it by accident that these two incidents took place at the same spot? David at once saw that this was the place for the Temple. " This is the house of the Lord God, and this is the altar of the burnt-offering for Israel." Here God had pardoned his sin on the ground of grace, and had accepted him in the person of his burnt-offering; and he begins immediately to make preparation for building, having purchased not only the threshing floor, as in 2 Sam. xxiv. 24, but the whole place, as in 1 Chron. xxi. 25.

The Temple was actually built by Solomon, "in Mount Moriah, where the Lord appeared unto David his father" (2 Chron. iii. 1), and where Jehovah-Jireh revealed Himself to Abraham. There the altar of burnt-offering was placed and innumerable sacrifices offered. As Abraham and Isaac went "both of them together" up the slopes of Mount Moriah, Isaac said, " Behold the fire and the wood; but where is the lamb for the burnt-offering?" That question seems to cover the whole of the Old Testament times. On the opening page of the Gospel we have John saying, " Behold the Lamb!" and as we look back to Calvary, we may ask, " Where is the fire?" It has expended itself; it has said, "It is enough" (Prov. xxx. 16).

When this greatest of all burnt-offerings was offered, God once more answered from heaven; this time not by actual fire, or by a voice, but by rending the vail in the Temple.

We find linked with Mount Moriah, three examples of costly giving : Abraham spared not his only son ; David at great expense purchased the whole place, and all it contained, saying, " Neither will I offer burnt-offerings unto the Lord my God of that which doth cost me nothing "; and the Lord sitting over against the treasury noted the widow's gift, how "she of her want did cast in all that she had, even all her living."

There is another "green hill far away, without a city wall," which is a very sacred spot. Our Lord often trod *the Mount of Olives* ; and it is closely connected with many incidents in His life. He must have loved that hill overlooking the city, which was really "the city of the great King," but which yet refused to own allegiance to Him. It seems a specially hallowed place, because it was the last on which His feet stood, when, leading His disciples over its brow "as far as to Bethany," "He was taken up ; and a cloud received Him out of their sight." But this is not all : it will be the very next spot on earth's soil where those once pierced feet will stand ; for the two men who appeared to the disciples said, "This same Jesus, which is taken up from you into heaven, shall so come in like manner as ye have seen Him go into heaven." It may be that this verse is applicable to both events in the Lord's coming—His return to the air for His Church, and His return to the earth with His Church. It will be "in like manner," on both occasions. "A cloud received Him out of their sight"; and a cloud will restore Him when "the dead in Christ shall rise first ; then we which are alive and remain shall be caught up together with them in the clouds, to meet the Lord in the air." His own saw Him go, and it will be to His own that He will return.

It will be especially "in like manner" that He will return to the earth in His glory ; for not only will the clouds again give Him back to the earth, when "they shall see the Son of Man coming in the clouds of heaven, with power and great glory," but "His feet shall stand . . . upon the Mount of Olives, which is before Jerusalem on the east ; and the Mount of Olives shall cleave in the midst thereof toward the east and toward the west, and there shall be a very great valley" (Zech. xiv. 4). Our Lord's ascension from, and His return to, the Mount of Olives seems to be foretold by the prophet Ezekiel. The glory was seen by him to leave the city and stand upon "the mountain which is on the east side of the city" (Ezek. xi. 23) ; and later on he sees that "The glory of the God of Israel came from the way of the east, . . . by the way of the gate whose prospect is toward the east" (Ezek. xliii. 2, 4).

The Mount of Olives would be a place of deep interest to

us if we merely traced out the different occasions on which He stood upon its slopes ; but it is still more so when we see that many of them were foreshadowed in the life of David. One little word in Samuel links together David and David's greater Son, for it tells us that there David "was wont to worship God"; while in Luke we read that on that sad night, the saddest in all His life, the Lord "went as He was wont to the Mount of Olives" (2 Sam. xv. 32 R.V., *marg.* ; Luke xxii. 39, 40). It was the familiar resort of each when they would pour out their heart to God ; and it may have been under the shade of the very olives that grew in that garden, where our Lord poured out His soul in agony, "the place" mentioned in Luke, that David, inspired by the Holy Spirit, uttered the Psalms so wondrously expressing the thoughts of the Man of Sorrows. The Lord Jesus afterwards explained to His disciples all that was "written in the Psalms concerning" Himself; and we may well believe that some of them were truly the language of His heart during the hours He spent there.

The heading of Psa. cii. tells us that it is "a prayer of the afflicted, when he is overwhelmed, and poureth out his complaint before the Lord"; and some of it has been thought specially applicable to that scene in the garden. We are told in Heb. i. that vers. 25, 26 were actually addressed to the Lord Jesus; and it may have been that they were literally spoken to Him at this time by the angel, the "ministering spirit," that came to Him and strengthened Him (Luke xxii. 43). The twenty-fourth verse may have been His language then : " I said, O my God, take me not away in the midst of my days"; and the angel's answer, "Thy years are throughout all generations. Of old hast Thou laid the foundation of the earth, and the heavens are the work of Thy hands. They shall perish, but Thou shalt endure ; yea, all of them shall wax old like a garment ; as a vesture shalt Thou change them, and they shall be changed. But Thou art the same, and Thy years shall have no end."

There are twenty-eight verses in the Psalms which are quoted in forty-six passages in the New Testament as referring to the Lord ; and sixteen of these He applied to Himself, while many more seem to express His thoughts.

It is as the rejected king that we read of David in connection with the Mount of Olives. Absalom, who had slain his brother, had stolen the hearts of the people, and they had anointed him king, as their descendants did long years afterwards when they "denied the Holy One and the Just, and desired a murderer to be granted" unto them. David was obliged to leave his city ; and we read that "the king went forth, and all the people after him, and tarried in a place that was far off." This is what the great Son of David has done. His own people, Israel, have said, "We will not have this man to reign over us" ; and He, too, has had to leave His city, and He is now "as a man taking a far journey" (Mark xiii. 34). But He has not left His city for ever : it is true that He has gone into a "far country," but He intends "to return" (Luke xix. 12), and so, like David, He is only tarrying in the place that is far off. Very soon " He that shall come will come, and will not tarry." Meanwhile He has said to Jerusalem, " Ye shall not see Me henceforth, till ye shall say, Blessed is He that cometh in the name of the Lord."

The little scene between David and Ittai is very beautiful. The king said to him, "Wherefore goest thou also with us ? return to thy place, . . for thou art a stranger, and also an exile. Whereas thou camest but yesterday, should I this day make thee go up and down with us ?" But Ittai does not hesitate : it is true he has but just come to know David, but that is enough,—"As the Lord liveth, and as my lord the king liveth, surely in what place my lord the king shall be, whether in death or life, even there also will thy servant be." This is the language of every heart which has been taught by the Holy Ghost to " say that Jesus is the Lord." If they have enlisted " but yesterday," they will prefer to take their place with the

King in exile, rather than join the ranks of the usurper. David offers Ittai the choice, and draws from him this loyal response. When our Lord had opened the eyes of the blind man, He said unto him, "Go thy way"; but we read, "Immediately he received his sight, and followed Jesus in the way." He did not want a separate way from His : and so with each one who has had his eyes opened and has had a glimpse of the Lord Jesus. The language of his heart is, "Thy way, not mine, O Lord!"

David begins now his sorrowful journey over the Mount of Olives; and many things in this chapter link themselves with scenes which took place on the same mount in our Lord's life.

In 2 Sam. xv. 23 we read, "The king also himself passed over the brook Kidron"; and in John xviii. 1 we are told that Jesus "went forth with His disciples over the brook Kidron, where was a garden, into the which He entered, and His disciples." *Kidron* means "blackness"; and truly the King of Israel went down into blackness and darkness on that night in which He was betrayed.

As he stood there David spoke to his followers of his return, "If I shall find favour in the eyes of the Lord, He will bring me again, and shew me both it and His habitation." From the Mount of Olives he could look down on the city, and could doubtless see the tent in which the Ark had lodged, but which was now deserted for a time. David was leaving Jerusalem on account of his own sin—he was reaping what he had sown ; and thus the type is very imperfect. There was no "if" in our Lord's teaching to His disciples, as " He sat upon the Mount of Olives, over against the Temple," and told them of His return. The twenty-fourth and twenty-fifth chapters of Matthew and the thirteenth of Mark were delivered on the Mount of Olives.

We are told that "David went up by the ascent of Olivet, and wept as he went up," and the people with him followed his example ; and here we have a foreshadowing of our Lord, who wept over His rejection by Jerusalem on the very same spot.

The procession of which He was the central figure differed in many respects from the sorrowful one which we have been following in Samuel. The Lord was not leaving Jerusalem, but was going into the city ; and in Luke xix. 37 we read, " When He was come nigh, even now at the descent of the Mount of Olives, the whole multitude of the disciples began to rejoice and praise God with a loud voice " ; but we read in the forty-first verse, " When He was come near, He beheld the city, and wept over it." While His disciples were rejoicing, His heart was full of sorrow. The multitudes were shouting " Hosanna ! " ; but He knew that in a few days they would be crying, " Crucify Him ! crucify Him ! " The sorrow of David was shared by his servants, as they thought of the treatment he had received. The sorrow of our Lord was borne alone, for none understood His grief ; and He cries in the sixty-ninth Psalm, " I looked for some to lament with Me, but there was none ; and for comforters, but I found none." So it was, too, in the garden, when alone He poured out His soul in agony.

In the following chapter (2 Sam. xvi.), we still find David on the Mount of Olives ; and here he is met by an enemy, Shimei, who " went along on the hill's side over against him, and cursed as he went, and threw stones at him, and cast dust." David had to bear the cursing of Shimei, and his Lord the kiss of Judas ; but both forbade their followers to take vengeance. Abishai said unto the king, " Why should this dead dog curse my lord the king ? let me go over, I pray thee, and take off his head. And the king said, . . . So let him curse ; because the Lord hath said unto him, Curse David. Who shall then say, Wherefore hast thou done so ? . . . Let him alone, and let him curse ; for the Lord hath bidden him." Our Lord in the Garden of Gethsemane, on the slopes of Olivet, said, " The

cup which My Father hath given Me, shall I not drink it?"
and when Peter used his sword in his Master's defence, He
said, "Put up thy sword into his place."

We are told that "Shimei cast stones at David, and at all
the servants of King David; and all the people and all the
mighty men were on his right hand and on his left." We can
imagine how they would try and shield their lord, and we do
not hear that they deserted him. How different from the treatment which the Lord received when "they all forsook Him
and fled"!

We may, however, learn many practical lessons from the
conduct of David's followers in the time of his rejection.
They followed "after him" (xv. 17); and were "beside him"
(18); "with him" (30; and xvi. 14); and "on his right hand
and on his left" (xvi. 6).

Shimei "cast stones at David, and at all the servants of King
David," because they were his servants; and it is true now, as
our Lord said, "If the world hate you, ye know that it hated
Me before it hated you." If we are walking close to Him we
are sure to come in for some of the stones, or at least the dust.
We may be certain that when the kingdom was restored to
David, he took special delight in honouring those who had
been hit by the stones which were aimed at himself. He
reminds Solomon, his son, that he must honour those who
shared his rejection. "Show kindness unto the sons of
Barzillai, the Gileadite, and let them be of those that eat of
thy table: for so they came to me when I fled because of
Absalom." This is almost word for word the reward promised
by the Lord to those who had shared His earthly sorrows.
"Ye are they which have continued with Me in My temptations. And I appoint unto you a kingdom, as My Father hath
appointed unto Me: that ye may eat and drink at My table in
My kingdom" (Luke xxii. 28–30). To us who share His rejection now, it is promised that, "If we suffer, we shall also reign
with Him."

The true followers of David would not willingly remain in Jerusalem, for they could not have had any fellowship with the usurper's festivities ; their place was outside the city. Are not many of God's children trying to be in both places at once, friendly with Absalom's followers and yet professing to be on David's side ? We have to live amongst those who reject our Lord, and are in this respect like Mephibosheth, who could not leave the city ; but there was no doubt to which party he belonged. His grief at David's absence was unmistakable, and he certainly did not join with David's enemies. He "had neither dressed his feet, nor trimmed his beard, nor washed his clothes, from the day the king departed until the day he came again in peace " : and when he did welcome him back, his own affairs and his servants' misrepresentations were nothing to him. "Yea, let him take all," he said, "forasmuch as my lord the king is come again in peace unto his own house."

Ours is this twofold position : we have to live amongst the enemies of our King, but we must also take our place and walk beside Him in the path of His rejection. Though his own city had driven David forth into exile, there was a place on his journey of which we read "the king came weary, and refreshed" himself there. We are not told its name, but it reminds us of what Bethany was to our Lord : the place of rest and refreshment when Jerusalem rejected Him. Again and again He left the city to go thither. One of the meanings given to the name Bethany is "the House of the Lord's grace"; and whether we take the meaning of the name or not, it is a beautiful picture of how the Lord finds His home in the hearts of those who love Him, while He is an exile from His kingdom.

XIV

Typical Characters

THE Bible characters which foreshadowed the Lord Jesus Christ are very numerous; but they need to be studied very differently from such types as the Tabernacle, Temple, Offerings, etc. The latter were instituted for the one great purpose of uttering His glory, every detail being of Divine importance; and though we can only suggest the meanings of many smaller particulars which are unexplained, we may be quite certain that they had a typical significance. It is not so, however, when we take up the characters. They were not perfect men, and therefore they cannot be perfect types. In chronicling their histories the Holy Spirit has presented them as they were; not hiding their sins, but faithfully giving their portraits. For this reason some feel great reluctance in acknowledging them to be types; but the fact that they are quoted in the New Testament as foreshadowing some truth about the Lord Jesus proves to us that they are intended as such. In many of them there is a double teaching, by contrast as well as by likeness; and their very failings serve to intensify the perfections of the great Antitype.

The first character presented in the Bible prefigures our Lord Jesus Christ in several ways; and yet he was the one through whom "sin entered into the world." In the eighth Psalm David was probably referring to *Adam* in the first instance. "Thou madest him to have dominion over the works of Thy hands"; but we know that it was also a prophecy of the Lord Jesus Christ, for it is quoted thus in the Epistle to the Hebrews. Then again he foreshadows Christ as the head of a race; and in 1 Cor. xv. Paul compares and contrasts the two. " For as in Adam all die, even so in Christ shall all be made alive." Death has come upon all the members of the first family because their father died ; those who belong to the second live because the Head of their race has been made alive. The first "all" includes the whole of mankind—all the descendants of the first Adam ; the second, all believers, those who are united to the last Adam.

Later on in the same chapter the two are again contrasted : " The first man Adam was made a living soul ; the last Adam was made a quickening spirit." In the former there was life ending in death ; in the latter there was death bringing forth life. " The first man is of the earth earthy ; the second man is the Lord from heaven "—and thus Paul compares the destiny of their descendants, the character of the life they possess, and their origin. In another epistle, as we have seen already, he points out that in his relationship to Eve the first Adam is a type of Christ ; for in Eph. v., quoting from Gen. ii., he adds, " This is a great mystery ; but I speak concerning Christ and the Church."

Many other points might be noticed, especially the contrast between their temptations. Satan in both cases came in to try and spoil God's work immediately after He had expressed His approval. In Genesis, after the creation, God had pronounced all " very good." In the Gospels, at the baptism of the Lord Jesus, He had proclaimed, " This is My beloved Son, in whom I am well pleased." The devil at once appeared on the scene ; but how different was the result ! The first Adam fell, and " by one man sin entered into the world, and death by sin " ; but the last Adam vanquished His foe : and the latter part of the Psalm which Satan so artfully quoted to Him was really fulfilled, " Thou shalt tread upon the lion and adder ; the young lion and the dragon shalt thou trample under feet." In quoting—or rather, misquoting—the preceding verses, " He shall give His angels charge over Thee," Satan did not add those which prophesied his own defeat under the three-fold simile of the lion, the serpent, and the dragon. In both temptations the object was to make God's Word and His goodness to be doubted. To Eve he put the question, " Yea, hath God said ? " to the Lord he said, " If Thou be the Son of God "—though God's voice had just been heard from heaven, saying, " This is My beloved Son." In the first, the lie was believed ; but in the second, it was not listened to for a moment. Thus we see in Adam a Bible character who in some respects is a type of Christ, and in others by contrast teaches us precious lessons about Him.

While some only typify Him in certain particulars, there are a few which seem to do so in almost every detail of their lives. Of these, Joseph, Moses, Aaron, Joshua, David, and Elisha, seem to be the most complete, though the disobedience of Moses, the golden calf of Aaron, and the terrible sin of David, mar the pages of their history. Three of them, *Joseph*, *Moses*, and *David*, foreshadow both the sufferings and glory of the Lord ; and may thus be linked together. Though their circumstances were very different, they all beautifully pre-figured the rejected One ; while if the three are placed side by side, each adds touches to the picture which are not given by the others.

In Acts vii. Stephen compares the histories of Joseph, Moses, and Israel's Messiah, showing how the two former had been re-jected by their brethren, but were afterwards received ; but that He whom they foreshadowed had been betrayed and murdered. His hearers did not allow him to finish his address, or to urge them to own their Deliverer ; yet his dying vision was a fitting close to that wonderful summary of history and type, when "he, being full of the Holy Ghost, looked up steadfastly into heaven, and saw the glory of God, and Jesus standing on the right hand of God, and said, Behold, I see the heavens opened, and the Son of Man standing on the right hand of God "—stand-ing as though to listen for their answer; standing as though ready to return. Stephen's last words were also prophetic of the day when the Son of Man should be no longer the rejected One.

The thirteen chapters of Genesis which tell us the beautiful story of Joseph's life are full of Christ ; and as verse after verse gives the familiar Old Testament picture we may compare with them many New Testament passages describing the life and character of the One of whom Joseph is such a marvellous type.* He is loved by his father, clothed by him, and sent forth on an errand to his brethren. By them he is hated and envied ; they refuse allegiance, conspire against him, strip him, and deliver him into the hands of the Gentiles. The sorrows, suffering, and shame, through which he passed are depicted in a series of pictures ; and the pit, the price of the purchase, Potiphar's house, and the prison, show how Joseph was led, step by step, down the path of humiliation. The pit reminds us of how the Lord cries in the sixty-ninth Psalm, " I sink in deep mire, where there is no standing. . . . Let not the pit shut her mouth upon me." The price paid for Joseph when he was sold into slavery was twenty pieces of silver ; while the Lord Jesus was betrayed for thirty pieces of silver, the price of a slave (Exod. xxi. 32). Next Joseph becomes a servant in the house of Potiphar, the captain of the guard ; and is like Him of whom we read in Isa. xlix. 7, 8, " Him whom man despiseth ; . . . Him whom the nation abhorreth ; . . . a servant of rulers."

There is one more step in his degradation. Falsely accused, he is thrust into the prison, and numbered with the transgressors. He is brought lower and lower ; but here the type fails, for though the shame of the cross is foreshadowed, Joseph did not have to lay down his life. We read in Psa. cv. 18, " Whose feet they hurt with fetters ; he was laid in iron " ; but the crucified One cried, " They pierced My hands and My feet." In Gen. xl. we see that, like Him of whom Joseph was a type, " there were also two other, malefactors," with him ;

* See Appendix, p. 169.

and to one he gives a message of life, to the other a message of doom. The one goes from the prison to the king's palace and the king's table; the other is led forth to death. So it was on Calvary "where they crucified Him, and two other with Him, on either side one, and Jesus in the midst." To one of these also He gave a message of life: "To-day shalt thou be with Me in Paradise." The language of the dying thief was very similar to that of the chief butler when he stood before Pharaoh. The latter said, "I do remember my faults this day"; and went on to speak of Joseph. The former said, "We indeed justly: for we receive the due reward of our deeds; but this Man hath done nothing amiss."

Joseph makes a threefold request of the chief butler: "Think *on* me; . . and show kindness *unto* me; and make mention *of* me": but his request was long forgotten; for we read "yet did not the chief butler remember Joseph, but forgat him." The Lord asks all those who have received the message of life from Himself to do these three things. Alas! that it should ever be said of Him, as of the poor wise man in Solomon's parable, who "by his wisdom delivered the city; yet no man remembered that same poor man. . . The poor man's wisdom is despised, and his words are not heard." Joseph's character throughout is very beautiful. He resists temptation to sin; and those whom he serves recognise that the Lord is with him, that he is blessed and others with him, and that he is to be entirely trusted. "The Lord made all that he did to prosper in his hand"; like the One of whom it is said, "The pleasure of the Lord shall prosper in his hand." That which was put into Joseph's hand was absolutely safe. The experience of the captain of the guard and of the keeper of the prison agreed; and we, too, can say with Paul, "I know whom I have believed, and am persuaded that He is able to keep that which I have committed unto Him against that day."

Joseph's history does not, however, close in the prison. There is another side to the picture; and Stephen tells us that God "delivered him out of all his afflictions," as we read in Psa. xxii., "He hath not despised nor abhorred the affliction of the afflicted." Joseph was brought out of the dungeon by Pharaoh, and "he made him lord of his house, and ruler of all his possession" (Psa. cv. 21, *marg.*). Here we are reminded of another of Solomon's parable prophecies, of the poor and wise child in Eccles. iv. 13–15 (R.V.), who is "better . . than an old and foolish king. . . For out of prison he came forth to be king : yea, even in his kingdom he was born poor."

The story of Joseph may be compared with Phil. ii. : for we see him stripped of his robe, becoming a servant to his brethren, having been made a slave and numbered with the transgressors, and then being exalted and given a name of honour—all being commanded to "bow the knee" before him. In Phil. ii. we are told of the One who voluntarily emptied Himself and "made Himself of no reputation, and took upon Him the form of a servant"; but the Antitype went far lower than the type: "He humbled Himself, and became obedient unto death, even the death of the cross." For this we have no parallel in Joseph's life. The Lord went far below Joseph in His humiliation, and He also rose far above him in His exaltation : "Wherefore also God highly exalted Him, and gave unto Him the name which is above every name : that in the name of Jesus every knee should bow, of things in heaven and things on earth and things under the earth, and that every tongue should confess that Jesus Christ is Lord, to the glory of God the Father" (R.V.). It was "the gospel of the glory" that changed Saul of Tarsus into Paul the Apostle ; and it was the glad news that Joseph was yet alive and sitting on the throne that brought Jacob to Goshen.

Almost everything that is said by Pharaoh concerning Joseph is true of One greater than he. "Can we find such a one as this is, a man in whom the Spirit of God is ? . . . There is none so discreet and wise as thou art ; thou shalt be over my house ; and according unto thy word shall all my people be ruled." And to the hungry ones who came for food, Pharaoh said, "Go unto Joseph ; what he saith to you, do."

Then we may also trace out wonderful foreshadowings in his dealing with his brethren, noting how he told them that God had sent him before them to save their lives by a great deliverance ; how he gradually led them to confess their sin in their treatment of himself ; forgave them, and acknowledged them as his brethren ; how in the time of famine he fed them, gave them as much as they could carry, and provision for the way ; and when they had obeyed his invitation of " Come unto me," nourished them, telling them to come and live near himself, lest they came to poverty. Reference has already been made to his inexhaustible storehouses, and his treatment of the famine-stricken people who came to buy ; and also to the special Jewish application of the story.

We see from Stephen's address that *Moses* was another deliverer who was a type of the Lord Jesus, both in his rejection and when recognised by the people as their leader. Whilst Joseph was hated by his brethren, Moses was misunderstood. " He supposed his brethren would have understood " ; but, like the Lord Himself, " He came unto His own, and His own received Him not." They said, " Who made thee a ruler and a judge over us ? " These are almost the very words used by our Lord when one came and said, " Master, speak to my brother, that he divide the inheritance with me. And He said unto him, Man, who made Me a judge or a divider over you ? " It may be that He was comparing Himself to Moses. If " His brethren would have understood," He would indeed have been their King and their Ruler ; but they refused Him ; and if He had consented then to arbitrate between them, He would have been treated as Moses. But we read, " This Moses, whom they refused, saying, Who made thee a ruler and a judge ? the same did God send to be a ruler and a deliverer " ; and Peter said, " Therefore let all the house of Israel know assuredly, that God hath made that same Jesus, whom ye have crucified, both

Lord and Christ." Though Israel has not yet acknowledged Him, they will by-and-by say, "Blessed is He that cometh in the name of the Lord."

Joseph was taken from his home and his father's love into loneliness, slavery, and captivity; but what was the love he had received from Jacob compared to that of which the Lord spake in John xvii., "Thou lovedst Me before the foundation of the world"? Moses gave up the pleasures and riches of Pharaoh's court, and his high position there; but what was it all, compared with the glory to which our Lord refers, "the glory which I had with Thee before the world was," of which He emptied Himself when He became of no reputation? "Ye know the grace of our Lord Jesus Christ, that though He was rich, yet for your sakes He became poor." The son of Pharaoh's daughter held high rank in the court of Egypt; but what must have been the position of Him whom Jehovah calls "the Man that is My Fellow," who even in His humiliation had but to pray to His Father, and He would at once have given Him "more than twelve legions of angels"?

During the time that they were strangers to their brethren, both Joseph and Moses took to themselves brides from a strange people. Asenath and Zipporah have therefore been taken to represent the Church during the present dispensation, espoused while Israel is a stranger to their Deliverer. We see that all through this time of separation the hearts of Joseph and Moses were full of love to their own brethren. The beautiful picture of Joseph's tenderness and love shows how his heart yearned over them; and Moses names his son "Gershom; for he said, I have been a stranger in a strange land." He had not forgotten his kindred who were toiling amongst the brick-kilns.

Throughout the whole history of Moses there is much typical teaching. He was full of wisdom, and "mighty in words and in deeds"; he was "very meek, above all the men which were upon the face of the earth," till He came who could say "I am meek and lowly in heart." He worked miracles which

were rightly ascribed to " the finger of God " (Exod. viii. 19 ;
Luke xi. 20) ; and it might have been said of him, " What
manner of man is this, that even the winds and the sea obey
him ? " In both these cases, however, he was only God's
human instrument ; while the Lord Jesus Christ manifested
His own Divine power. " There arose not a *prophet* since in
Israel like unto Moses, whom the Lord knew face to face," till
God raised up the One whom He had promised to send "like
unto Moses " (Deut. xviii. 15–19), " Unto Him ye shall
hearken " ; " Hear ye Him " (Matt. xvii. 5). In Psalm xcix. 6
Moses is mentioned as a *priest*, and we know that " he was
king in Jeshurun," and *shepherd, judge,* and *leader,* of the
people ; but it is as the *intercessor* that he so pre-eminently
reminds us of the Lord Jesus. When God was angry with
them, " Moses, His chosen, stood before Him in the breach,
to turn away His wrath " (Psa. cvi. 23). When they were fighting against their enemies he went up to the top of the hill, and
sat there as the intercessor : " And it came to pass, when Moses
held up his hand, that Israel prevailed ; and when he let down
his hand Amalek prevailed." He tells them in Deut. v. 5, " I
stood between the Lord and you . . . to shew you the word
of the Lord " ; and when difficulties arose, he " brought their
cause before the Lord." Thus he prefigured the " one Mediator between God and men, the Man Christ Jesus " ; the
" Advocate with the Father " ; the One who " ever liveth to
make intercession " for us. He indeed stood in the breach
when " He was wounded for our transgressions, He was
bruised for our iniquities." When beset by temptation, He
prays for His people, that their faith fail not, as He prayed for
Peter. He is Himself the Word ; and we have an example of
the way in which He presents our cause to His Father in John
xvii. Not only is Moses a type by comparison, but also by
contrast ; for as the representative of the law, he is in the
New Testament again and again compared with Him by whom
grace and truth came.

While Joseph was an exile from home, and Moses from kindred, *David* represents another aspect ; for he was an exile from his throne.   Joseph was the deliverer from famine ; Moses from Egypt's bondage ; David from the power of the enemy.   It would be difficult in comparing this wonderful trio to say which is the most complete type of our Lord.

The first mention of David is in his genealogy at the close of the Book of Ruth, reminding us of the opening of the Gospels of Matthew and Luke.   His birth at Bethlehem, and the lowly place of submission in the home ; then his anointing as God's chosen one—like the baptism of the Lord Jesus, when the voice from heaven proclaimed, " This is My beloved Son, in whom I am well pleased "—followed by his encounter with the enemy, all remind us of the Gospel story.   Forty days had the foe been menacing the people when David went forth and overcame him ; and the temptation in the wilderness was for forty days.   David vanquished the giant with one of his five smooth stones from the brook ; the Lord, the champion of His people, conquered the enemy by a threefold quotation from Deuteronomy, one of the five books of Moses.   The shepherd's bag or scrip, from which David took the stone, would be used " for carrying materials for healing or binding up lame sheep," or for the shepherd's food ; and we also are provided in the Word with healing for sick and wounded sheep, food for the shepherd, and stones for the enemy.   David compared Goliath to the lion that had taken the lamb out of his flock, and had roared against himself ; and we see that he was indeed a type of " our adversary the devil," who " as a roaring lion, walketh about, seeking whom he may devour." There are many beautiful thoughts concerning David in 1 Sam. xviii., where we have the description of the poor wise man lightly esteemed, who so wonderfully delivered the people (14, 15, 23, 30 ; Eccles. ix. 15), and whose name was in consequence " much set by," or " precious."

In the story of Joseph we saw a series of pictures representing various steps in his humiliation and exaltation ; in Moses we saw different official relationships ; and in David's history we have accounts of various characters who were attracted to his person, and became his friends, mighty men and servants, especially during the waiting time that preceded his coronation as king. Each one seems to give us a different picture of the sinner and his Lord. First we have the story of *Jonathan's* devotion. His heart goes out to David on account of the deliverance he has wrought. His soul "was knit with the soul of David"; he "loved him as his own soul"; "delighted much" in him ; "stripped himself" of his robe, his garments, and his precious sword, the second in the kingdom (1 Sam. xiii. 22), and was content to yield the throne to David, "that in all things he might have the pre-eminence." But David did not only win kings' sons. In *the cave of Adullam* he made himself captain over any who were willing to come to him—those in distress, in debt, and discontented, were welcomed as they were. He was very different from his predecessor, for "when Saul saw any strong man, or any valiant man, he took him unto him "; but in Saul's company they did not become stronger, but "followed him trembling."

The followers of David in the cave of Adullam—the audience to whom he addressed the thirty-fourth Psalm—became under his training some of the mighty men who are so beautifully described in 1 Chron. xii. Separated unto David, they became strong, skilful, and swift, devoted to his service and able to do exploits. The love of his mighty men was such that he had but to express a longing for water from the well of Bethlehem, and three of them at once were willing to hazard their lives to satisfy that desire. It was not a great victory, but it was great love ; and, therefore, they were his three mightiest. Our work will be tested, not as to what *size* it is, but as to "what *sort* it is."

Then there is the account of *the Egyptian* whom they found in the field. He was in a deplorable condition, sick, starving, and deserted by his old master, the Amalekite, when no longer useful ; but brought to David, fed, revived, and saved to serve. The conversation between him and David is most suggestive.

" Though fully restored he was unable to act with David until possessed with the full assurance of life and liberty (Rom. vi.). The believer needs to know his entire emancipation from the dominion of his old master, the flesh, before ever he can with confidence apply himself to the service of Christ."*

In *Abigail*, another of the brides of Scripture, we have a picture of one who recognised the Lord's anointed, even when he was the poor fugitive. Her prayer (1 Sam. xxv. 31), "When the Lord shall have dealt well with my lord, then remember thine handmaid," reminds us of the prayer of the dying thief, " Lord, remember me when Thou comest in Thy kingdom" (R.V.). In the one case the answer was, "See, I have hearkened to thy voice, and have accepted thy person "; and afterwards, " David sent and communed with Abigail to take her to him to wife "; while the other received the wonderful answer, " To-day shalt thou be with Me in Paradise."

The story of *Mephibosheth* is a beautiful illustration of the way in which the poor sinner is received by the Lord. Lame, and helpless; a fugitive in the far country; dwelling in Lodebar, the place of "no pasture"; hiding from one of whom he has wrong thoughts, and on whom he looks as an enemy—he is at last fetched by David. He comes into his presence expecting the worst; but the gracious greeting, " Fear not," falls upon his ear. He feels himself unfit for the king's presence; but David gives him a place at his table where his lameness is hidden.

All this is but a faint picture of how the Lord " brings a poor vile sinner into His house of wine "; each one thus brought in is seated at His table, not merely " as one of the king's sons," but having been actually born into the family. " Behold, what manner of love the Father hath bestowed upon us, that we should be called the sons of God: and such we are." The last mention of Mephibosheth shows that the enmity was all gone, and its place taken by true heart-devotion to David.

Many other of David's servants and friends, such as *Ittai* and *Barzillai*, might well be considered ; while *Joab's* history

* C. H. M.

is full of solemn warning. The foremost in the battle, the leader against the foe, the nearest to the king, yet not really true to him, deliberately disobeying his commands and ending his life in rebellion. There could not have been real love to his king, though there was so much activity in his service. All his great victories counted for nothing without this : they were like the wood, hay, and stubble ; while the devotion of the three mighty men who fetched the water from Bethlehem's well was like the gold, silver, and precious stones.

When our Lord would speak of Old Testament characters who typified His sufferings and glory, He linked together the two who foreshadowed the deepest depths of sorrow and the greatest heights of exaltation—*Jonah*, who said, " All Thy billows and Thy waves passed over me " ; and *Solomon*, whose glory attracted the stranger from the far country. He was greater than the prophet in his suffering ; greater than the king in his glory ; and earlier in the chapter He had proved Himself greater than all the priests, for He was " greater than the Temple " itself (Matt. xii. 6, 40, 42).

Besides the many who are directly referred to in the New Testament as pointing to Him, there is another class of types from which we may learn many lessons ; viz., those who by their offices or occupations speak to us of Him. They may not be mentioned as types ; but they clearly foreshadow Him in these various particulars.

Thus we are not distinctly told that *Boaz* was a type of Christ ; but in his relationship to Ruth the Moabitess as kinsman and redeemer there is no doubt that he beautifully foreshadows the Lord : and seeing this, the whole Book of Ruth becomes full of typical teaching. It has been pointed out that Boaz is a type in a seven-fold aspect—as the lord of the harvest, the near kinsman, the supplier of wants, the redeemer of the inheritance, the man who gives rest, the wealthy kinsman, and the bridegroom.

Types of Christ as the Shepherd

THE various aspects of our Lord's work for His people are brought before us in many different ways. One character alone would not be sufficient to give us any idea of His many-sided official relationships ; so He appears as Prophet, Priest, King, Leader, Commander, Conqueror, Saviour, Surety, and Shepherd. And in studying any one of these aspects it is helpful to group together the Bible characters who thus typify our Lord's work.

As an illustration of this method—taking the last-named of these offices—we have a beautiful cluster of types in the records of the Old Testament shepherds ; and it will be seen as in other groups that each separate type seems to emphasize some special point, so that together they give a complete picture of the character, duties, and devotion of the shepherd.

Abel, the first shepherd, as we know from Heb. xii., is a type of Christ : " The blood of sprinkling speaketh better things than that of Abel." We know very little about Abel except in connection with his sacrifice and his death. God said to Cain, " The voice of thy brother's blood crieth unto Me from the ground." It cried out for vengeance on the murderer ; but "the blood of, sprinkling," referred to in Hebrews, called, not for vengeance, but for pardon. This passage does not clearly state to which of the Levitical types reference is made, for the blood of Abel is here shown to be a type of a type ; but it points probably to the sin-offerings, where alone the blood was sprinkled on the earth itself. At the slaying of the red heifer the blood was sprinkled before the Tabernacle (Num. xix.) ;

in the sin-offering for the priest and congregation, the blood was sprinkled before the vail; and on the great Day of Atonement, before the mercy-seat. All these were sin-offerings, and in each case the blood was sprinkled on the ground. It spoke of forgiveness and cleansing, and typified the blood that would be shed on Calvary when the good Shepherd gave His life for the sheep.

Abel had himself offered a lamb from his flock to atone for his own sin, and thus the lamb died for the shepherd; but on Calvary the Shepherd died for the lambs.

We learn another lesson about the shepherd in Gen. xxiv., where we see that the wealth of the shepherd lies in his flocks. The servant of Abraham who had been sent to find a bride for Isaac says to Rebekah and her friends, "The Lord hath blessed my master greatly, and he is become great; and He hath given him flocks and herds." The Great Shepherd of the sheep looks on His flock as His choicest possession; and thus the Apostle Paul prayed for the Ephesian saints, that they might know what were "the riches of the glory of His inheritance in the saints." "The Lord's portion is His people"; and so precious were they in His sight, that He became poor in order that He might purchase them with His blood.

Jacob, in speaking to Laban of his twenty years of service, shows something of what a shepherd's duties involve. There is the responsibility of the shepherd. He says, "That which was torn of beasts I brought not unto thee; I bare the loss of it; of my hand didst thou require it, whether stolen by day, or stolen by night." The shepherd was personally responsible for the safety of every one of the sheep; and the Good Shepherd in John x. tells us that He has made Himself responsible for every one who has been given into His care—"They shall never perish, neither shall any man pluck them out of My hand." Jacob could not thus secure Laban's flock—many of them probably perished; but the Lord Jesus could say, "Of them which Thou gavest Me have I lost none." He has pledged Himself to keep the feeblest lamb ; and with Paul we can say, " I know whom I have believed, and am persuaded that He is able to keep that which I have committed unto Him against that day."

Then, too, we learn from Jacob the endurance of the shepherd. He adds, " Thus I was : in the day the drought consumed me, and the frost by night; and my sleep departed from mine eyes." The Lord knew what it was to suffer thus Twice over we read of His asking for something to quench His thirst. In John iv., He says to the woman of Samaria, " Give Me to drink " ; and on the cross He cries, " I thirst." We do not hear of that request being granted, and His bodily thirst was unsatisfied ; but He that said, " I have meat to eat that ye know not of," on both occasions found refreshment by giving the water of life to thirsty ones—the woman who took her first draught, and hurried away to bring others to Him ; and the dying thief who recognised Him as Lord.

The work of the shepherd in the East involves careful guarding by night as well as by day ; and thus the shepherds of Bethlehem kept watch over their flocks by night. It must have been literally true of our Lord that sleep departed from His eyes. He had not where to lay His head, and He spent the night hours in prayer for His flock. During the stormy night when the disciples were tossing on the Sea of Galilee, He was alone on the mountain praying, and " saw them toiling in rowing." And this is still true, for " He that keepeth thee will not slumber : behold, He that keepeth Israel shall neither slumber nor sleep." He will watch over His flock all through the hours of darkness and danger, " till the day break, and the shadows flee away." There will then be no more danger from the roaring lion, for it is in the night that " all the beasts of the forest do creep forth. The young lions roar after their prey. . . . The sun ariseth; they gather themselves together, and lay them down in their dens " ; and God's flock at the sunrise will be safe from all their enemies.

In Jacob's answer to Esau we see the care of the shepherd (Gen. xxxiii. 13): "If men should overdrive them one day, all the flock will die": reminding us of Him of whom it is said, "He shall feed His flock like a shepherd; He shall gather the lambs with His arm, and carry them in His bosom, and shall gently lead those that are with young."

In his early youth we read of *Joseph* feeding the flock with his brethren; and the thought emphasized in his history is the hatred of the other shepherds. Those who should have loved and protected him, hated him, and were filled with envy, and said, "Shalt thou indeed reign over us? or shalt thou indeed have dominion over us?"

When the Lord Jesus was here upon earth, those who should have been shepherds of God's sheep hated Him without a cause : they themselves were like the shepherds mentioned in Ezek. xxxiv., who neglected the flock, so that when the Lord Himself, the Good Shepherd came, His heart was moved with compassion, because He saw the people "as sheep, having no shepherd." In John ix., we see how these shepherds treated one who came to Him—they "cast him out." The Lord at once goes on to show in the tenth chapter that He leadeth out His own sheep—He putteth them forth. They may be cast out of the fold by men, but it is really He Himself that is putting them forth; for the word in verse 4 is the same as that used in chap. ix. 35. In chap. x. 16, He says, "Other sheep I have, which are not of this fold : them also I must bring, . . . and there shall be one flock (R.V.), and one Shepherd." Nothing stirred the hatred of the false shepherds so much as to hear that He was turning away from the fold of Judaism and calling Gentiles into the flock; and, like Joseph's brethren, they said, "We will not have this man to reign over us."

Moses is the next shepherd-type of whom we read. For forty years he kept the flock of Jethro, his father-in-law, as a preparation for the last forty years of his life, when he was to shepherd God's flock, as we read in Isa. lxiii. 11, 12. In his history we have the thought of the leading of the shepherd. We are told in Exod. iii. that "he led the flock to the backside of the desert, and came to the mountain of God, even to Horeb"; and in the twelfth verse God says, "When thou hast brought forth the people out of Egypt, ye shall serve God upon this mountain." A short time afterwards he led the whole flock of the children of Israel to the same desert and to the same mountain; and where he had first heard God speaking to him out of the burning bush, the Lord spake once more "in Horeb out of the midst of the fire." The Lord still makes His own people to go forth, and guides them in the wilderness like a flock; and He leads them on safely, so that they fear not. And thus Moses speaks to us of the Good Shepherd, of whom we read that He leadeth out His sheep, and "goeth before them, and the sheep follow Him."

David, the shepherd-king, like Moses, was keeping the sheep when God called him to shepherd his people; so that God could say, "I took thee from the sheepcote, even from following the sheep, that thou shouldest be ruler over My people Israel" (1 Chron. xvii. 7). The incident which David himself relates to Saul, tells of deliverance by the shepherd. At the risk of his own life he rescued the lamb from the mouth of the lion and the bear (1 Sam. xvii. 34). Only one of the flock seems to have been in danger; but that was enough for the shepherd. Like the man in Luke xv., who left the ninety and nine to go after that which was lost, so David left those who were in safety to rescue the one that was in such sore peril. Our "adversary the devil, as a roaring lion," seeketh whom he may devour; but the Shepherd has conquered him. The Lord might have said with David, "He arose against Me"; for his enmity was against the Lord Jesus Christ, and he had to cry in Psalm xxii., "Save me from the lion's mouth." It seemed on Calvary as if Satan had indeed conquered; for though "He saved others, Himself He cannot save"—the Good Shepherd must give His life for the sheep. In this respect David, as a shepherd, falls far short of the Antitype.

When David was sent by his father to enquire after his brethren, " he left the sheep with a keeper." Eliab asked him, "With whom hast thou left those few sheep in the wilderness ? " but David had seen that they were safe before he left them. The Chief Shepherd has had to leave His little flock in the wilderness ; but He has left them in the care of the "other Comforter," and has commissioned His servants to feed His flock : so that Paul says, " Take heed therefore unto yourselves and to all the flock, over the which the Holy Ghost hath made you overseers, to feed the Church of God which He hath purchased with His own blood."

It is interesting to trace in the Psalms of David and in his after-history the influence of his earlier years amongst the flocks. God's people in all ages have abundant reason to bless him for the precious Psalm where he puts himself amongst the flock and says, " The Lord is my Shepherd." It has often been pointed out that the twenty-second Psalm tells of "the Good Shepherd " that died ; the twenty-third of the " Great Shepherd " that rose and now cares for His flock ; and the twenty-fourth of the " Chief Shepherd " that shall appear. When God's judgment fell on account of David's sin in numbering the people, he pleaded for the flock, and said, " Lo, I have sinned, and I have done wickedly ; but these sheep, what have they done ? " God's judgment on Calvary did indeed fall on the Shepherd, that the sheep might be delivered ; for we read in Zechariah, " Awake, O sword, against My Shepherd, and against the Man that is My Fellow, saith the Lord of Hosts : smite the Shepherd, and the sheep shall be scattered." He was "smitten of God and afflicted " ; not for His own sin, as in David's case, but " He was wounded for our transgressions." In this passage (Zech. xiii. 7), we see "the Good Shepherd that giveth His life for the sheep"; while in xi. 17, in the "idol shepherd that leaveth the flock," we have "the hireling" spoken of by our Lord, who "fleeth, because he is an hireling." David, who interceded for the sheep and begged that the stroke might fall upon himself, is like the former; but Saul reminds us of the hireling that "careth not for the sheep." When he had disobeyed the Lord, he tried to put all the blame on the people. "Yea, I have obeyed the voice of the Lord; . . . but the people took of the spoil." How different from the man after God's own heart!

A picture of one of the duties of the shepherd is given in 1 Chron. iv. Certain princes of the sons of Simeon went forth "to seek pasture for their flocks. And they found fat pasture and good; and the land was wide, and quiet, and peaceable"; and having utterly destroyed the enemies that were found there, "they dwelt in their rooms, because there was pasture there for their flocks." The sheep have not to find their own pasture. This, the shepherd is engaged to do : and our Shepherd has won the pasture-land from the enemy, and now He makes us "to lie down in green pastures." The sheep will not rest till they are satisfied ; but where He leads His flock there is an abundant supply. The sheep of His pasture "go in and out and find pasture." Sometimes, alas! the sheep try and find it for themselves ; and wandering away from the Shepherd, are lost for a time, till He goes after them and brings them back from the wilderness or the mountain. In Matt. xviii., the lost sheep is represented as having gone astray among the mountains ; and, as one has said, God's sheep often wander by getting up too high. The pasture is very poor on the mountain tops, and there are many dangers—so we read in Hos. xiii. 6 : "According to their pasture, so were they filled : they were filled, and their heart was exalted : therefore have they forgotten Me." The Good Shepherd, if need be, "goeth into the mountains and seeketh that which is gone astray."

Thus in these groups of Old Testament shepherds, so different in character and history, we have brought before us the death of the shepherd in Abel; the wealth of the shepherd in Isaac ; the responsibility, endurance, and care of the shepherd in Jacob ; the hatred of other shepherds in Joseph ; the leading of the shepherd in Moses ; the deliverance by the shepherd in David ; and the pasture of the shepherd in the sons of Simeon. Though all falling far short of the Antitype, together they give us a beautiful picture of Him who will shepherd the flock till the time when His sheep " shall hunger no more, neither thirst any more ; neither shall the sun strike upon them, nor any heat : for the Lamb which is in the midst of the throne shall be their Shepherd, and shall guide them unto fountains of waters of life : and God shall wipe away all tears from their eyes " (R.V.). The green pastures of earth will then be exchanged for the richer fields of heaven, and the still waters for these living fountains. In the earthly fields of the promised land He will yet shepherd His people Israel, when " He that scattered Israel will gather him, and keep him, as a shepherd doth his flock."

XVI

Types of the Holy Spirit

IN looking at the typical substances of Scripture we have already noticed some that prefigured the Holy Spirit, such as *oil, water,* etc.; and there are also others which must not be omitted in this brief survey of the types. On the very opening page of the Bible we have a mention of the Spirit; and the word which is used reminds us of one of the symbols or types of Himself. Where we are told in Gen. i. that the Spirit moved on the face of the waters, the word is one, it is said, which applies to a bird brooding. We know the bird which symbolizes the Spirit; for we are told in the Gospels that at the time of our Lord's baptism, "He saw the Spirit of God descending like *a dove* and lighting upon Him."

The Spirit brooded as a dove over earth's darkness when God first said, "Let there be light"; and He again appeared as a dove when He who was the light of the world was entering upon His work and was about to shine on those who "sat in darkness." Throughout the Bible the dove is a type of the Holy Spirit, and of those who are indwelt by Him.

A beautiful picture is given in the twenty-fourth of Genesis of the work of the Holy Spirit. Isaac is, as we know, a type of Christ. The promises to Abraham concerning his seed are shown in Galatians to have referred to the Lord Himself, though they had their first fulfilment in Isaac. He was the only begotten son of the father, his well-beloved; and we have seen how the scene on Mount Moriah foreshadowed the love of Him who "spared not His own Son, but delivered Him up for us all," and thus became Jehovah-Jireh, for with Him He freely gives us all things. In this chapter we have an account of the father sending *his servant* to find a wife for his son—the one who in figure has already passed through death and resurrection; and this servant is a wonderful type of the Holy Ghost, who is now calling out a people for His name. First we have the charge to the servant. The bride of Isaac is to be brought right up out of the land in which she dwells. There is no mistake about the directions. The servant suggests that perhaps she will want to remain in her own home, and will not come to Isaac; is he then to bring Isaac down to her? But Abraham is very decided—Isaac's place is not there. As Mr. Spurgeon has said on this verse, "The Lord Jesus Christ heads that grand emigration party which has come right out of the world."

In the tenth verse we are told that the servant does not go empty-handed, but takes with him samples of the riches of Abraham and Isaac—"all the goods of his master were in his hand." When the Holy Spirit came down, He, too, brought with Him an earnest of the inheritance which they who listen to His message would receive, for He Himself is the earnest.

In the beautiful Eastern picture of the scene at the well we have the servant, having been led to the one whom God had appointed for Isaac, asking if there is room for him in her father's house. Had she refused, he would never have been able to tell her about Isaac. When he is admitted, his first thought is of his errand: "I will not eat until I have told mine errand." He never forgets it; and his object, like that of Him whom he foreshadows, is to speak of the one who sent him. "When the Comforter is come, whom I will send unto you from the Father, even the Spirit of truth, which proceedeth from the Father, He shall testify of Me." "He shall not speak of Himself."

So Abraham's steward tells about his master, his master's son, and all his possessions; and gives to Rebekah some of the precious things which he has brought. "The Lord hath blessed my master greatly, and he is become great": and unto his son "hath he given all that he hath." In John we read, "The Father loveth the Son, and hath given all things into His hand"; and again, "All things that the Father hath are Mine." But there was one more thing that Isaac needed : he could not enjoy these things alone ; as God had said of Adam, "It is not good that the man should be alone : I will make him an helpmeet for him," and the servant's business was to fetch Rebekah. He therefore took that which was Isaac's and showed it unto Rebekah, to prove the truth of his words about his riches. "He shall receive of Mine, and shall show it unto you." He also promised blessing to her in Isaac, and he showed her things to come.

Her friends would have detained her, but there must be no delay—"Hinder me not," he says to them, when they suggest her waiting at least ten days. "The Holy Ghost saith, To-day" (Heb. iii. 7). "Behold, now is the accepted time." The question is put to Rebekah. Does she believe what she has heard ? Is she satisfied that Isaac really wants her to go to him ? Is she willing to trust herself to the guidance of the one who has come to fetch her ? "Wilt thou go ? " she is asked ; and her answer is, "I will go."

She believes the report he has brought her ; and forgetting the things which are behind, and reaching forth unto those things which are before, she presses toward the mark for the prize of the high calling—which is, that she shall be the bride of Isaac.

She leaves the old home, and forgetting also her own people and her father's house (Psa. xlv. 10), she commences the desert journey under the guidance of the servant. We read in Gen. xxiv. 61 that she "followed the man ; and the servant took Rebekah, and went his way." It was the right way, we may be sure, for he knew just the best road to take, having travelled that way before ; and it was not likely that Rebekah tried to choose her own path—she was satisfied to be guided. Thus we also are being led by the Spirit of God.

We can imagine that during the journey, and at the various stopping places, she would question him about Isaac, and would want to learn more about the one to whom she was going. We are not told anything about those conversations, only one question and answer are given ; but they are characteristic of the whole. " What man is this ? " asks Rebekah. " My master," is the answer. From first to last this is the servant's one theme. He does not speak of himself ; but only speaks well of Isaac, and at last is able to bring her right into his presence. The type is so plain that none can fail to see its beauty. We, too, who have believed the message are being led by the faithful Guide through the desert journey, till by-and-by we shall see Him face to face.

> Oh, the blessed joy of meeting—
> All the desert past !
> Oh, the wondrous words of greeting
> He shall speak at last !

Isaac, meanwhile, was waiting for his bride ; and we are told two things about him : the one, that he came to meet her from the well Lahai-roi, where was his dwelling-place (Gen. xxiv. 62 ; xxv. 11), "the well of Him that liveth and seeth me" (Gen. xvi. 14, *margin*) ; the other, that as she journeyed he went out into the field at evening to meditate, or to pray (*margin*).

The words of Isaac's prayer are not given ; but we have the record of another prayer, offered by One who ever dwelt in the presence of God, and who pleads for those who are journeying to Him through the wilderness. " Holy Father, keep through Thine own name those whom Thou hast given Me." " The glory which Thou gavest Me I have given them." " Father, I will that they also, whom Thou hast given Me, be with Me where I am, that they may behold My glory."

The chapter ends with the assurance of Isaac's satisfaction and love—" He loved her." The story falls far short of the Antitype, for Isaac did not have to bear anything in order to win her for his bride ; but He whom he foreshadows " shall see of the travail of His soul and shall be satisfied." The very expression in Revelation, " the bride, the Lamb's wife," tells us of the Lamb that had to be slain, that He might have her for Himself.

There is another in Genesis who also seems to foreshadow the work of the Spirit. If Joseph is a type of Christ, and there is no doubt of it, the interpreter through whom he talked to his brethren, and *the ruler of his house*, speak to us of the Holy Ghost. He said to his steward, " Bring these men home, and slay and make ready ; for these men shall dine with me at noon. And the man did as Joseph bade ; and the man brought the men into Joseph's house" (Gen. xliii. 16, 17). Joseph called them, and his steward brought them. It is the Spirit Himself who brings us home, so that by faith we enter into the house of the Lord and feast at His table ; and soon, guided by the Spirit, we shall in very deed be " at home with the Lord."

In their trouble Joseph's brethren came to the steward, and "they communed with him at the door of the house." His reply reminds us of the way in which the "other Comforter" speaks peace to troubled hearts; for he said, " Peace be to you ! fear not." " Ye have not received the spirit of bondage again to fear ; but ye have received the Spirit of adoption, whereby we cry, Abba, Father." " The fruit of the Spirit is . . . peace." And He fills with " all joy and peace in believing, that ye may abound in hope, through the power of the Holy Ghost."

Again, we are told that he brought them to Joseph's house (ver. 24), "and gave them water and they washed their feet " ; so that they were ready to meet Joseph, and present themselves and their offering to him. In the following chapter we read that the steward, or ruler of his house, was commanded by Joseph to test his brethren, that their sin might be brought to their remembrance. In great sorrow they hastened back into Joseph's presence, saying, " How shall we clear ourselves ? God hath found out the iniquity of thy servants."

They called to mind their treatment of Joseph; and our Lord tells us that when the Spirit is come, " He will convince the world of sin, and of righteousness, and of judgment"; of sin against Christ; of the righteousness of Christ; and of judgment by Christ.

In these two chapters in Genesis, Joseph's steward speaks with all the authority of Joseph himself. "I had your money," and "he with whom it (the cup) is found shall be my servant."

There is another important type of the Holy Spirit to which we must refer. In 1 Cor. x. 1, 2, the Apostle says, " All our fathers were under the cloud, and all passed through the sea ; and were all baptized unto Moses in the cloud and in the sea." We have seen that passing through the Red Sea signified passing through the waters of death ; and it appears from this passage that *the pillar of cloud* typified the Holy Ghost—for " by [or, in] one Spirit are we all baptized into one body." It was not a mere cloud ; but a symbol of God's presence amongst them, overshadowing, protecting, and guiding, and so also prefiguring the work of Him who guides us through the desert. In Exodus xiii. 21, 22 we read, " The Lord went before them by day in a pillar of a cloud, to lead them the way; and by night in a pillar of fire, to give them light ; to go by day and night " ; and in the following chapter we are told that "the angel of God, which went before the camp of Israel, removed and went behind them ; and the pillar of the cloud went from before their face, and stood behind them." It was God Himself, the angel of His presence, that dwelt in the cloud. And in Heb. iii., "The Holy Ghost saith, . . . Your fathers tempted Me, proved Me, and saw My works forty years. Wherefore I was grieved with that generation, and said, They do alway err in their heart : and they have not known My ways." The Holy Ghost Himself was there, as we see from Neh. ix. 20 ; and the pillar of cloud and fire was the visible emblem of His presence.

Redemption had been accomplished, the paschal lamb had

been slain, and the blood sprinkled; and now the blood-bought people delivered from Egypt must have a guide. They needed the pillar by day and by night, for the people could not find their way alone. As one has said, "We need leading in the brightest of nature's day, as well as in the darkest of nature's night." When once God had given the pillar of cloud, it remained with them for the rest of the journey. "He took not away the pillar of the cloud by day, nor the pillar of fire by night, from before the people." And so our Lord said of the Guide whom He promised, He shall "abide with you for ever." The Holy Spirit is given "upon believing," and can never be taken away. We are "sealed with that Holy Spirit of promise, which is the earnest of our inheritance, until the redemption of the purchased possession." If the seal could be broken after having been affixed, it would not be "until the redemption of the purchased possession." It might be said of every soul that trusts in the Lord Jesus, "The King sealed it with his own signet, . . . that the purpose might not be changed." The way by which the pillar led seemed strange to the children of Israel, and when they found themselves hemmed in by the sea in front and the enemy behind, they thought they had been brought in a wrong direction; but their guide led them by the right way, and very soon they understood that it was so. There was another road into the land, and it seemed an easier and quicker one; but if they had gone by the way of the Philistines, they would have seen war at once, and God knew that they were not yet ready to fight. Besides this, we are told that "all these things happened unto them for ensamples"; and therefore they must pass through the Red Sea, which would cut them off from all return.

When they were in this difficulty, the pillar went behind them and remained there all night, between them and the Egyptians; enshrouding their enemies in darkness, but giving light to the children of Israel. All through their journey they were never in the dark; and those who are guided by the Spirit

"shall not walk in darkness, but shall have the light of life."
That which was brightness to Israel was darkness to their foes;
and so it is now.   God has given to us a Guide, "even the
Spirit of truth; whom the world cannot receive, because it
seeth Him not, neither knoweth Him."   The Word of God,
illuminated by the Spirit, is bright and clear; but "the
natural man receiveth not the things of the Spirit of God—for
they are foolishness unto him : neither can he know them,
because they are spiritually discerned."   It is true now that
"men see not the bright light which is in the clouds."

The path of the Israelites was like "the path of the just,
as the shining light, that shineth more and more unto the
perfect day"; whilst that of the Egyptians was like "the way
of the wicked, as darkness, they know not at what they
stumble."   They followed the children of Israel, and did not
discover that they were in the bed of the Red Sea till they
were overwhelmed by its waters; and that which was "life
unto life" to Israel was "death unto death" to Pharaoh's
host.

When God would talk with Moses we read that He
"descended in the cloud, and stood with him there, and
proclaimed the name of the Lord" (Exod. xxxiv. 5; Num.
xi. 25; xii. 5; Deut. xxxi. 15).   He spoke out of the cloud.
It is through the Spirit that God speaks now and reveals
Himself.   In Exod. xvi. 10 we read that the children of Israel
"looked toward the wilderness, and, behold, the glory of the
Lord appeared in the cloud."   With their back upon Egypt
they could see the glory; but this was not always their attitude:
for Stephen tells us that they "in their hearts turned back
again into Egypt."   If we are looking longingly towards the
world, we shall miss the sight of the glory; but we shall not
desire to go back into Egypt if "we all, with unveiled face
beholding as in a glass the glory of the Lord, are changed
into the same image from glory to glory, even as by the Spirit
of the Lord."

In Num. ix. we have a beautiful description of the two-fold position held by the cloud in the camp of Israel. When they journeyed it went first; when they encamped it was in the midst.

In our study of God's dwelling places we have seen how the cloud filled the Tabernacle, and afterwards the Temple, and abode there. We, too, are the dwelling-place of God. " Know ye not that ye are the temple of God, and that the Spirit of God dwelleth in you?" and thus we are commanded to " be filled with the Spirit." But it is not only individually that it should be so. It was in the midst of the congregation of the people. If the Spirit were at all times manifestly in the midst of the Church to-day, what power would there be! " So it was alway," we read; but alas, it does not " alway" appear to be so now !

Another expression is also used, for we are told that the cloud rested, or abode, upon the Tabernacle : and thus Peter wrote in his epistle, " The Spirit of glory and of God resteth upon you" (1 Pet. iv. 14).

Then as to the guidance, they never thought of journeying unless the pillar moved ; but abode in their tents and journeyed not, "whether it were two days, or a month, or a year." We never hear of them going on in front of the cloud ; and of God having to speak to them out of the cloud with "a word behind, . . . saying, This is the way, walk ye in it."* This happened to Israel afterwards ; and it often is the case now. We sometimes hear people praying that they may hear the voice behind them ; but we want rather to follow our Guide—not to go on in front with our backs toward Him, and have to be called back "when ye turn to the right hand, and when ye turn to the left." This is very different from the description in Num-ix., where the people learnt to rest in their tents, when the pillar rested ; seven times over we are told that it was " at the

---

* In Numbers xiv. 44, they presumed to go up into the land when forbidden, and were in consequence smitten by Amalek.

commandment of the Lord "—and that commandment was revealed to them by the cloud. We now are "led by the Spirit," as they were led by the pillar; and we are commanded to "walk in the Spirit," as they were to walk in the shadow of the cloud. It may be that the very cloud that guided them hid the next bit of their path. We cannot see what lies before us, but we know that the Guide will lead us aright. He always went first; for we read in Deut. i. 33, "Who went in the way before you, to search you out a place to pitch your tents in, in fire by night, to shew you by what way ye should go, and in a cloud by day"; and in Nehemiah we are told that it was "to give them light in the way wherein they should go."

Many of God's children are perplexed on the subject of God's guidance; but God has not left us in the dark now, He has promised to direct our paths. If the pillar does not move, let us rest; if it journeys, let us follow.

Reference has already been made more than once to the rivers of *water* that flowed *from the smitten rock* as a type of the Holy Spirit. The God-given waters satisfied the thirst of the people, so that they could say to the king of Edom and to the king of the Amorites in passing through their lands, "We will not drink of the water of the wells." In both cases these words were spoken immediately after God had given them water, first from the smitten rock, and then from *the well* (Num. xx. 8, 11, 17, and xxi. 16, 17, 22); and thus we have a beautiful illustration of our Lord's words, "Whosoever drinketh of the water that I shall give him shall never thirst; but the water that I shall give him shall be in him a well of water springing up into everlasting life." It is so also when the well of the fourth of John becomes the overflowing river of the seventh chapter. Those who have this water springing up in them, and flowing out from them, do not need to drink of the world's wells.

But often in the experience of believers, who have come to Christ to drink of the water that He gives, the well does not seem to go on springing up till it becomes the rivers of living water. Perhaps their well has become like those of which we read in Gen. xxvi. 18, 19, where we are told that " Isaac digged again the wells of water which they had digged in the days of Abraham his father : for the Philistines had stopped them, . . . And Isaac's servants digged in the valley, and found there a well of living water" (*marg.*). The world comes in and chokes the well ; and it is little wonder that there is no overflowing stream of blessing for others.

"*The river of God*, which is full of water," is throughout Scripture a beautiful type of the Holy Spirit, and has often been traced through Scripture. " In Eden it took its rise in the earth to water the garden, and from thence to wander in divers streams over the earth. In the wilderness, the smitten rock was its source, and every path of the camp of God its channel. In Canaan, afterwards, the waters of Shiloah flowed softly ; Jehovah watered the land from His own fountains, and made it to drink of the rain of heaven. The river will also rise under the sanctuary for the watering of Jerusalem and the whole land (Ezek. xlvii. ; Joel iii. ; Zech. xiv. ; Psa. xlvi. 4 ; lxv. 9)."* In the book of Revelation we see it proceeding out of the throne of God and of the Lamb, while in Ezekiel the waters issue from under the threshold of the house. In both there is a description of the trees growing on either side of this river ; for wherever it goes the result is sure to be fruitfulness (Ezek. xlvii. 12 ; Rev. xxii. 2). Where the river flows now, there will be all manner of fruit all the year round—the fruit of the Spirit, which is described in Gal. v. 22, 23.

Another emblem of the Holy Spirit is referred to by the Lord Jesus. "*The wind* bloweth where it listeth, and thou hearest the sound thereof, but canst not tell whence it cometh and whither it goeth ; so is every one that is born of the Spirit," or of the wind. In Ezek. xxxvii. we read how it was the wind, or breath, that gave life to the dry bones ; and at

---

* J. G. Bellett.

Pentecost at the giving of the Holy Spirit there is the sound of a rushing mighty wind. Twice there is a direct prayer to the Spirit, and in both cases it is a cry to the wind. The one passage is in Ezek. xxxvii., and the other in Song of Solomon iv. 16, "Awake, O north wind; and come, thou south; blow upon my garden, that the spices thereof may flow out." As Mr. Spurgeon has said, "The prayer is *blow*, the result is *flow*." What would the garden do without the water and the wind? But it has both. The preceding verse in the Song tells us of the well and the river. "A fountain of gardens, a well of living waters, and streams from Lebanon"; and so we have here both symbols of the Holy Spirit. The south wind quieteth the earth (Job xxxvii. 17); is followed by heat (Luke xii. 55); and blows softly (Acts xxvii. 13); but it comes by His power (Psa. lxxviii. 26). Cold comes out of the north (Job xxxvii. 9); and it bringeth forth rain (Prov. xxv. 23, *marg.*), "to satisfy the desolate and waste ground; and to cause the bud of the tender herb to spring forth." Both the strong north wind and the gentle south wind are needed in their turn to make the garden fruitful.

It is not possible in the scope of these pages to do more than touch on a few of the wonderful types in God's Word. We have but presented a few nuggets found close to the surface of this inexhaustible gold country. If some to whom it has been hitherto an unexplored land are prompted to search, they will find themselves well repaid. It is a dominion in which every one is free to dig; there are plenty of "claims" for all; there is no fear of famine: for, unlike the gold regions of earth, the precious ore we find not only enriches, but at the same time satisfies hunger and thirst. "The gold of that land is good."

May He open our eyes that we may behold wondrous things out of His law, and be as those who find therein "great spoil"!

XVII

The Majesty in the Heavens
"Our God is a consuming fire"

WE have often dwelt with thankfulness on the wonderful contrast in Heb. xii., "Ye are not come unto the mount that might be touched, and that burned with fire, nor unto blackness, and darkness, and tempest (vers. 18–21); . . . but ye are come unto Mount Sion, . . . and to Jesus the Mediator of the new covenant" (vers. 22–24). Our eyes are directed first to the terrors of dark Sinai, and then to the full sunshine of grace, the glories of present and future privilege. But the passage does not close with these contrasted pictures. They are used to emphasise the solemn warning which immediately follows. If *they* escaped not who rebelled, then much more *we* shall not. The pronouns are emphatic. Although we do not need to fear "a palpable and kindled fire" (ver. 18, R.V. marg.), "our God is a consuming fire." These words are quoted from Deut. iv., the very chapter which tells of the burning mountain. He is still the same. We delight to quote the words in the next chapter, "the Same yesterday, and to-day, and for ever"; but do we remember that they are true of the holiness of God as much as of the grace of our Lord Jesus Christ? The holiness of God is not less because grace is reigning.

Men have tried to teach that the God of the Old Testament is a different Being from the God of the New Testament; but we know that it is not so. If, therefore, we would understand His character, we must study the two; and must remember that the incidents related in the Old Testament Scriptures form part of "the oracles of God," because by them God revealed Himself.

Too often have we forgotten the reverence and godly fear which should characterise every approach into His presence.

There are seven instances of sudden judgment falling upon

155

men in connection with the Tabernacle or the Temple, with its worship or its holy vessels; and when we study these together, we have a solemn picture of the majesty of God and the awfulness of His presence. The place on which we stand is holy ground whenever we draw near to Him, and we may learn many lessons from these incidents.

The seven are as follows:

i. Nadab and Abihu (two sons of Aaron) offer strange fire (Lev. x.).

ii. Korah (a Levite) and Dathan and Abiram (sons of Reuben), and "two hundred and fifty princes of the assembly, famous in the congregation, men of renown," offer incense (Num. xvi.).

iii. The Philistines carry away the Ark (1 Sam. v.).

iv. The men of Bethshemesh look into the Ark (1 Sam. vi. 19, 20).

v. Uzzah, the son of Abinadab (probably a Levite), takes hold of the Ark (2 Sam. vi. 1–11; 1 Chron. xiii. 1–14).

vi. Uzziah (king of Judah) offers incense (2 Chron. xxvi. 16–23).

vii. Belshazzar (king of Babylon) uses the candlestick and other vessels from the temple at his feast (Dan. v.).

Three of these have to do with the offering of *incense*, three have to do with the *Ark*, and one with the *candlestick*.

The Philistines are smitten with pestilence and destruction; Uzziah with leprosy, leading to death; and in all the other cases death falls in judgment upon those who recklessly and presumptuously put forth their hands to these holy things.

i. Nadab and Abihu were probably the very first to die in the wilderness. "There was not one feeble person" among the tribes of the children of Israel when they left Egypt (Psa. cv. 37). Strong and healthy they started, and at the first numbering soon after their journey began, the total was 603,550 '(Ex. xxxviii. 26; Num. i. 46); exactly the same as at the numbering of the people on the first day of the second

month of the second year.   The Levites were not included
in either of these numberings, and the figures prove that no
one had died in all the other tribes of Israel.   Nadab and
Abihu were the first; and it was their death that had defiled
their cousins Mishael and Elzaphan, who carried their dead
bodies out of the Tabernacle (Lev. x. 4, 5), and were therefore
debarred from keeping the passover (Num. ix. 6, 7).   See
Blunt's *Coincidences*.

Nadab and Abihu were the sons of Aaron, and, next to
Moses and Aaron, had been the most highly privileged of
all the redeemed people.   They were singled out to accom-
pany Moses and their father, when with seventy of the elders
of Israel they were called to "come up unto the Lord" (Ex.
xxiv. 1, 9–11).   "Nadab and Abihu . . . saw the God of
Israel; and there was under His feet as it were a paved work
of a sapphire stone, and as it were the body of heaven in his
clearness.   And upon the nobles of the children of Israel He
laid not His hand; also they saw God and did eat and drink."
And yet, a few months after, they attempted to do what was
forbidden, and they died before the Lord.

In the eighth and ninth chapters of Leviticus we have an
account of the consecration of Aaron and his sons, and the
commencement of their priesthood.   A wonderful eight days'
experience had been theirs—a week of consecration, a day of
ministry, and then sudden death !

The Tabernacle itself had only just been set up.   In the
chapter which describes how, on the first New Year's Day
after leaving Egypt the work was completed, the words are
repeated seven times, "as the Lord commanded Moses."   It
was made according to the pattern; and when all was
finished, the "cloud covered the tent of the congregation, and
the glory of the Lord filled the Tabernacle" (Ex. xl. 34).
But there must be just as close adherence to the commands
of the Lord in the setting apart of those who are to serve in
the Tabernacle as in the meeting-place itself; and so we find
the same words, "as the Lord commanded Moses," repeated

again and again in Lev. viii. and ix. And again God signifies
His approval by a visible sign, " the glory of the Lord
appeared unto all the people," and fire fell upon the altar and
consumed the offerings (Lev. ix. 23, 24).

Nadab and Abihu, with their two brothers, were brought
nigh with Aaron, they were clothed in priestly raiment and
anointed as he had been. They remained for seven days at
the door of the Tabernacle, and on the eighth day helped
him to offer for the first time the offerings that are described
in the opening chapters of Leviticus—a sin-offering and a
burnt-offering for Aaron and his sons; and sin-offering,
burnt-offering, peace offerings, and meat-offering for the
people. They stood by and shared in the blessing that was
pronounced upon the people by Moses and Aaron, they
witnessed the fire fall on the altar. They, too, must have
been filled with awe at the sight. And then—how quickly
the scene changes ! We do not know exactly what their sin
was; but moved perhaps by a false zeal, excited, it may be,
by strong drink (Lev. x. 9), they did something that had been
expressly forbidden. They offered strange fire before the
Lord, which He commanded them not. It may be that they
not only lit the fire themselves instead of taking it from the
altar, but mixed a strange incense of their own. This is forbidden in Ex. xxx. 9, 10. Had they become too familiar
with their sacred privileges? Did they think to improve on
God's plan? Or did they think that it did not matter what
they did, as long as they were in earnest? We cannot tell;
but surely we may learn the solemn lesson. We live in a day
of grace and not of law, and therefore sudden death does not
fall on those who attempt to approach other than in His own
appointed way; but the God we worship is the same who
dwelt between the cherubim. Those who have had the
highest privileges are probably in the greatest danger of trans-
gressing after the manner of Nadab and Abihu; and who can
tell what blessings have been lost because of such things !

ii. Korah, Dathan, and Abiram (Num. xvi.). The next

miraculous display of God's majesty in connection with the Tabernacle Service is shown in the terrible judgment that fell upon Korah and his company.

> "The Kohathites upon their shoulders bear
> The holy vessels covered with all care."

Korah was not satisfied with this the service allotted to his family, but sought "the priesthood also." He wished to offer incense, and this belonged only to the priests. He was joined in his rebellion by two sons of Reuben, the tribe whose tents were pitched near those of the Kohathites; and "two hundred and fifty princes of the assembly, famous in the congregation, men of renown" (ver. 2). When Moses called upon God to show forth His power, Dathan and Abiram, refusing to stand at the door of the Tabernacle, remained outside their own tents; and there the earth opened its mouth and swallowed them and their families. Korah and the rest of his companions perished as Nadab and Abihu had done, by a fire from the Lord. And this was not all. The people of Israel murmured against Moses and against Aaron; and in the plague that followed, 14,700 people died. The rebellion started with one man; but nearly 15,000 were involved in the judgment that followed—affording us another solemn lesson as to the majesty of God, and the solemnity of approach into His presence.

The next three events on the list have to do with the history of the Ark, and have already been noticed (pp. 67–69).

iii. Judgment fell on the Philistines who had carried the Ark into their own country;

iv. Upon the men of Bethshemesh who looked into the Ark, and (v.) upon Uzzah who touched it. It is remarkable that the Ark was three days in the temple of Dagon (1 Sam. v. 2–4). On two successive "morrows" we read that the idol fell before it, and on the second occasion was broken in pieces. It is not likely that the Philistines allowed it to remain longer in the temple, and we know how they were obliged to send it back at last.

We cannot doubt that as Jonah's "three days and three nights in the whale's belly" were a type of the "three days and three nights spent by the Lord Himself 'in the heart of the earth'" (Matt. xii. 40), so also were the three days spent by the Ark in the house of the fish-god.

v. The Ark had been in the home of Abinadab for twenty years; and it is sad indeed that at last that home should be plunged into sorrow on account of Uzzah's presumption. Had the Ark by long familiarity lost its sacredness to him?

vi. The leprosy of Uzziah. This again has to do with the offering of incense. Uzziah the king, like Korah the Levite, wished to offer incense. He was of the tribe of Judah, "of which tribe Moses spake nothing concerning priesthood," and "no man gave attendance at the altar." Uzziah sought for increased honour; but the high priest withstood him, and told him "neither shall it be for thine honour from the Lord God." "The leprosy even rose up in his forehead before the priests in the house of the Lord from beside the incense altar." "They thrust him out from thence"; but it was not necessary for them to do so, for, covered with shame, "himself hasted also to go out." He remained a leper to the day of his death.

We learn therefore from these three solemn scenes, that it is no light thing to approach into the presence of God, for this was typified by the offering of incense; and God will not permit men presumptuously to draw near in any way but that which He has ordained.

The other three which have to do with the Ark, teach us something concerning the power that dwells in the Lord Himself, and the reverence with which He should be treated. The lesson is concerning the sacredness of His Person.

vii. The handwriting on the wall. The last on our list is a scene in Babylon, and it is closely associated with the candlestick. Belshazzar sought to decorate his table with the vessels which had been taken from the Temple. The sacred candlestick stood against the wall, and shed its light on the scene of revelry. And "in the same hour came forth fingers of a Man's hand, and wrote *over against the candlestick*" the sentence of judgment. In Daniel's indictment of Belshazzar, he mentions as a proof of his having lifted up himself against the Lord of heaven that he had made use of these sacred vessels. That which is consecrated to the Lord must not be used for the service of the world.

In view of these solemn pictures, with what joy do we turn to the words of Heb. vii. 24, 25, "This Man . . . hath an unchangeable priesthood. Wherefore He is able also to save them to the uttermost that come unto God by Him, seeing He ever liveth to make intercession for them"—coming unto God as worshippers, for the word is translated in chap. x. 22, "draw near." The Majesty in the heavens is the same as in the days of old; but we have "such an High Priest" who is set on the right hand of the throne.

But there is another series of brighter pictures which we may place side by side with these seven.

i. Aaron the high priest, in full acceptance, offers on the day of atonement in the holiest of all the right kind of incense and the right kind of fire (Lev. xvi. 12, 13). As though to mark the contrast, the chapter opens with a mention of the death of Nadab and Abihu.

ii. In Luke i. 8–11, we have an example of a priest offering incense. "According to the custom of the priest's office, his (Zacharias') lot was to burn incense"; and while doing so, "there appeared unto him an angel of the Lord, standing on the right side of the altar of incense"—not in order to smite with judgment, but to give a promise of blessing. Though Korah might not offer, God had His chosen priests who were called to the service.

iii. In Josh. vi. we read how the Ark, borne round Jericho on the shoulders of the priests, brings victory to the people of the Lord instead of pestilence and death, as in the case of the Philistines. The walls fall at His presence, as Dagon fell afterwards; but the Ark brought no death among those who carried it.

iv. When the people passed over Jordan, the Ark was in the midst of the river, covered with the vail of the Tabernacle, the badgers' skins, and the cloth of blue. There was no looking into it. And that which afterwards brought death to the men of Bethshemesh, brought safety to Israel.

v. The house of Obed-edom was blessed by the presence of the Ark; whereas the house of Abinadab had been devastated. We can picture with what reverence and godly fear it was treated; it was the savour of life unto life in one home, and death unto death in the other.

vi. We read in Isaiah vi. that it was "in the year that King Uzziah died" that the wonderful vision was given to Isaiah. The reference was evidently intended, as in the case of Lev. xvi. 1, to emphasise the contrast. Isaiah saw "the Lord sitting upon a throne, high and lifted up, and His train filled the Temple." He saw the seraphim, he heard their voices; and as he remembered the judgment that had fallen on Uzziah, he felt that he too was a leper before God. "I am a man of unclean lips," he cried, comparing himself to the leper who put a covering upon his lip and cried, "Unclean, unclean" (Lev. xiii. 45). But in the very place where Uzziah was struck with leprosy, Isaiah received cleansing by the "live coal . . . from off the altar."

> And so the two went forth—
> The king to living death, and lonely pain;
> The prophet to the errands of His Lord.

vii. The call of the child Samuel is associated with the candlestick of the Tabernacle; for we are told, the voice of the Lord came to him "ere the lamp went out." What a different scene from that depicted in Daniel! The candlestick was in its right place, serving its right purpose; and instead of a handwriting of judgment, came a call to God's young servant.

Typical Verbs

Note to Chart on p. 86, and to Chapter V

EVEN in the minute details of the various typical ceremonies which God enjoined, we may recognise many foreshadowings of the Cross by the very verbs which are employed. For instance, it is not by accident that, in connection with the offerings, blood was to be *poured out*; certain things were to be *pierced*, or *parted in pieces*; or again, that the rock was to be *smitten*, and the serpent *lifted up*.

Attention has already been called to the *bruising* or *beating* of many substances (pp. 29, 30), but many other typical verbs may be studied.

One such gives us the key to an important truth in connection with the Meal-offering, which has not generally been noticed. While it is quite true that there was no shedding of blood in this offering (p. 90), the death of the Lord Jesus is clearly foreshadowed. It does not merely typify His spotless life, though this is the most prominent characteristic. At the end of the chapter (Lev. ii.) the oblation of the first-fruits is included with the Meal-offering. Surely there must be some mention of His death between the description of His life in vers. 1, 2, and of the resurrection, typified by the first-fruits in ver. 14 (see p. 47). In ver. 6 we find it shining forth in one little verb. The cake or loaf of fine flour, unleavened and mingled with oil, was to be *parted in pieces*. Broken bread! Where could we find a clearer type of His death? Can we not hear Him saying, as He did long years after, when He broke the bread at the institution of the memorial

163

feast, "This is My body, which is given for you"? The usual interpretation of the Meal-offering, as stated on the Chart (p. 86), is that it is "Typical of the Lord Jesus as Man, presenting to God an unblemished life." This is true, but it is not complete. It would be better to state it thus, "The Lord Jesus, in life, death and resurrection, presenting to God an unblemished manhood." *

In the same way the word used for the cakes in Lev. ii. 4 is derived from the verb *pierced* or *wounded* (see Newberry's Bible); and thus we have another foreshadowing of the death on the cross.

It was in view of the coming crucifixion that the words of Deut. xxi. 23, quoted in Gal. iii. 13, were written : "Cursed is every one that hangeth on a tree"; "the Scripture fore-seeing" the very "death He should die," when He was "hanged on a tree" (Acts v. 30; x. 39), that He might be "made a curse for us." With terrible appropriateness "Judas, which had betrayed Him . . went and hanged himself" (Matt. xxvii. 3–5); for the very method by which he thus committed suicide was but a symbol of his spiritual death, as he brought himself under the curse. He became, as it were, a forerunner of that company of all who, by re-jecting the substitutionary death of Christ, refuse to have any share in the blessing.

By overlooking these important typical verbs, some have failed to see the completeness of the picture, and have even denied that the Cross was in the Old Testament. But when we put the various verbs together, we see how accurate are the smallest details. It is not by accident that each word is used in its place by the Holy Spirit, when He would "signify" (Heb. ix. 8) something fresh about the very form of the death which the Lamb of God would suffer.

---

* As revised in *Outline Studies of the Tabernacle.*

Moses, a Type of Christ

" Like unto me "
Type parallel and contrast

His servant ... ... Psa. cv. 26 ...	"My Servant ... ... Matt. xii. **18**.
His chosen ... ... Psa. cvi. **23** ...	Whom I have chosen " Isa. xlii. **1**.
The prophet ... Deut. xviii. **15–19** ...	The Prophet John vi. **14**; Lu. vii. **16**.
Priest ... ... Psa. xcix. 6 ...	Priest ... ... Heb. vii. **24**.
King ... ... Deut. xxxiii. 4, 5 ...	King ... ... Acts xvii. 7.
Judge ... ... Ex. xviii. 13 ...	Judge ... John v. **27**; Acts xvii. **31**.
Shepherd ... Ex. iii. **1**; Isa. lxiii. **11** ...	Shepherd ... ... John x. **11**, **14**.
Leader Isa. lxiii. **12**, **13**; Psa. lxxvii. 20 ...	Leader ... ... Isa. lv. 4.
Mediator ... ... Ex. xxxiii. 8, 9 ...	One Mediator ... ... **1** Tim. ii. 5.
Intercessor ... ... Num. xxi. 7 ...	Intercessor ... ... Rom. viii. **34**.
Deliverer ... ... Acts vii. **35** ...	Deliverer Rom. xi. **26**; **1** Thess. i. **10**.
Ruler ... ... ,, ,, ,, ...	Ruler ... ... Micah v. 2.

"Pharaoh charged all his people, saying, Every son that is born ye shall cast into the river" Ex. i. **22**; Acts vii. **19** } ... { "Herod . . . sent forth and slew all the children that were in Bethlehem." Matt. ii. **13-16**.

"A goodly child" Ex. ii. **1**, 2; Heb. xi. **23** "Fair to God ... Acts vii. 20 (Marg.) } ... { "Jesus increased in wisdom and stature, and in favour with God and man." Luke ii. **40**, **52**.

"Refused to be called the son of Pharaoh's daughter" (thus refusing a kingdom). Heb. xi. **24**, **25** } ... { "The devil . . . sheweth Him all the kingdoms of the world, and the glory of them" ... Matt. iv. **8-10**.

"Greater riches than the treasures in Egypt" ... ... Heb. xi. **26** } ... { "Though He was rich, yet for your sakes He became poor" 2 Cor. viii. 9.

"Had respect unto the recompence of the reward" ... ... Heb. xi. **26** } ... { "For the joy that was set before Him" ... ... Heb. xii. 2,

"By faith he forsook Egypt." Heb. xi. **11**, **27** } ... { "Out of Egypt have I called My Son." Matt. ii. **15**.

"He endured as seeing Him who is invisible" ... ... Heb. xi. **27** } ... { "He that hath sent Me is with Me." John viii. **29**.

"He supposed his brethren would have understood . . . but they understood not" ... ... Acts vii. **25** } ... { "His own received Him not." John i. **10**, **11**.

"Who made thee a ruler and a judge over us?"... ... ... ,, **27** } ... { "Who made Me a judge or a divider over you?" Luke xii. **14**. (Was He reminding them how Moses had been treated?)

"This Moses whom they refused . . . the same did God send to be a ruler and a deliverer" ... ,, **35** } ... { "God hath made that same Jesus, whom ye have crucified, both Lord and Christ"... ... Acts ii. **36**.

"He sat down by a well" Ex. ii. **15** ... { "Jesus therefore, being wearied with His journey, sat thus on the well" John iv. 6.

"All the men are dead which sought thy life" ... Ex. iv. 19	... {"They are dead which sought the young child's life" ... Matt. ii. 20.
"He looked on their burdens." "Ye make them rest from their burdens" ... Ex. ii. 11; v. 5	... {"Come unto Me, all ye that labour and are heavy laden, and I will give you rest" ... ... Matt. xi. 28.
"Let My people go" ... Ex. ix. 13	... {"To proclaim liberty to the captives." Isa. lxi. 1.
"All these . . . shall bow down themselves unto me" ... ... xi. 8	... {"That at the Name of Jesus every knee should bow" ... Phil. ii. 10.
"How long shall this man be a snare unto us" ... ... x. 7	... {"A stone of stumbling and a rock of offence" ... ... 1 Pet. ii. 8.
"He went out from Pharaoh in a great anger" ... ... xi. 8	... {"He looked round about on them with anger, being grieved for the hardness of their hearts" ... Mark iii. 5.
"Speak thou . . . all that I say unto thee" ... ... vi. 29	... {"I have not spoken of Myself . . . as the Father said unto Me, so I speak.' John xii. 49, 50.
"Certainly I will be with thee" iii. 12	... {"He that hath sent Me is with Me" John viii. 29.
"This is the finger of God" ... viii. 19	... {"If I with the finger of God cast out devils" ... ... Luke xi. 20.
"About midnight . . . there shall be a great cry" ... ... xi. 4, 6	... {"At midnight there was a cry made" Matt. xxv. 6.
"The Lord smote all the first-born . . . and there was not a house where there was not one dead" ... ... Ex. xii. 29, 30	... {"They shall look upon Me whom they have pierced; and they shall mourn for Him . . . as one that is in bitterness for his first-born" Zech. xii. 10.
"Learned in all the wisdom of the Egyptians, and was mighty in words and deeds" ... ... Acts vii. 22	... {"Whence hath this Man this wisdom and these mighty works?" Matt. xiii. 54; Mark vi. 2.
"Moses stretched out his hand over the sea; and the Lord caused the sea to go back by a strong east wind." Ex. xiv. 21	... {"What manner of Man is this, that even the winds and the sea obey Him?" ... ... Matt. viii. 27.
"The people thirsted there for water" ... ... xvii. 3	... {"If any man thirst, let him come unto Me, and drink" ... John vii. 37.
"Almost ready to stone me" ... ,, 4	... {"Then took they up stones to cast at Him" ... ... John viii. 59.
"Spring up, O well" Num. xxi. 16–18	... {"The water that I shall give him shall be in him a well of water springing up" ... ... John iv. 14.
"Moses brought their cause before the Lord" ... Num. xxvii. 5	... {"An Advocate with the Father." 1 John ii. 1.
"The Lord did according to the word of Moses" ... ... Ex. viii. 13	... {"That the saying might be fulfilled which He spake" ... John xviii. 9.
"Thou hast found grace in My sight, and I know thee by name" ... ... iii. 17	... {"This is My beloved Son in whom I am well pleased" ... Matt. xvii. 5.

"When Moses held up his hand, Israel prevailed"   ... Ex. xvii. 11 } ... { "More than conquerors through Him that loved us"   ... Rom. viii. 37.

"His hands were steady until the going down of the sun"   ... ,, 12 } ... { "He ever liveth to make intercession for them"   ...   ... Heb. vii. 25.

"I stood between the Lord and you at that time, to shew you the word of the Lord"... Deut. v. 5; Ex. xx. 19 } ... { "Hath in these last days spoken unto us by His Son"   ... Heb. i. 2.

"Who is on the Lord's side? let him come unto me"   ... Ex. xxxii. 26 } ... { "He that is not with Me is against Me"...   ...   ... Matt. xii. 30.

"Miriam and Aaron spake against Moses"   ...   ... Num. xii. 1 } ... { "Neither did His brethren believe in Him"   ...   ... John vii. 5.

"The man Moses was very meek" ,, 3 ... { "I am meek and lowly in heart." Matt. xi. 29.

"Wherefore then were ye not afraid to speak against My servant Moses?",, 8 } ... { "That all men should honour the Son, even as they honour the Father." John v. 23.

"They envied Moses also in the camp." Psa. cvi. 16 } ... { "He knew that the chief priests had delivered Him for envy" Mark xv. 10.

"Moses wist not that the skin of his face shone while he talked with Him." Ex. xxxiv. 29, 30 } ... { "His face did shine as the sun." Matt. xvii. 2.

"When the people saw that Moses delayed to come down out of the Mount, the people said . . . as for this Moses we wot not what has become of him." Ex. xxxii. 1 } ... { "My Lord delayeth His coming." Matt. xxiv. 48-50. "Where is the promise of His coming?" 2 Pet. iii. 3, 4.

"I took twelve men of you." Deut. i. 23 } ... { "And He ordained twelve, that they might be with Him, and that He might send them forth." Mark iii. 13, 14.

"Seventy men of the elders of the people"   ... Num. xi. 16, 24 } ... { "The Lord appointed other seventy also"...   ...   ... Luke x. 1.

"Behold the blood of the covenant"   ...   ... Ex. xxiv. 8 } ... { "This cup is the new covenant in My blood"   ...   ... Luke xxii. 20.

"So Moses finished the work" xl. 33 ... { "I have finished the work which Thou gavest Me to do" ... John xvii. 4, 5.

"It went ill with Moses for their sakes." Psa. cvi. 32 } ... { "He was wounded for our transgressions"   ...   ... Isa. liii. 5.

"I have pardoned according to Thy word"   ... Num. xiv. 17–20 } ... { "Even as God for Christ's sake hath forgiven you"   ... Eph. iv. 32.

"Had not Moses His chosen stood before Him in the breach" Psa. cvi. 23 } ... { "Awake, O sword, against My Shepherd"   ...   ... Zech. xiii. 7.

"There arose not a prophet since in Israel . . . whom the Lord knew face to face in all the signs and wonders." Deut. xxxiv. 10, 11 } ... { "As the Father knoweth Me, even so know I the Father" John x. 15. "If I had not done among them the works which none other man did." John xv. 24.

'According to all that the Lord com-
manded him so did he"   Ex. xl. 16 } ... { "Even as I have kept My Father's
commandments" ...   John xv. 10.

"As also Moses was faithful in all his
house" ...   .   Heb. iii. 2 } ... { "Who was faithful to Him that appointed Him"   ...   Heb. iii. 2.

"He made known His ways unto
Moses" ...   .   Psa. ciii. 7 } ... { "The Father loveth the Son, and
sheweth Him all things that Himself
doeth"   ...   ...   John v. 20.

A parting blessing   ... Deut. xxxiii. 1 } ... { "While He blessed them He was
parted from them" Lu. xxiv. 50, 51.

"Let the Lord set a man over the congregation which may . . . lead them
out, and which may bring them in ;
that the congregation of the Lord be
not as sheep which have no shepherd."
Num. xxvii. 16, 17. } ... { "I will pray the Father, and He shall
give you another Comforter, that He
may abide with you for ever . . . I
will not leave you comfortless."
John xiv. 16-18.

"Contending with the devil, he disputed
about the body of Moses" ... Jude 9 } ... { "Pilate said unto them . . . Make it
as sure as ye can." Matt. xxvii. 65.

"The children of Israel went on dry land
in the midst of the sea. And Miriam
. . . took a timbrel . . . and all the
women . . . after her with timbrels."
Ex. xv. 19, 20 } ... { "And I saw as it were a sea of glass
. . . and them that had gotten the
victory . . . stand on the sea of glass,
having the harps of God."
Rev. xv. 2.

"Then sang Moses and the children of
Israel this song unto the Lord."
Ex. xv. 1 } ... { "They sing the song of Moses, the
servant of God, and the song of the
Lamb"   ...   ...   Rev. xv. 3.

CONTRASTS.

The law given by Moses   John i. 17 } ... { "Grace and truth came by Jesus
Christ"   ...   ...   John i. 17.

Fading glory   ...   ...   2 Cor. iii. 7 ... Glory that excelleth ... 2 Cor. iii. 6.

When Moses' face shone the people
feared   ...   .   Ex. xxxiv. 3 } ... { When the Lord's face shone they ran
to Him   ...   ...   Mark ix. 15.

Moses' first recorded act—slaying a man
Ex. ii. 12 } ... { Christ's first act in Mark—healing a
man ...   .   Mark i. 25, 26.

First plague, water turned into blood,
emblem of a curse   ...   Ex. vii. 20 } ... { First miracle, water turned into wine,
emblem of joy   ...   John ii. 1-10.

Unable to save   ...   ...   Jer. xv. 1 } ... { "Able to save to the uttermost."
Heb. vii. 25.

"Moses verily as a servant" Heb. iii. 5 } ... { "But Christ as a Son over His own
house"   ...   ...   Heb. iii. 6.

The law broken in his hands.
Ex. xxxii. 19 ; Deut. ix. 17 } ... { The law perfectly kept in His heart.
Psa. xl. 8.

Bread that sustained life John vi, 31, 49 ... Bread that gives life. John vi. 33, 50, 51.

Praying for a leper   ... Num. xii. 13 ... Healing a leper   ...Matt. viii. 2, 3.

The first passover   ... Heb. xi. 28 ... The last passover   ... Luke xxii. 15.

Willing to be a substitute.
Ex. xxxii. 30, 34 } ... { Actually a substitute.
1 Pet. ii. 24 ; Isa. liii. 4-6.

Forty days in the mount Ex. xxxiv. 28 ... Forty days in the wilderness. Matt. iv. 2.

An incomplete exodus Deut. iii. 25-27 } ... { An exodus accomplished (decease, *lit.*
exodus)   ...   ...   Luke ix. 31.

Joseph, a Type of Christ

Feeding the flock ... Gen. xxxvii. 2 ...	The Good Shepherd ... John x. 11, 14.
Their evil report ... ... ,, 2 ...	Their deeds evil ... John iii. 19, 20.
Loved (by his father) ... ... ,, 3 ...	My beloved Son ... Matt. iii. 17.
Hated (by his brethren) ... ,, 4, 5 ...	Hated without a cause John xv. 25.
Not believed ... ... ,, 5 ...	Neither did His brethren believe in Him ... ... John vii. 5.
Obeisance ... ... ,, 7, 9 ...	In all things the pre-eminence. Col. i. 18.
Shalt thou indeed reign over us? ,, 8 ...	We will not have this man Lu. xix. 14.
Envied ... ... ,, 11 ...	Delivered for envy ... Mark xv. 10.
His father observed the saying ,, 11 ...	His mother kept all these sayings in her heart... ... ... Lu. ii. 51.
Sent to his brethren ... ... ,, 13 ...	I will send my beloved Son Lu. xx. 13.
Here am I ... ... ,, 13 ...	Lo, I come ... ... Psa. xl. 7, 8.
Bring me word again ... ... ,, 14 ...	Now come I to Thee... John xvii. 13.
Out of the vale of Hebron (fellowship) ... ... ,, 14 } ... {	The glory which I had with Thee. John xvii. 5, 24.
He came to Shechem ... ... ,, 14 ...	To a city of Samaria which is called Sychar (or Shechem) John iv. 4, 5.
Wandering in the field ... ,, 15 ... {	The field the world ... Matt. xiii. 38. Not where to lay His head Lu. ix. 58.
I seek my brethren ... ... ,, 16 ...	Come to seek and to save Lu. xix. 10
Went after his brethren ... ,, 17 ...	Going after that which is lost Lu. xv. 4.
They conspired against him ... ,, 18 ...	Took counsel against Him. Matt. xxvii. 1 ; John xi. 53.
We shall see ... ... ,, 20 ...	That we may see ... Mark xv. 32.
Stripped ... ... ,, 23 ...	They stripped Him ... Matt. xxvii. 28.
The pit ... ... ,, 24 ...	The horrible pit Psa. xl. 2; lxix. 2, 14, 15.
They sat down... ... ... ,, 25 ...	Sitting down they watched Him there. Matt. xxvii. 36.
Twenty pieces of silver ... ,, 28 ...	Thirty pieces of silver. Matt. xxvi. 15; xxvii. 9; Ex. xxi. 32.
Into Egypt ... ... ,, 36 ...	Out of Egypt have I called My Son. Matt. ii. 14, 15.
Servant to Potiphar, an officer of Pharaoh, captain of the guard. Gen. xxxix. 1 ; Psa. cv. 17 } ... {	A servant of rulers ... Isa. xlix. 7. The form of a servant Phil. ii. 7.

The Lord with Joseph. Gen. xxxix. 2, 21, 23 ...	The Father is with Me	John xvi. 32.
The Lord made all that he did to prosper in his hand ... Gen. xxxix. 3	The pleasure of the Lord shall prosper in His hand	Isa. liii. 10.
All put into his hand ... ... ,, 4, 8 ...	Hath given all things into His hand.	John iii. 35.
Blessed for Joseph's sake ... ,, 5 ...	Blessed in Christ	Eph. i. 3; iv. 32.
Left all in Joseph's hand ... ,, 6 ...	Able to keep	2 Tim. i. 12.
A goodly person ... ... ,, 6 ...	Altogether lovely	Song of Sol. v. 16.
Well favoured ... ... ,, 6 ...	Increased . . . in favour with God and man	Lu. ii. 52.
How can I do this great wickedness ? ... ... ,, 9 ...	Yet without sin	Heb. iv. 15.
Where the king's prisoners were bound ... ... ,, 20 ...	When they had bound Him, they led Him away	Matt. xxvii. 2.
Whose feet they hurt with fetters. Psa. cv. 18, 19. ...	They pierced My hands and My feet.	Psa. xxii. 16.
Two of Pharaoh's officers . . . in the place where Joseph was bound. Gen. xl. 2, 3 ...	There were also two other, malefactors.	Lu. xxiii. 32.
(To one a message of life.) Yet within three days shall Pharaoh lift up thine head and restore thee unto thy place ... ... ,, 13	To-day shalt thou be with Me in Paradise	Lu. xxiii. 43.
I do remember my faults this day: . . . and there was with us a young man, an Hebrew. Gen. xli. 9, 12 ...	We receive the due reward of our deeds: but this Man hath done nothing amiss.	Lu. xxiii. 41.
He served them ... ... Gen. xl. 4 ...	I am among you as He that serveth.	Lu. xxii. 27.
Wherefore look ye so sadly to-day? ,, 7 ...	What manner of communications are these that ye have one to another, as ye walk, and are sad?	Lu. xxiv. 17.
Think on me, ... ,, 14 ...	This do in remembrance of Me.	1 Cor. xi. 24.
Show kindness, I pray thee, unto me, ... ,, 14 ...	Inasmuch as ye have done it unto one of the least of these My brethren, ye have done it unto Me ...	Matt. xxv. 40.
Make mention of me ... ... ,, 14 ...	Whosoever therefore shall confess Me before men, him will I confess also before My Father ...	Matt. x. 32.
Yet did not the chief butler remember Joseph, but forgat him ... ... ,, 23 ...	Yet no man remembered that same poor man	Eccl. ix. 15.
Here also have I done nothing that they should put me into the dungeon ... ... ,, 15 ...	Which of you convinceth Me of sin?	John viii. 46.
Out of the dungeon ... ... xli. 14 ...	Out of prison He cometh to reign.	Eccl. iv. 14.

The king sent and loosed him.	Psa. cv. 20	... { Whom God hath raised up, having loosed the pains of death. Acts ii. 24.
It is not in me ... ... Gen. xli. 16		The Son can do nothing of Himself, but what He seeth the Father do.
God hath shewed Pharaoh ... ,, 25		... { John v. 19.
A man in whom the Spirit of God is ... ... ,, 38		... { Anointed with the Holy Ghost and with power ... ... Acts x. 38.
God hath showed thee all this ,, 39		... The Father loveth the Son, and sheweth Him all things that Himself doeth. John v. 20.
None so discreet and wise ... ,, 39		... All the treasures of wisdom and knowledge ... ... Col. ii. 3.
Over my house ... ... ,, 40		... As a Son over His own house; whose house are we ... . Heb. iii. 6.
According unto thy word shall all my people be ruled ... ,, 40		... { The government shall be upon His shoulder ... ... Isa. ix. 6, 7.
Without thee shall no man lift up his hand or foot ... ... ,, 44		... { Without Me ye can do nothing. John xv. 5.
Bow the knee ... ... ,, 43		... That in the name of Jesus every knee should bow ... ... Phil. ii. 10.
Thirty years old ... ... ,, 46 Num. iv. ; 2 Sam. v. 4.		... About thirty years of age Lu. iii. 23.
Joseph gathered corn . . . very much . . . without number ,, 49		... { The unsearchable riches of Christ. Eph. iii. 8.
Manasseh—forgetting ... ... ,, 51		... He shall see of the travail of His soul and shall be satisfied ... Isa. liii. 11.
Ephraim—fruitful ... ... ,, 52		... Much fruit ... ... John xii. 24.
As Joseph had said ... ... ,, 54		... His disciples remembered that He had said this ... ... John ii. 22.
Go unto Joseph ... ... ,, 55		... Lord, to whom shall we go? John vi. 68.
What he saith to you, do ... ,, 55		... Whatsoever He saith unto you, do it. John ii. 5.
Famine over all the face of the earth ... ... ,,56,57		... { A mighty famine in that land Lu. xv. 14.
The famine waxed sore ... ,, 56		... Not a famine of bread, . . . but of hearing the words of the Lord. Amos. viii. 11.
Joseph opened all the storehouses ... ... ,, 56		... { The windows of heaven ... Mal. iii. 10. While He opened to us the Scriptures. Lu. xxiv. 27, 32.
All countries came to buy ... ,, 57		... My salvation unto the end of the earth. Isa. xlix. 6.
He it was that sold ... ... xlii. 6		... { Blessing upon the head of him that selleth it ... ... Pro. xi. 26. None other name ... Acts iv. 12.
He knew them ... ... ,, 7, 8		... He knew all men ... John ii. 24, 25.
But they knew not him ... ,, 8		... The world knew Him not. He came unto His own and His own received Him not ... ... John i. 10, 11.

Joseph made himself strange unto them, and spake roughly unto them. He put them altogether into ward three days ... ... Gen. xlii. 7, 17 ... { If they be bound in fetters, and be holden in cords of affliction ; then He sheweth them their work, and their transgressions, that they have exceeded. He openeth also their ear to discipline.
Job xxxvi. 8–10.

His blood is required ... ... ,, 22 ... His blood be on us, and on our children.
Matt. xxvii. 25.

They knew not that Joseph understood them ... ... ,, 23 } ... Of quick understanding ... Isa. xi. 3.

He spake unto them by an interpreter ... ... ,, 23 } ... { He shall receive of Mine and shall shew it unto you ... John xvi. 13, 14.
Ambassadors for Christ   2 Cor. v. 20.

He turned himself about from them and wept * ... ... ,, 24 } ... { He beheld the city and wept over it.
Lu. xix. 41.

Joseph commanded to fill their sacks with corn ... ... ,, 25 } ... { Filleth thee with the finest of the wheat.
Psa. cxlvii. 14.
Of His fulness have all we received.
John i. 16.

To restore every man's money into his sack ... ... ,, 25 } ... { Without money, and without price.
Isa. lv. 1.

To give them provision for the way ... ... ,, 25 } ... All your need ... ... Phil. iv. 19.

Thus did he unto them ... ,, 25 ... All came to pass. Josh. xxi. 45; xxiii. 14.
As much as they can carry ... xliv. 1 ... As much as they would ... John v.. 11.
Bring these men home... ... xliii. 16 ... Compel them to come in   Lu. xiv. 23
Make ready ... ... ,, 16 ... All things are ready ... Matt. xxii. 4
The men were afraid ... ... ,, 18 ... Perfect love casteth out fear 1 John 4,18.
They came near to the steward, and they communed with him ,, 19 } ... { He shall teach you all things.
John xiv. 26.
Other money have we brought down ... ... ,, 22 } ... { Going about to establish their own righteousness... ... Rom. x. 3.
Peace be to you ! Fear not ... ,, 23 ... { All joy and peace in believing . . . through the power of the Holy Ghost.
Rom. xv. 13.

They drank, and were merry with him ... ... ,, 34 } ... { They began to be merry.   Lu. xv. 24.
God hath found out the iniquity of thy servants ... ... xliv. 16 } ... { He will convince the world of sin.
John xvi. 8, 9.
Joseph made himself known ... xlv. 1 ... Their eyes were opened, and they knew Him ... ... Lu. xxiv. 31.
At the second time ... Acts vii. 13 } ... { They shall look upon Me whom they have pierced, and they shall mourn for Him ... ... Zech. xii. 10.
They were troubled at his presence ... ... Gen. xlv. 3
I am Joseph your brother whom ye sold... ... ... ,, 4 } ... { I am Jesus whom thou persecutest.
Acts ix. 5.
Come near to me ... ... ,, 4 ... Made nigh ... ... Eph. ii. 13.
God did send me ... ... ,, 5, 7 ... God sent His only begotten Son.
1 John iv. 9.

* It is mentioned seven times that Joseph wept : Gen. xlii. 24 ; xliii. 30 ; xlv. 2, 14 ; xlvi. 29 ; l. 1, 17.

A great deliverance ...	Gen. xlv. 7 ...	Who delivered us from so great a death. 2 Cor. i. 10.
Not you, . . . but God ...	,, 8 ...	By the determinate counsel and fore-knowledge of God ... Acts ii. 23.
Tarry not	,, 9 ...	Behold, now is the accepted time. 2 Cor. vi. 2.
There will I nourish thee ...	,, 11 ...	He that cometh to Me shall never hunger ... ... John vi. 35.
Joseph nourished . . . all his father's household, with bread, as a little child is nourished xlvii. 12 (*marg.*).	...	The Lord is my Shepherd, I shall not want ... ... Psa. xxiii. 1.
Behold your eyes see that it is my mouth that speaketh unto you ... ... xlv. 12	...	Behold, My hands and My feet, that it is I Myself; handle Me and see. Lu. xxiv. 39.
Ye shall tell my father of all my glory ... ... ,, 13	...	The gospel of the glory of Christ. 2 Cor. iv. 4.
His brethren talked with him . ,, 15 ...		Jesus Himself drew near, and went with them ... ... Lu. xxiv. 15.
Come unto me ... ... ,,18,19 ...		Come unto Me ... ... Matt. xi. 28.
Regard not your stuff, for the good of all the land of Egypt is yours ... ... ,, 20	...	Forgetting those things which are behind, and reaching forth unto those things which are before. Phil. iii. 13, 14.
Joseph is yet alive ... ... ,,26,28 ...		One Jesus, . . . whom Paul affirmed to be alive ... ... Acts xxv. 19.
Jacob's heart fainted, for he believed them not ... ... ,, 26	...	They believed not for joy Lu. xxiv. 11, 41.
Now let me die since I have seen thy face ... ... xlvi. 30	...	Now lettest thou Thy servant depart in peace, . . . for mine eyes have seen Thy salvation... ... Lu. ii. 29, 30.
My brethren ... xlvi. 31 ; xlvii. 1 ...		Not ashamed to call them brethren. Heb. ii. 11.
Why should we die in thy presence ?... ... ... xlvii. 15, 19	...	I am the Resurrection and the Life. John xi. 25.
Our money is spent ... ... ,, 18 ...		When he had spent all. Lu. xv. 14 ; Mark v. 26. Nothing to pay... ... Lu. vii. 42.
There is not ought left . . . but our bodies ... ... ,, 18	...	Present your bodies ... Rom. xii. 1.
I have bought you this day ... ,, 23 ...		Bought with a price ... 1 Cor. vi. 20.
Lo, here is seed for you, and ye shall sow the land ... ... ,, 23	...	Seed to the sower, and bread to the eater Isa. lv. 10, 11; 2 Cor. ix. 10.
When Joseph's brethren saw that their father was dead . . . they sent a messenger unto Joseph, saying, Forgive, &c. And Joseph wept ... l. 15-17	...	Have I been so long time with you, and yet hast thou not known Me? John xiv. 9.

God meant it unto good . . . to save much people alive Gen. l. 20 } ... {	In bringing many sons unto glory. Heb. ii. 10.
Now therefore fear ye not, . . . and he comforted them ,, 21 } ... {	Let not your heart be troubled. John xiv. 1.
Joseph is a fruitful bough . . . whose branches run over the wall xlix. 22 } ... {	I am the vine, ye are the branches. John xv. 5.
A fruitful bough by a well ,, 22 ...	In him a well of water ... John iv. 14.
The archers have sorely grieved him, and shot at him, and hated him ,, 23 } ... {	A man of sorrows, and acquainted with grief ... ... Isa. liii. 3.
His bow abode in strength, and the arms of his hands were made strong by the hands of the mighty God of Jacob ... ,, 24 } ... {	I have laid help upon One that is mighty. Psa. lxxxix. 19.
From thence is the Shepherd ,, 24 ...	That great Shepherd of the sheep. Heb. xiii. 20.
The stone of Israel ... ... ,, 24 ...	The stone which the builders rejected, the same is become the head of the corner ... ... Matt. xxi. 42.
Let the blessing come upon the head of Joseph. Deut. xxxiii. 16 ; Gen. xlix. 25, 26 } ... {	Therefore God, thy God, hath anointed thee with the oil of gladness above thy fellows... ... ... Ps. xlv. 7.
Separate from his brethren ,, 26 ...	Separate from sinners ... Heb. vii. 26.
The birthright was Joseph's 1 Chron. v. 2 ...	The firstborn among many brethren. Rom. viii. 29.
Not grieved for the affliction of Joseph. Amos vi. 6 } ... {	Is it nothing to you, all ye that pass by ? Lam. i. 12.
A new king . . . which knew not Joseph. Ex. i. 8 } ... {	Which none of the princes of this world knew ... ... 1 Cor. ii. 8.
The house of Joseph shall abide in their coasts ... ... Jos. xviii. 5 } ...	Abide in Me, and I in you John xv. 4.
Joshua spake unto the house of Joseph, . . . saying, Thou art a great people and hast great power ... ... xvii. 17 } ... {	I can do all things through Christ which strengtheneth me ... Phil. iv. 13.
I am a great people forasmuch as the Lord hath blessed me hitherto ... ... ,, 14 } ... {	Blessed with all spiritual blessings. Eph. i. 3.
The hand of the house of Joseph prevailed... ... Judges i. 35 } ... {	More than conquerors through Him that loved us ... ... Rom. viii. 37.

INDEX

Part II

PRIESTS AND LEVITES
A Type of the Church

PREFACE

IN the following pages the Word of God has been allowed to speak for itself, and to show, by comparison and contrast, in how remarkable a manner the Priests and Levites were a type of the Church.

In many cases other New Testament passages will probably suggest themselves to the reader as being more truly the antitype of the Old Testament scripture, and for this reason a wide margin has been left, that Bible students may make their own additions and corrections.

These pages have been the result of some years' study, and the thought of publication was only entertained at the request of several friends, who urged that others, who perhaps had less time for study, should be allowed to have the benefit of the work.

Though feeling that it is still very imperfect, I have ventured to send it forth, trusting that it will lead some to see how much teaching there is on the subject in the Word, and what a wonderful position all believers have, as associated with their great High Priest in the worship and service of the Lord.

"WHAT human pen can bring out the marvellous instruction contained in the inspired account of the tribe of Levi? . . .

"The Levites were a separated people—God's special possession. They took the place of all the firstborn in Israel—of those who were saved from the sword of the destroyer by the blood of the lamb. They were typically a dead and risen people, set apart to God, and by Him presented as a gift to Aaron the High Priest, to do the service of the tabernacle. . . . In all this the Levites were a striking type of God's people now. It is not merely that we are pardoned, justified, accepted : all this is true ; but we are called to the high and holy work of bearing through this world the Name, the testimony, the glory of our Lord Jesus Christ. . . .

"A true Levite of old could say, 'To me to live is the Tabernacle'; and a true Christian now can say, 'To me to live is Christ.'

"As priests we are privileged to worship, but as Levites we are responsible to serve ; and our service is to carry through this desert scene the antitype of the Tabernacle, and that Tabernacle was the figure of Christ."

Notes on Numbers   BY C. H. M.

I

Introduction

" IN the beginning God." These are the first words that we read as we
open our Bibles, and in studying the history of the Levites, or any
other subject in the Word, we cannot do better than commence here. It
was God's free grace that chose the Levites from the other tribes, just as it
was His grace that called Abraham from Ur of the Chaldees, and that calls
us "out of darkness into His marvellous light." There was nothing in Levi
to commend him to God; on the contrary, we should have said, in reading
Genesis xlix., that Levi was one of the worst of Jacob's sons, but God in
His sovereign grace could say, "The Lord thy God hath chosen him out
of all the tribes." (Deut. xviii. 5.) "God commendeth His love toward us,
in that, while we were yet sinners, Christ died for us." The Levites must
have been amongst those who stood afar off when the law was given from
Sinai, but God says to Aaron, "Bring the tribe of Levi near" (Num. iii. 6),
and we "who sometimes were far off, are made nigh by the blood of Christ."

As we study the history of the tribe of Levi in relation to Aaron the
great High Priest, we are taught many beautiful lessons.

There is no more striking type of Christ than Aaron, from the very
earliest mention of him, in Exodus, to the last, in Hebrews. He is first
spoken of in Exodus iv., where God says to Moses, "Is not Aaron the Levite
thy brother? I know that he can speak well." After He, who "sticketh closer
than a brother," had come to dwell in human flesh, God's first declaration
was, "This is my beloved Son, in whom I am well pleased"; while on the
Mount of Transfiguration He added, "Hear ye Him"; and those who did
hear Him were bound to confess that "never man spake like this Man."

The work of Aaron in the tabernacle, in his garments for glory and beauty
wonderfully prefigures Him who, crowned with glory and honour, still walks
in the midst of the golden candlesticks. The high priest bore upon the

shoulder-pieces and breastplate the names of the children of Israel, as our High Priest bears us upon the shoulder of His power and the breast of His never-failing love. Within that wonderful breastplate, and thus suspended from the shoulder-pieces, were the Urim and Thummim, the lights and perfections, by which God's will was revealed to Israel. "Of Levi he said, Let thy Thummim and thy Urim be with thy holy one." (Deut. xxxiii. 8.) The lights and perfections are still with Him "in whom are hid all the treasures of wisdom and knowledge"; but while He said of Himself, "I am the Light of the world," He also says to His followers, "Ye are the light of the world," and "Be ye therefore perfect, even as your Father which is in heaven is perfect." It is His will now that the lights and perfections should be seen in His followers, but it is only as dwelling in the Lord's bosom and sustained by His power, that this can be possible. The Urim and Thummim were the indications of the mind of God, and the world should be able to learn it now through the lives of His people.

In the time of Ezra some of the priests were unable to prove their parentage; they believed themselves to be Aaron's sons, but could not show it. "These sought their register among those that were reckoned by genealogy, but they were not found; therefore were they, as polluted, put from the priesthood. And the Tirshatha said unto them, that they should not eat of the most holy things, till there stood up a priest with Urim and with Thummim." (Ezra ii. 62, 63.) We have not to wait as they had for a High Priest to appear, but may rejoice because our names are written in heaven, and that "the foundation of God standeth sure, having this seal, The Lord knoweth them that are His."

The numbering of the Levites brings before us a point of great interest, and shows how in association with their great High Priest they were entirely separated from the other tribes, and were spared from the condemnation that fell upon the rest of Israel.

It is generally stated that of all those who came out of Egypt, Caleb and Joshua alone were allowed to go into the promised land, but by carefully studying the history of the Levites it appears that they also were exempt from the general wilderness ruin. The reasons which lead to this conclusion are as follows:

I. The tribe of Levi sent no spy to view the land (see Num. xiii. 1–16), and the curse fell because of the evil report of the spies and the consequent murmuring of the people. "Your carcases shall fall in this wilderness; and all that were numbered of you, according to your whole number, from twenty years old and upward, which have murmured against me. . . . After the number of the days in which ye searched the land, even forty days, each day for a year, shall ye bear your iniquities, even forty years; and ye shall know my breach of promise. . . . And the men which Moses sent to search the land, who returned, and made all the congregation to murmur against him, by bringing up a slander upon the land, even those men, that did bring up the evil report upon the land, died by the plague before the Lord. But Joshua the son of Nun, and Caleb the son of Jephunneh, which were of the men that went to search the land, lived still." (Num. xiv. 29, 34, 36–38.)

II. As already stated in the above passage, those who thus fell in the wilderness were numbered from twenty years old and upward, and are further described as "all the men of war." "Surely none of the men that came up out of Egypt, from twenty years old and upward, shall see the land which I sware unto Abraham, unto Isaac, and unto Jacob; because they have not wholly followed me; save Caleb the son of Jephunneh the Kenezite, and Joshua the son of Nun; for they have wholly followed the Lord." (Num. xxxii. 11, 12.) "For the children of Israel walked forty years in the wilderness, till all the people that were men of war, which came out of Egypt, were consumed, because they obeyed not the voice of the Lord." (Jos. v. 6.) "And the space in which we came from Kadesh-Barnea, until we were come over the brook Zered, was thirty and eight years; until all the generation of the men of war were wasted out from among the host, as the Lord sware unto them." (Deut. ii. 14.)

III. But that the Levites were not numbered amongst the men of war is very clearly shewn in the first chapter of Numbers, where we are told that "the Lord spake unto Moses in the wilderness of Sinai . . . saying, Take ye the sum of all the congregation of the children of Israel, . . . from twenty years old and upward, all that are able to go forth to war in Israel: thou and Aaron shalt number them by their armies." This was done, and at the close of the chapter we read, "But the Levites after the tribe of their fathers were not numbered among them. For the Lord had spoken unto Moses, saying, Only thou shalt not number the tribe of Levi, neither take the sum of them among the children of Israel." (Num. i. 1–3 and 47–49; also ii. 33.)

The Levites were numbered separately, "from a month old and upward; for they were not numbered among the children of Israel, because there was no inheritance given them among the children of Israel." (Num. xxvi. 62), and the last clause in this passage also explains why their tribe was not represented by a spy.

IV. The children of Israel who were thus to die without entering the land were those numbered in the wilderness of Sinai, when, as we have seen, the Levites were not included. Just before the people went over Jordan the sum was again taken, not by Moses and Aaron, but "by Moses and Eleazar the priest, who numbered the children of Israel in the plains of Moab, by Jordan near Jericho. But among these there was not a man of them whom Moses and Aaron the priest numbered, when they numbered the children of Israel in the wilderness of Sinai; for the Lord had said of them, They shall surely die in the wilderness. And there was not left a man of them, save Caleb the son of Jephunneh, and Joshua the son of Nun." (Num. xxvi. 63–65.)

V. Eleazar and Phinehas went into the land. The former with Joshua divided the inheritance amongst the tribes (Num. xxxiv. 17); while Phinehas was sent as one of the messengers to the children of Reuben, Gad, and the half tribe of Manasseh, and yet neither were mentioned as exceptions in the general condemnation. Eleazar, at least, if not his son, must have been more than twenty years old when they came out of Egypt.

The passages on the above subject have been quoted at some length, that the position of the Levites may be clearly seen; and if the conclusion is correct, that they were indeed exempt from the curse that fell upon the rest of the children of Israel, we see in them, as in so many other particulars, a striking picture of the position of true believers. The sentence of death is on all around them, but "there is, therefore, now no condemnation to them which are in Christ Jesus." (Rom. viii. 1.) "He that believeth on Him is not condemned: but he that believeth not is condemned already, because he hath not believed in the name of the only-begotten Son of God." (John iii. 18.) "Verily, verily, I say unto you, He that heareth my word, and believeth on Him that sent me, hath everlasting life, and shall not come into condemnation; but is passed from death unto life." (John v. 24.)

The position of the Levites was different to that of the rest of the children of Israel in many respects. Two portions having been given to Joseph, and his sons being reckoned as sons of Jacob, Levi formed the thirteenth tribe, and thus, as it has been pointed out, held a position amongst them like that of Paul amongst the apostles.

When the Levites were numbered from a month old and upwards, they were numbered in their weakness (Num. iii.); and, as one has said, we learn from this that their position in the tribe depended not on what they had done for God, but on what He had done for them. In the following chapter they are numbered according to the days of their strength, from thirty years old and upward—the age of Joseph when he stood before Pharaoh, of David when he began to reign, and of our Lord Himself when He entered upon His public ministry. This was the age for the commencement of the Levitical service in the wilderness period, but after that, when the work would require less bodily strength but more ministers, the age was twenty-five; and David, in 1 Chron. xxiii. 24–27, changes it to twenty.

There is a great contrast between the history of the tribe of Levi before they were brought out of Egypt, and subsequently. In the olden days it was said by Jacob, "Simeon and Levi are brethren; instruments of cruelty are in their habitations" (Gen. xlix. 5); but afterwards they kept "all the instruments of the tabernacle of the congregation." (Num. iii. 8.) He said also, "O my soul, come not thou into their secret; unto their assembly, mine honour, be not thou united." But after they had crossed the Red Sea, God said to Aaron, "Thy brethren also of the tribe of Levi, the tribe of thy father, bring thou with thee, that they may be joined unto thee." (Num. xviii. 2.) Levi had been a cause of shame to Jacob, but now he is called of God to this place of high privilege in association with the great High Priest. The meaning of the name Levi is "joined," as we see from Genesis xxix. 34, and it is as joined to Aaron that he is thus blessed.

The story of cruelty and bloodshed to which Jacob refers is in Genesis xxxiv., when all the men of the city of Shechem were murdered. But how different is the picture in John iv., where it is said to the men of the same city, who were no better than those in the time of Simeon and Levi, "Come, see a man, which told me all things that ever I did: is not this the Christ? then they went out of the city, and came unto Him." John himself, the beloved disciple, evinced something of the spirit of these sons of Jacob when he wished to call down fire from heaven on the Samaritans; and the Master rebuked him, and said, "Ye know not what manner of spirit ye are of. For the Son of Man is not come to destroy men's lives, but to save them."

Simeon and Levi were cursed for their cruelty and their sin, and the punishment was thus pronounced, "I will divide them in Jacob and scatter them in Israel." This sentence was literally carried out, but the curse was changed into a blessing, and though scattered amongst the tribes, and receiving no inheritance in the land, the reason afterwards given, tells of matchless grace, and a promise takes the place of the sentence of judgment. They were separated "to bear the ark of the covenant of the Lord, to stand before the Lord . . . and to bless in His name. . . . Wherefore Levi hath no part nor inheritance with his brethren: the Lord is his inheritance, according as the Lord thy God promised him." (Deut. x. 8, 9.) We, too, were once under a curse on account of our sin; but "Christ hath redeemed us from the curse of the law, being made a curse for us," and now we are blessed "with all spiritual blessings in heavenly places in Christ." The sentence pronounced upon us for our sin was, "Thou shalt surely die." But He has taken the sting from death, so that we can say with Paul, "To me to live is Christ, and to die is gain."

We have also a striking contrast in the occupations of the Levites at these two periods in their history. In the land of Egypt they, with the rest of the children of Israel, were made "to serve with rigour," and the Egyptians "made their lives bitter with hard bondage, in mortar, and in brick, and in all manner of service in the field: all their service, wherein they made them serve, was with rigour." (Ex. i. 13, 14.) Building the treasure cities for Pharaoh was no easy task; but how different was their life afterwards, when "the Levites were appointed unto all manner of service of the tabernacle of the house of God" (1 Chron. vi. 48), and "were over the storehouses and treasuries of the house of God." (1 Chron. ix. 26, marg.)

Then, too, the work was done for a very different Master, and under very different supervision. The Egyptians "set over them taskmasters, to afflict them with their burdens." (Ex. i. 11.) But Aaron was no cruel taskmaster, and it was he who in the wilderness journey appointed them "every one to his service and to his burden" (Num. iv. 19), and afterwards they were under the King's commandment.

The burdens of Egypt were heavy and made their lives bitter, so that they cried unto God "by reason of the bondage," and He removed their "shoulder from the burden." (Ps. lxxxi. 6.) But He gave instead an easy burden when "the children of the Levites bare the ark of God on their shoulders" (1 Chron. xv. 15), reminding us of the loving invitation that our Lord gives in Matthew xi. 28 to all who are heavy laden, to come to Him and rest, and then to take upon their shoulders His easy yoke and His light burden.

Thus, in their early history, as well as in the days after they were appointed to the service and worship of God, the Levites were a type of the royal priesthood that has been called "out of darkness into His marvellous light," and "from the power of Satan unto God."

THE PRIESTS AND LEVITES A TYPE OF THE CHURCH

IN RELATION TO GOD

By Possession

The Levites shall be mine.—*Numb. viii. 14.*

For they are wholly given unto me from among the children of Israel.—*Num.* viii. 16.

Even instead of the firstborn of all the children of Israel, have I taken them unto me.—*Num.* viii. 16.

And I, behold, I have taken the Levites from among the children of Israel instead of all the firstborn.—*Num.* iii. 12.

For they are thine. And all mine are thine, and thine are mine ; and I am glorified in them.—*John* xvii. 9, 10.

Whether we live therefore, or die, we are the Lord's.—*Rom.* xiv. 8.

To take out of them a people for his name.—*Acts* xv. 14.

The general assembly and church of the firstborn, which are written in heaven.—*Heb.* xii. 23.

By Covenant and Oath

Thus saith the Lord ; If ye can break my covenant of the day, and my covenant of the night, and that there should not be day and night in their season ; then may also my covenant be broken with David my servant, that he should not have a son to reign upon his throne ; and with the Levites the priests, my ministers.—*Jer.* xxxiii. 20, 21.

That my covenant might be with Levi, saith the Lord of hosts.—*Mal.* ii. 4.

Wherein God, willing more abundantly to shew unto the heirs of promise the immutability of His counsel, confirmed it by an oath: That by two immutable things, in which it was impossible for God to lie, we might have a strong consolation, who have fled for refuge to lay hold upon the hope set before us.—*Heb.* vi. 17, 18.

But now hath he obtained a more excellent ministry, by how much also he is the mediator of a better covenant, which was established upon better promises.—*Heb.* viii. 6.

By Choice

For the Lord thy God hath chosen him out of all thy tribes.—*Deut.* xviii. 5.

For them the Lord thy God hath chosen to minister unto him, and to bless in the name of the Lord.—*Deut.* xxi. 5.

Them hath the Lord chosen to carry the ark of God.—1 *Chron.* xv. 2.

For the Lord hath chosen you to stand before him, to serve him, and that ye should minister unto him, and burn incense.—2 *Chron.* xxix. 11.

And with them Heman and Jeduthun, and the rest that were chosen.—1 *Chron.* xvi. 41.

I have chosen you out of the world.—*John* xv. 19.

But ye are a chosen generation, a royal priesthood, an holy nation, a peculiar people ; that ye should shew forth the praises of him who hath called you out of darkness into his marvellous light.—1 *Peter* ii. 9.

For he is a chosen vessel unto me, to bear my name before the Gentiles, and kings, and the children of Israel.—*Acts* ix. 15.

According as he hath chosen us in him before the foundation of the world, that we should be holy and without blame before him in love.—*Eph.* i. 4.

And he goeth up into a mountain, and calleth unto him whom he would : and they came unto him. And he ordained twelve, that they should be with him, and that he might send them forth.—*Mark* iii. 13, 14.

Who were expressed **by name.**—1 *Chron.* xvi. 41.

He calleth his own sheep **by name,** and leadeth them out.—*John* x. 3.

By Position

And the Lord spake unto Moses, saying, Bring the tribe of Levi **near.**—*Num.* iii. 5, 6.

And he hath brought thee **near** to him.—*Num.* xvi. 10.

But now in Christ Jesus ye who sometimes were far off are made **nigh** by the blood of Christ.—*Eph.* ii. 13.

For through him we both have **access** by one Spirit unto the Father.—*Eph.* ii. 18.

ASSOCIATION WITH AARON
Relationship

Thy brethren also of the tribe of Levi, the tribe of thy **father.**—*Num.* xviii. 2.

That they may be **joined** unto thee (Levi = joined).—*Num.* xviii. 2.

He is not ashamed to call them **brethren.** —*Heb.* ii. 11.

My **Father** and your **Father.**—*John* xx. 17.

He that is **joined** unto the Lord is one spirit.—1 *Cor.* vi. 17.

For we are **members** of his body, of his flesh, and of his bones.—*Eph.* v. 30.

Gift

And **I** have **given** the Levites as a gift to Aaron.—*Num.* viii. 19.

They are **wholly given** unto him out of the children of Israel.—*Num.* iii. 9.

And I, behold, I have taken your brethren the Levites from among the children of Israel : to you they are given as a gift **for the Lord.** —*Num.* xviii. 6.

Thine they were, and thou **gavest** them me.—*John* xvii. 6.

Father, I will that they also, whom thou hast **given** me, be with me where I am.—*John* xvii. 24.

I kept them in thy name : those that thou gavest me I have **kept,** and none of them is lost.—*John* xvii. 12.

Presentation
(*To Him.*)

Present them before Aaron the priest.— *Num.* iii. 6.

That he might **present** it to himself a glorious church, not having spot, or wrinkle, or any such thing ; but that it should be holy and without blemish.—*Eph.* v. 27.

(*By Him.*)

And Aaron shall offer the Levites before the Lord for an **offering** of the children of Israel.—*Num.* viii. 11.

And Aaron offered them as an **offering** before the Lord.—*Num.* viii. 21.)

That the **offering** up of the Gentiles might be acceptable, being sanctified by the Holy Ghost.—*Rom.* xv. 16.

Now unto him that is able to keep you from falling, and to **present** you faultless before the presence of his glory with exceeding joy. —*Jude* 24.

Worship

And the sons of Aaron brought the blood unto him. . . . And he slew the burnt offering ; and Aaron's sons presented unto him the blood, which he sprinkled round about upon the altar. —*Lev.* ix. 9, 12.

Having therefore, brethren, boldness to enter into the holiest by the blood of Jesus, by a new and living way, which he hath consecrated for us, through the veil, that is to say, his flesh ; and having an high priest over the house of God ; let us draw near with a true heart in full assurance of faith, having our hearts sprinkled from an evil conscience, and our bodies washed with pure water.— *Heb.* x. 19-22.

With Him in Separation

And take thou unto thee Aaron thy brother, and his sons with him, from among the children of Israel.—*Exodus* xxviii. 1.

Dead with Christ.—*Col.* ii. 20.

Risen with Christ. . . . For ye are dead, and your life is hid with Christ in God. When Christ, who is our life, shall appear, then shall ye also appear with him in glory— *Col.* iii. 1, 3, 4.

With Him in Service

(*Unto the Lord.*)

That he may minister unto me in the priest's office, even Aaron, Nadab and Abihu, Eleazar and Ithamar, Aaron's sons.—*Exodus* xxviii. 1.

And greater works than these shall he do ; because I go unto my Father.—*John* xiv. 12.

For without me ye can do nothing.—*John* xv. 5.

(*Unto Aaron.*)

That they may minister unto him.—*Num.* iii. 6.

And many women were there beholding afar off, which followed Jesus from Galilee, ministering unto him.—*Matt.* xxvii. 55.

For God is not unrighteous to forget your work and labour of love, which ye have shewed toward his name, in that ye have ministered to the saints, and do minister. —*Heb.* vi. 10.

Verily I say unto you, Inasmuch as ye have done it unto one of the least of these my brethren, ye have done it unto me.—*Matt.* xxv. 40.

With Him Brought Nigh

Thy brethren also of the tribe of Levi . . . bring thou with thee.—*Num.* xviii. 2.

In bringing many sons unto glory.—*Heb.* ii. 10.

For Christ also hath once suffered for sins, the just for the unjust, that he might bring us to God.—1 *Peter* iii. 18.

With Him Clothed

And thou shalt make holy garments for Aaron thy brother for glory and for beauty. And thou shalt put them upon Aaron thy brother, and his sons **with him.**—*Exodus* xxviii. 2, 41.

It doth not yet appear what we shall be : but we know that, when he shall appear, we shall be **like him ;** for we shall see him as he is.—1 *John* iii. 2.

With Him Anointed

And thou shalt anoint them, **as** thou didst anoint their father.—*Exodus* xl. 15.

For God giveth not the Spirit by measure unto him.—*John* iii. 34.

But ye have an **unction** from the Holy One, and ye know all things.—1 *John* ii. 20.

With Him Sanctified

I will **sanctify** also both Aaron and his sons, to minister to me in the priest's office. —*Exodus* xxix. 44.

And for their sakes I **sanctify** myself, that they also might be **sanctified** through the truth.—*John* xvii. 19.

With Him Consecrated

And thou shalt **consecrate** * Aaron and his sons.—*Exodus* xxix. 9.

* Margin, "fill the hand of."

For in him dwelleth all the **fulness** of the Godhead bodily. And ye are **complete** in him.—*Col.* ii. 9, 10.

With Him in Obedience

So Aaron and his sons did all things which the Lord commanded by the hand of Moses. —*Lev.* viii. 36.

If ye keep my **commandments**, ye shall abide in my love ; even as I have kept my Father's **commandments**, and abide in his love.—*John* xv. 10.

With Him in Resurrection

And thou shalt write Aaron's name upon the rod of Levi : for one rod shall be for the head of the house of their fathers . . . And it came to pass, that on the morrow Moses went into the tabernacle of witness ; and, behold, the rod of Aaron **for the house of Levi** was budded, and brought forth buds, and bloomed blossoms, and yielded almonds.—*Num.* xvii. 3, 8.

But now is Christ risen from the dead, and become the **firstfruits** of them that slept.— 1 *Cor.* xv. 20.

And God hath both **raised** up the Lord, and will also **raise** up us by his own power.— 1 *Cor.* vi. 14.

But if the Spirit of him that raised up Jesus from the dead dwell in you, he that raised up Christ from the dead shall also **quicken** your mortal bodies by his Spirit that dwelleth in you.—*Rom.* viii. 11.

With Him Lights and Perfections

And of Levi he said, Let thy Thummim and thy Urim be with thy holy one.—*Deut.* xxxiii. 8.

These sought their register among those that were reckoned by geneology, but they were not found : therefore were they, as polluted, put from the priesthood. And the Tirshatha said unto them, that they should not eat of the most holy things, till there stood up a priest with Urim and with Thummim.—*Ezra* ii. 62, 63.

I am the light of the world.—*John* viii. 12.

In whom are hid all the treasures of wisdom and knowledge.—*Col.* ii. 3.

Nevertheless the foundation of God standeth sure, having this seal, The Lord knoweth them that are his.—2 *Tim.* ii. 19.

Rejoice, because your names are written in heaven.—*Luke* x. 20.

LEVITICAL AND PRIESTLY CHARACTERISTICS

Life and Peace

My covenant was with him of **life** and **peace.**—*Mal.* ii. 5.

To be spiritually minded is **life** and **peace.** —*Rom.* viii. 6.

The Fear of the Lord

And I gave them to him for **the fear** wherewith he **feared** me, and was afraid before my name.—*Mal.* ii. 5.

Let us have grace, whereby we may serve God acceptably with reverence and godly **fear.**—*Heb.* xii. 28.

Truth

The law of **truth** was in his mouth.— *Mal.* ii. 6.

Speaking the **truth** in love.—*Eph.* iv. 15.

Purity of Speech

Iniquity was not found in his **lips.**—*Mal.* ii. 6.

Laying aside all malice, and all guile, and hypocrisies, and envies, and **all evil speakings.**—1 *Peter* ii. 1.

Knowledge

For the priest's **lips** should keep **knowledge,** and they should seek the law at his mouth.—*Mal.* ii. 7.

But **speak** thou the things which become sound doctrine.—*Titus* ii. 1.

Filled with all **knowledge.**—*Rom.* xv. 14.

Fellowship

He walked **with me** in peace and equity. —*Mal.* ii. 6.

And truly our **fellowship** is with the Father, and with his Son Jesus Christ.— 1 *John* i. 3.

Holiness

In their set office they sanctified themselves in **holiness.**—2 *Chron.* xxxi. 18.

Perfecting **holiness** in the fear of God.— 2 *Cor.* vii. 1.

Uprightness

The Levites were more **upright** in heart to sanctify themselves than the priests.—2 *Chron.* xxix. 34.

That ye may approve things that are excellent ; that ye may be **sincere** and without offence till the day of Christ.—*Phil.* i. 10.

Therefore let us keep the feast, not with old leaven, neither with the leaven of malice and wickedness ; but with the unleavened bread of **sincerity** and truth.—1 *Cor.* v. 8.

Wholeheartedness

Who said unto his father and to his mother, I have not seen him ; neither did he acknowledge his brethren, nor knew his own children.—*Deut.* xxxiii. 9.

If any man come to me, and hate not his father, and mother, and wife, and children, and brethren, and sisters, yea, and his own life also, he cannot be my disciple.—*Luke* xiv. 26.

And every one that hath forsaken houses, or brethren, or sisters, or father, or mother, or wife, or children, or lands, for my name's sake, shall receive an hundredfold, and shall inherit everlasting life.—*Matt.* xix. 29.

Obedience

For they have **observed** thy word, and **kept** thy covenant.—*Deut.* xxxiii. 9.

Teaching them to **observe** all things whatsoever I have commanded you. — *Matt.* xxviii. 20.

If a man love me, he will **keep** my words. *John* xiv. 23.

Strength

Able men for **strength** for the service.— 1 *Chron.* xxvi. 8.

Able ministers of the new testament.— 2 *Cor.* iii. 6.

Be **strong** in the Lord, and in the power of his might.—*Eph.* vi. 10.

Separation

Thus shalt thou **separate** the Levites from among the children of Israel.—*Num.* viii. 14.

Seemeth it but a small thing unto you, that the God of Israel hath **separated** you from the congregation of Israel, to bring you near **to himself.**—*Num.* xvi. 9.

They (the Israelites) have corrupted themselves, their spot is not the spot of his children : they are a **perverse** and **crooked** generation.—*Deut.* xxxii. 5.

Wherefore come out from among them, and be ye **separate,** saith the Lord, and touch not the unclean thing ; and I will **receive** you.—2 *Cor.* vi. 17.

That ye may be blameless and harmless, the sons of God, without rebuke, **in the midst** of a **crooked** and **perverse** nation.— *Phil.* ii. 15.

Diversity

As well the small as the great, the teacher as the scholar.—1 *Chron.* xxv. 8.

But now are they many members, yet but one body. And the eye cannot say unto the hand, I have no need of thee : nor again the head to the feet, I have no need of you. Nay, much more those members of the body,

which seem to be more feeble, are necessary :
. . . Now ye are the body of Christ, and
members in particular.—1 *Cor.* xii. 20–22, 27.

Abstaining from Wine

And the Lord spake unto Aaron, saying,
Do not drink **wine** nor strong drink, thou,
nor thy sons with thee, when ye go into the
tabernacle of the congregation, lest ye die : it
shall be a statute for ever throughout your
generations.—*Lev.* x. 8, 9.

(*Wine* typical of intoxicating pleasures, &c.)

And be not drunk with **wine,** wherein is
excess ; but be filled with the Spirit. *Eph.*
v. 18.

Love not the **world,** neither the things that
are in the world. If any man love the world,
the love of the Father is not in him. • For all
that is in the world, the lust of the flesh, and
the lust of the eyes, and the pride of life, is
not of the Father, but is of the world. And
the world passeth away, and the lust thereof :
but he that doeth the will of God abideth for
ever.—1 *John* ii. 15–17.

PREPARATION FOR SERVICE
Birth into the Family

None ought to carry the ark of God but the
Levites.—1 *Chron.* xv. 2.

Ye must be born again.—*John* iii. 7.
So then they that are in the flesh cannot
please God.—*Rom.* viii. 8.

Atonement

Aaron made an **atonement** for them to
cleanse them.—*Num.* viii. 21.

And not only so, but we also joy in God,
through our Lord Jesus Christ, by whom we
have now received the **atonement.**—*Rom.*
v. 11.

Identification with the Sacrifices

And the Levites shall **lay their hands**
upon the heads of the bullocks : and thou
shalt offer the one for a **sin-offering,** and the
other for a **burnt-offering,** unto the Lord, to
make an atonement for the Levites.—*Num.*
viii. 12.

If the priest that is anointed do sin according to the sin of the people ; then let him
bring for his sin, which he hath sinned, a
young bullock without blemish unto the Lord
for **a sin-offering.**—*Lev.* iv. 3.

(*With the Sin-offering.*)
Who loved me, and gave himself for me.—
Gal. ii. 20.
(*With the Burnt-offering.*)
Accepted in the beloved.—*Eph.* i. 6.

For if the blood of bulls and of goats, and
the ashes of an heifer sprinkling the unclean,
sanctifieth to the purifying of the flesh : how
much more shall the blood of Christ, who
through the eternal Spirit offered himself
without spot to God, purge your conscience
from dead works to serve the living God?—
Heb. ix. 13, 14.

Cleansing

Take the Levites from among the children
of Israel, and **cleanse** them. And thus shalt
thou do unto them, to cleanse them : Sprinkle
water of purifying upon them, and let them
shave all their flesh, and let them wash their

Having our hearts sprinkled from an evil
conscience, and our bodies washed with pure
water.—*Heb.* x. 22.
But let a man examine himself.—1 *Cor.* xi. 28.
Having therefore these promises, dearly

clothes, and so make themselves clean.—*Num.* viii. 6, 7.

beloved, let us **cleanse** ourselves from all filthiness of the flesh and spirit.—*2 Cor.* vii. 1.

Purifying

And the Levites were **purified,** and they washed their clothes.—*Num.* viii. 21.

That he might redeem us from all iniquity, and **purify** unto himself a peculiar people, zealous of good works.—*Tit.* ii. 14.

Purging

And he shall sit as a refiner and purifier of silver : and he shall purify the sons of Levi, and **purge** them as **gold** and **silver,** that they may offer unto the Lord an offering in right-eousness.—*Mal.* iii. 3.

But in a great house there are not only vessels of **gold** and of **silver,** but also of wood and of earth ; and some to honour, and some to dishonour. If a man therefore **purge** himself from these, he shall be a vessel unto honour, sanctified, and meet for the master's use, and prepared unto every good work.—2 *Tim.* ii. 20, 21.

That the trial of your faith, being much more precious than of **gold** that perisheth, though it be **tried** with fire, might be found unto praise and honour and glory at the appearing of Jesus Christ.—1 *Pet.* i. 7.

Public Confession

Then Moses stood in the gate of the **camp,** and said, Who is on the **Lord's side ?** let him come unto me. And all the sons of Levi gathered themselves together unto him.—*Ex.* xxxii. 26.

He that is not **with** me is against me.—*Luke* xi. 23.

Let us go forth therefore unto him without the **camp,** bearing his reproach.—*Heb.* xiii. 13.

Washing

And shalt **wash** them with water.—*Ex.* xxix. 4.

But ye are **washed.**—1 *Cor.* vi. 11.

Christ also loved the church, and gave himself for it ; that he might sanctify and cleanse it with the **washing** of **water** by the word.—*Eph.* v. 25, 26.

Washing of Hands and Feet

And he set the laver between the tent of the congregation and the altar, and put water there, to wash withal. And Moses and Aaron and his sons washed their **hands** and their **feet** thereat : when they went into the tent of the congregation, and when they came near unto the altar, they washed; as the Lord com-manded Moses.—*Ex.* xl. 30-32.

Jesus saith to him, He that is washed needeth not save to wash his **feet,** but is clean every whit.—*John* xiii. 10.

Clothing *

And thou shalt bring his sons, and put **coats** upon them.—*Exodus* xxix. 8.

But **put ye on** the Lord Jesus Christ.—*Rom.* xiii. 14.

* See also "With Him clothed" (p. 17) and "Future Rest and Service" (p. 63).

And the priest that offereth any man's burnt offering, even the priest shall have to himself the **skin of the burnt offering** which he hath offered.—*Lev.* vii. 8.

And thou shalt gird them with **girdles**, Aaron and his sons, and put the **bonnets** on them.—*Exodus* xxix. 9.

Let thy priests be clothed with **righteousness.**—*Psalm* cxxxii. 9.

I will also clothe her priests with **salvation.** —*Psalm* cxxxii. 16.

Put on therefore, as the elect of God, holy and beloved, bowels of mercies, kindness, humbleness of mind, meekness, longsuffering. . . . And above all these things **put on** charity, which is the bond of perfectness.— *Col.* iii. 12, 14.

To the praise of the glory of his grace, wherein he hath made us **accepted** in the beloved.—*Eph.* i. 6.

Stand therefore, having your loins **girt** about with **truth.**—*Eph.* vi. 14.

Jesus saith unto him, I am the way, the **truth,** and the life.—*John* xiv. 6.

For an **helmet,** the hope of salvation.— I *Thess.* v. 8.

Having on the breastplate of **righteousness.**—*Eph.* vi. 14.

And this is his name whereby he shall be called, THE LORD OUR **RIGHTEOUS-NESS.**—*Jer.* xxiii. 6.

But of him are ye in Christ Jesus, who of God is made unto us wisdom, and **righteousness,** and sanctification, and redemption.— I *Cor.* i. 30.

The Lord is my light and my **salvation.**— *Psalm* xxvii. 1.

For mine eyes have seen thy **salvation.** — *Luke* ii. 30.

For as many of you as have been baptized into Christ have **put on Christ.**—*Gal.* iii. 27.

Anointing

Thou shalt **anoint** them, and consecrate them.—*Exodus* xxviii. 41.

He which . . . hath **anointed** us, is God. —2 *Cor.* i. 21.

The **anointing** which ye have received of him abideth in you.—I *John* ii. 27.

Sanctification and Sprinkling

And **sanctify** them, that they may minister unto me in the priest's office.—*Exod.* xxviii. 41.

And Moses took of the anointing **oil,** and of the **blood** which was upon the altar, and **sprinkled** it upon Aaron, and upon his garments, and upon his sons, and upon his sons' garments with him ; and **sanctified** Aaron, and his garments, and his sons, and his sons' garments with him.—*Lev.* viii. 30.

And the very God of peace **sanctify** you wholly.—I *Thess.* v. 23.

Elect according to the foreknowledge of God the Father, through **sanctification** of **the Spirit,** unto obedience and **sprinkling** of the **blood** of Jesus Christ.—I *Peter* i. 2.

The blood of **sprinkling,** that speaketh better things than that of Abel.—*Heb.* xii. 24.

Dedication

Then shalt thou kill the ram, and take of his blood, and put it upon the tip of the right ear of Aaron, and upon the tip of the right ear of his sons, and upon the thumb of their right hand, and upon the great toe of their right foot.—*Exodus* xxix. 20.

I beseech you therefore, brethren, by the mercies of God, that ye present your **bodies** a living sacrifice, holy, acceptable unto God, which is your reasonable service.—*Rom.* xii. 1.

What? know ye not that your **body** is the temple of the Holy Ghost which is in you, which ye have of God, and ye are not your own? For ye are bought with a price: therefore glorify God in your **body**, and in your spirit, which are God's.—1 *Cor.* vi. 19, 20.

Readiness for Service

And **after that** went the Levites in to do their service in the tabernacle of the congregation before Aaron, and before his sons: as the Lord had commanded Moses concerning the Levites, so did they unto them.—*Num.* viii. 22.

Being then made free from sin, ye became the servants of righteousness.—*Rom.* vi. 18.

PRIESTLY PROVISION

Atonement

And they shall eat those things wherewith **the atonement** was made, to consecrate and to sanctify them; but a stranger shall not eat thereof, because they are holy.—*Exodus* xxix. 33.

Whoso eateth my flesh, and drinketh my blood, hath eternal life; and I will raise him up at the last day. For my flesh is meat indeed, and my blood is drink indeed. He that eateth my flesh, and drinketh my blood, dwelleth in me, and I in him. As the living Father hath sent me, and I live by the Father: so he that eateth me, even he shall live by me.—*John* vi. 54–57.

The Meat Offering

And the remnant of **the meat offering** shall be Aaron's and his sons': it is a thing most holy of the offerings of the Lord made by fire.—*Lev.* ii. 3.

And Moses spake unto Aaron, and unto Eleazar and unto Ithamar, his sons that were left, Take the meat offering that remaineth of the offerings of the Lord made by fire, and eat it without leaven **beside the altar:** for it is most holy: and ye shall eat it in the holy place, because it is **thy due**, and thy son's due, of the sacrifices of the Lord made by fire: for so I am commanded.—*Lev.* x. 12, 13.

And every meat offering, mingled with oil, and dry, shall all the sons of Aaron have, **one as much as another.**—*Lev.* vii. 10.

Truly our fellowship is with the Father, and with his Son Jesus Christ.—1 *John* i. 3.

We have an **altar,** whereof they have no right to eat which serve the tabernacle.—*Heb.* xiii. 10.

Do ye not know that they which minister about holy things live of the things of the temple? and they which wait at the altar are partakers with the altar? Even so hath the Lord ordained that they which preach the gospel should live of the gospel.—1 *Cor.* ix. 13, 14.

And of his fulness have **all we** received, and grace for grace.—*John* i. 16.

The Peace Offering

For the wave **breast*** and the heave **shoulder** have I taken of the children of Israel from off the sacrifices of their **peace offerings**, and have given them unto Aaron the priest and unto his sons by a statute for ever from among the children of Israel.—*Lev.* vii. 34.

* *The breast* indicating the place of affection ; *the shoulder* the place of power.

That Christ may dwell in your hearts by faith ; that ye, being rooted and grounded in love, may be able to comprehend with all saints what is the breadth, and length, and depth, and height : and to know **the love** of Christ, which passeth knowledge, that ye might be filled with all the fulness of God. —*Eph.* iii. 17-19.

And what is the exceeding greatness of his **power** to us-ward who believe, according to the working of his mighty power.—*Eph.* i. 19.

In the Holy Place

And it shall be Aaron's and his sons' ; and they shall eat **it in the holy place :** for it is most holy unto him of the offerings of the Lord made by fire by a perpetual statute.— *Lev.* xxiv. 9.

They shall come near to **my table.** *Ezekiel* xliv. 16.

And hath raised us up together, and made us sit together **in heavenly places** in Christ Jesus —*Eph.* ii. 6.

Ye cannot be partakers of **the Lord's table** and of the table of devils.—1 *Cor.* x. 21.

The Firstfruits

‹ And whatsoever is **first ripe** in the land, which they shall bring unto the Lord, shall be thine ; every one that is clean in thine house shall eat of it.—*Num.* xviii. 13.

Christ the **firstfruits.** But now is Christ risen from the dead, and become the **first-fruits** of them that slept.—1 *Cor.* xv. 23, 20.

Who was delivered for our offences, and was **raised again** for our justification.— *Rom.* iv. 25.

Every Dedicated Thing

Every dedicated thing in Israel shall be their's.—*Ezekiel* xliv. 29.

Every thing devoted in Israel shall be thine. —*Num.* xviii. 14.

For **all** things are yours ; whether Paul, or Apollos, or Cephas, or the world, or life, or death, or things present, or things to come ; **all** are yours ; and ye are Christ's ; and Christ is God's.—1 *Cor.* iii. 21-23.

Enough and Plenty Left

Then Hezekiah questioned with the priests and the Levites concerning the heaps. And Azariah the chief priest of the house of Zadok answered him, and said, Since the people began to bring the offerings into the house of the Lord, we have had **enough** to eat, and have **left plenty :** for the Lord hath blessed his people ; and that which is left is this great store.—2 *Chron.* xxxi. 9, 10.

Bread enough and to spare.—*Luke* xv. 17.

And they did all eat, and were filled : and they took up of the fragments that remained twelve baskets full.—*Matt.* xiv. 20.

But I have all, and abound.—*Phil.* iv. 18.

Satisfied

And I will **satiate** the soul of the priests with fatness, and my people shall be **satisfied** with my goodness, saith the Lord.—*Jer.* xxxi. 14.

And Jesus said unto them, I am the bread of life : he that cometh to me shall never hunger ; and he that believeth on me shall never thirst.—*John* vi. 35.

A Daily Portion

For it was the king's commandment concerning them, that a certain portion should be for the singers, due for **every day.**—*Neh.* xi. 23.

Give us **day by day** our daily bread.—*Luke* xi. 3.

For which cause we faint not ; but though our outward man perish, yet the inward man is renewed **day by day.**—2 *Cor.* iv. 16.

Not to be Eaten by

A Leper or the Unclean

What man soever of the seed of Aaron is a leper . . . he shall not eat of the holy things, until he be clean . . . The soul which hath touched any such shall be unclean until even, and **shall not eat** of the holy things, unless he wash his flesh with water. And when **the sun is down,** he shall be clean, and shall afterward eat of the holy things ; because it is his food.—*Lev.* xxii. 4, 6, 7.

And when he came to himself, he said, How many hired servants of my father's have bread enough and to spare, and I **perish with hunger !**—*Luke* xv. 17.

If we say that we have fellowship with him, and walk in **darkness,** we lie, and do not the truth : but if we walk in the light, as he is in the light, we have **fellowship** one with another, and the blood of Jesus Christ his Son cleanseth us from all sin.—1 *John* i. 6, 7.

A Stranger

There shall no **stranger** eat of the holy thing.—*Lev.* xxii. 10.

That at that time ye were without Christ, being aliens from the commonwealth of Israel, and **strangers** from the covenants of promise, having no hope, and without God in the world. . . . Now therefore ye are no more **strangers** and foreigners, but fellowcitizens with the saints, and of the household of God.—*Eph.* ii. 12-19.

A Sojourner

A **sojourner** of the priest.—*Lev.* xxii. 10.

They went out from us, but they were not of us ; for if they had been of us, they would no doubt have continued with us : but they went out, that they might be made manifest that they were not all of us.—1 *John* ii. 19.

A Hired Servant

Or an **hired servant** shall not eat of the holy thing.—*Lev.* xxii. 10.

Henceforth I call you not **servants** ; for the **servant** knoweth not what his lord doeth : but I have called you friends ; for all things that I have heard of my Father I have made known unto you.—*John* xv. 15.

I will arise and go to my father, and will say unto him, Father, I have sinned against heaven, and before thee, and am no more worthy to be called thy son : make me as one of thy **hired servants.**—*Luke* xv. 18, 19.

To be Eaten by

One Bought by the Priest

But if the priest **buy** any soul with his money, he shall eat of it.—*Lev.* xxii. 11.

For ye are **bought** with a price.—1 *Cor.* vi. 20.

Forasmuch as ye know that ye were not redeemed with corruptible things, as silver and gold, but with the precious blood of Christ, as of a lamb without blemish and without spot. —1 *Peter* i. 18, 19.

To **feed** the church of God, which he hath **purchased** with his own blood."—*Acts* xx. 28.

Or Born in His House

And he that is **born** in his house : they shall eat of his meat.—*Lev.* xxii. 11.

Being **born again,** not of corruptible seed, but of incorruptible, by the word of God, which liveth and abideth for ever.—1 *Peter* i. 23.

As **newborn** babes, desire the sincere milk of the word, that ye may grow thereby.— 1 *Peter* ii. 2.

THE APPOINTMENT OF SERVICE

The Pattern Given

And the **pattern** of all that he had by the spirit, of the courts of the house of the Lord, and of all the chambers round about, of the treasuries of the house of God, and of the treasuries of the dedicated things : also for the courses of the priests and the Levites, and for all the work of the service of the house of the Lord, and for all the vessels of service in the house of the Lord. All this, said David, the Lord made me understand in writing by his hand upon me, even all the works of this **pattern.**—1 *Chron.* xxviii. 12, 13, 19.

And he gave some, apostles ; and some, prophets ; and some, evangelists ; and some, pastors and teachers ; for the perfecting of the saints, for the work of the ministry, for the edifying of the body of Christ : till we all come in the unity of the faith, and of the knowledge of the Son of God, unto **a perfect man,** unto the measure of the stature of the fulness of Christ.—*Eph.* iv. 11-13.

For I have given you an **example,** that ye should do as I have done to you.—*John* xiii. 15.

The Appointment of Aaron

Aaron and his sons shall go in, and **appoint** them **every one** to his **service** and to his **burden.**—*Num.* iv. 19.

For the Son of man is as a man taking a far journey, who left his house, and gave authority to his servants, and **to every man his work,** and commanded the porter to watch.—*Mark* xiii. 34.

At **the appointment of Aaron** and his sons shall be all the **service** of the sons of the Gershonites, in all their **burdens,** and in all their service : and ye shall **appoint** unto them in charge all their burdens.—*Num.* iv. 27.

Their brethren also the Levites were appointed unto **all manner of service** of the tabernacle of the house of God.—I *Chron.* vi. 48.

For every man shall bear his own **burden.** —*Gal.* vi. 5.

For we are his workmanship, created in Christ Jesus unto good works, which God hath **before ordained** that we should walk in them.—*Eph.* ii. 10.

In every thing give thanks : for this is **the will of God** in Christ Jesus concerning you. —I *Thess.* v. 18.

And God hath set some in the church, first apostles, secondarily prophets, thirdly teachers, after that miracles, then gifts of healing, helps, governments, diversities of tongues.—I *Cor.* xii. 28.

The Commandment of the King

So the service was prepared, and the priests stood in their place, and the Levites in their courses, **according to the king's commandment.**—2 *Chron.* xxxv. 10.

According to the king's order * to Asaph, Jeduthun, and Heman.—I *Chron.* xxv. 6.

   * R. V. being *under the order of the king.*

And they departed not from **the commandment of the king** unto the priests and Levites concerning any matter, or concerning the treasures.—2 *Chron.* viii. 15.

But now hath God set the members every one of them in the body, **as it hath pleased him.**—I *Cor.* xii. 18.

He that hath **my commandments,** and keepeth them, he it is that loveth me.— *John* xiv. 21.

Ye are my friends, if ye do whatsoever I **command** you.—*John* xv. 14.

According to their Order

They waited on their office **according to their order.**—I *Chron.* vi. 32.

But all these worketh that one and the selfsame Spirit, dividing to every man severally **as he will.**—I *Cor.* xii. 11.

THE TIME OF SERVICE

Day and Night

For they were employed in that work **day and night.**—I *Chron.* ix. 33.

Always abounding in the work of the Lord.—I *Cor.* xv. 58.

Continually

To do **sacrifice continually.**—*Jer.* xxxiii. 18.

By him therefore let us offer the **sacrifice** of praise to God **continually,** that is, the fruit of our lips giving thanks to his name. But to do good and to communicate forget not : for with such **sacrifices** God is well pleased.—*Heb.* xiii. 15, 16.

Every Day's Work

So he left there before the ark of the covenant of the Lord, Asaph and his brethren, to minister before the ark continually, as **every day's work** required.—1 *Chron.* xvi. 37.

And they, continuing **daily** with one accord in the temple, and breaking bread from house to house, did eat their meat with gladness and singleness of heart, praising God, and having favour with all the people. And the Lord added to the church **daily** such as should be saved.—*Acts* ii. 46, 47.

No Departing

And the porters waited at every gate ; they **might not depart from their service.**— 2 *Chron.* xxxv. 15.

Blessed is that servant, whom his lord **when he cometh** shall find so doing.— *Matt.* xxiv. 46.

II

The Place of Service

WE do not expect types, as a rule, to give us a view of every side of their antitype, for they were but the "shadow of good things to come"; but the subject before us is so full that, by placing the pictures side by side, we seem to have an almost complete illustration of the believer's position. This is very noticeable when we study the Levites' place of service, for we find the priests and Levites in the *wilderness*, in the *land*, and in the *sanctuary*, thus giving us the threefold aspect of the place in which we are called to serve and worship; not some in the wilderness, some in the land, and some in the sanctuary, but every believer recognizing his position in each of these places at the same time.

It may be true that the forty years of wilderness wandering was not God's purpose for Israel. It is not mentioned in Hebrews xi. among the records of faith, for it was not "by faith" they wandered, but through unbelief; yet we are told that "all these things," even their constant failures, "happened unto them for ensamples" or types. If they had been so full of faith that but a few days had elapsed between the crossing of the Red Sea and the Jordan, we should have missed the beautiful picture we have in Numbers iv. of wilderness testimony, as each family of the tribe of Levi carried its own portion of the Tabernacle from place to place. We, too, are in the wilderness, and are called to journey through it "as strangers and pilgrims," not to settle down in it as though it were our home, but to pass on, guided by the pillar of cloud and fire, and, as we have it in another figure, finally to come up from the wilderness leaning upon our Beloved. But while by experience we are in the wilderness we are in another sense already in the land, and the type of the Levites does not fail us here. When the Jordan is passed we find them still bearing the ark, and outside the walls of Jericho the priests lead the victorious host, till, having compassed the city again and again, the walls of Jericho fall. Many of the hymns we sing speak of Jordan as death, and Canaan as heaven; but, as often shewn, the death prefigured by Jordan is our death with Christ, and Canaan is resurrection-ground, the heavenly places of Ephesians, where "we wrestle not against flesh and blood, but against principalities, against powers, against the rulers of the darkness of this world, against spiritual wickedness in high places," (margin heavenly). As priests and Levites there is work for us in the land as well as in the wilderness.

Then we have a third place to which we are called, and here our type fails except by contrast. The priests were indeed privileged to go into the holy place, but not into the holiest of all. Thither the high priest entered alone once a year; but now the veil has been rent, and we may have "boldness to enter into the holiest by the blood of Jesus, by a new and living way, which He hath consecrated for us through the veil; that is to say, His flesh." Thus, while as pilgrims we tread the wilderness, and as conquerors meet the enemies in the land, our hearts may be constantly before the throne of grace as suppliants and as worshippers.

The same many-sided picture is shown us in the dwelling-places of the Levites. In the wilderness they encamped "round about the tabernacle," and in after days in the land their time was in most cases divided between their own homes and lodging "round about the house of God." The forty-eight cities given to the Levites by the twelve tribes, were scattered in all parts of the land, and in order to serve in their courses they must lodge temporarily at Jerusalem, though the chief fathers dwelt there altogether.

Provision was, however, made for a Levite who so loved the house of his God that he was not satisfied with the short time of service allotted to him. He was to be allowed to give up his distant home, and come and make his abode in Jerusalem, ministering and feeding with those who served by course. We read in Deuteronomy xviii. 6, "If a Levite come from any of thy gates out of all Israel, where he sojourned, and come with all the desire of his mind unto the place which the Lord shall choose; then he shall minister in the name of the Lord his God, as all his brethren the Levites do, which stand there before the Lord. They shall have like portions to eat, beside that which cometh of the sale of his patrimony."

As we look at the list of cities belonging to the Levites, and study the meanings of these names, we find many suggestions of New Testament truths. They wonderfully prefigure the various aspects of the abiding place of the believer. This is especially the case with the six cities of refuge, according to the generally accepted meanings of their names. We have Kedesh—"holy," speaking to us of Christ the "Holy One"; Shechem—"shoulder," of Christ our strength; Hebron—"fellowship," of the One who calls us into fellowship with Himself; Bezer—"stronghold" or "rock," of the Lord who is our Rock and our Fortress; Ramoth—"exaltation," of Him whom God hath exalted with His right hand to be a Prince and a Saviour; and, lastly, Golan—"joy," telling us that abiding in our city of refuge His joy will remain in us, and our joy will be full. "In thy presence is fulness of joy."

But the priests and Levites must leave their homes, whether in these cities of refuge or other cities, in order to come up and take their turn in the service of the sanctuary; and here our type fails, for it is only as abiding in Christ that we can do anything. Separated from Him both service and worship will be fruitless.

THE PLACE OF SERVICE
Before the Lord

Continually **before** the Lord.—1 *Chron.* xxiii. 31.

Holy and without blame **before** him in love.—*Eph.* i. 4.

Before Aaron

And after that went the Levites in to do their service in the tabernacle of the congregation **before** Aaron.—*Num.* viii. 22.

And Eleazar and Ithamar ministered in the priest's office **in the sight of** Aaron their father.—*Num.* iii. 4.

That he would grant unto us, that we being delivered out of the hand of our enemies might serve him without fear, in holiness and righteousness **before him** all the days of our life.—*Luke* i. 74, 75.

Because we keep his commandments, and do those things that are pleasing **in his sight**. —1 *John* iii. 22.

With the King

And, behold, the courses of the priests and the Levites, even they shall be **with thee** for all the service of the house of God.—1 *Chron.* xxviii. 21.

And they went forth, and preached everywhere, the Lord **working with them,** and confirming the word with signs following.— *Mark* xvi. 20.

Lo, I am **with you** alway, even unto the end of the world.—*Matt.* xxviii. 20.

In the Sanctuary

They shall **enter** into my **sanctuary**.— *Ezek.* xliv. 16.

Having therefore, brethren, boldness to **enter** into the **holiest** by the blood of Jesus. —*Heb.* x. 19.

In the Wilderness

See Num. iv. &c.

As strangers and pilgrims.—1 *Peter* ii. 11.

In the Land

See Joshua iii., iv., vi., &c.

Blessed be the God and Father of our Lord Jesus Christ, who hath blessed us with all spiritual blessings in **heavenly places** in Christ.—*Eph.* i. 3.

See Joshua iii., iv., vi., &c.

For we wrestle not against flesh and blood, but against principalities, against powers, against the rulers of the darkness of this world, against spiritual wickedness **in high** * places.—*Eph.* vi. 12.

* Margin, heavenly.

THE LEVITES' DWELLING PLACES AND POSSESSIONS

Round About

And they shall minister unto it, and shall **encamp round about** the tabernacle.—*Num.* i. 50.

And they **lodged round about** the house of God.—1 *Chron.* ix. 27.

And exhorted them all, that with purpose of heart they would **cleave** unto the Lord.—*Acts* xi. 23.

There am I in the **midst** of them.—*Matt.* xviii. 20.

And **in the midst** of the seven candlesticks one like unto the Son of man.—*Rev.* i. 13.

At Jerusalem

These chief fathers of the Levites were chief throughout their generations ; these **dwelt** at Jerusalem.*—1 *Chron.* ix. 34.

* Or "floods of peace."

Abide in me, and I in you.—*John* xv. 4.

These things I have spoken unto you, that in me ye might have **peace**.—*John* xvi. 33.

No Inheritance

Wherefore Levi hath **no part** nor inheritance with his brethren.—*Deut.* x. 9.

Thou shalt have no **inheritance** in their land, neither shalt thou have any **part** among them.—*Num.* xviii. 20.

Ye shall give them **no possession** in Israel. —*Ezek.* xliv. 28.

For here have we **no continuing city,** but we seek one to come.—*Heb.* xiii. 14.

What **part** hath he that believeth with an infidel? (R.V., unbeliever).—2 *Cor.* vi. 15.

Knowing that of the Lord ye shall receive the reward of the **inheritance**.—*Col.* iii. 24.

As having nothing, and yet **possessing** all things.—2 *Cor.* vi. 10.

Neither said any of them that ought of the things which he **possessed** was his own.—*Acts* iv. 32.

They that buy, as though they **possessed** not.—1 *Cor.* vii. 30.

The Lord their Inheritance

I am thy part and thine **inheritance** among the children of Israel.—*Num.* xviii. 20.

The Lord is his **inheritance,** according as the Lord thy God promised him.—*Deut.* x. 9.

I am their **possession.**—*Ezek.* xliv. 28.

And if children, then heirs ; **heirs** of God, and joint-heirs with Christ.—*Rom.* viii. 17.

To an **inheritance** incorruptible, and undefiled, and that fadeth not away.—1 *Peter* i. 4.

In whom also we have obtained an **inheritance.**—*Eph.* i. 11.

My beloved is **mine,** and I am his.—*Song of Sol.* ii. 16.

Castles

Now these are their dwelling places throughout their **castles** in their coasts, of the sons of Aaron, of the families of the Kohathites.— 1 *Chron.* vi. 54.

The name of the Lord is a **strong tower :** the righteous runneth into it, and is safe. The rich man's wealth is his **strong city.**— *Prov.* xviii. 10, 11.

The unsearchable riches of Christ.—*Eph.* iii. 8.

Cities of Refuge

And among the cities which ye shall give unto the Levites there shall be six cities for **refuge,** which ye shall appoint for the manslayer, that he may flee thither : and to them ye shall add forty and two cities.—*Num.* xxxv. 6.

That by two immutable things, in which it was impossible for God to lie, we might have a strong consolation, who have fled for **refuge** to lay hold upon the hope set before us : which hope we have as an anchor of the soul, both sure and stedfast, and which entereth into that within the veil.—*Heb.* vi. 18, 19.

In the fear of the Lord is strong confidence: and his children shall have a place of **refuge.** —*Prov.* xiv. 26.

III

All Manner of Service

" A LL manner of service." Such indeed it appears, as we trace through
the Word the various occupations of the priests and Levites. Although
they held very different positions it is not always possible to make a distinction
between the work of Aaron's sons and the rest of the Levites, for though all
Levites were not priests, all priests were Levites, and are sometimes spoken
of as such.

As the Word itself loses sight of the distinction at times, we cannot too
rigidly enforce it.

It has been said that the work of the priests was unto the Lord, and that
of the Levites unto the people, but this is very much under-estimating the
high calling of even the least of the Levites. All their service was intended
to be unto the Lord, as truly as that of the priests, though the latter were
brought into His more immediate presence. He must be the object both
of service and worship. It is true that much of the ministry of the Levites
was to prepare for the priests, but it might as surely be "unto Him" as
may be a cup of cold water now, though only given to a disciple.

In the wilderness journey, and later in the temple service, there was no
independent work. It was all part of a great whole, which would have been
incomplete if the work of any Levite had been left undone. This is especially
noticeable in the account of the carrying of the Tabernacle, the details of
which are so minutely given in Numbers iv. If the Levites had failed in
their part, or had left any portion behind, the priests would have been
hindered in their higher service. Each had his own burden, and whether
it were a pin or a socket, a curtain or a board, all were needed. Is it not
so still in the service and testimony of the church? The helps are needed
as well as the pastors and teachers, and the little bits of humble service may

209

be as necessary in the uplifting of Christ as was the carrying of the seemingly insignificant portions of the Tabernacle by the Levites through the wilderness.

Each section of the tribe of Levi had its own work, and might not try and do that of another, or there would have been great confusion. As McCheyne wrote:

> "The Kohathites upon their shoulders bare
> The holy vessels covered with all care;
> The Gershonites receive an easier charge,
> Two waggons' full of cords and curtains large;
> Merari's sons four ponderous waggons' load
> With boards and pillars of the House of God."

In "the gainsaying of Core" we have an example of one who wished for different service than that which had been allotted to him. A Levite, but not a son of Aaron, he sought the priesthood also, and in the terrible account given in Numbers xvi. we read of the consequences of his discontent. The history of the sons of Korah forms a very interesting Bible study. When there came out a fire from the Lord, and consumed their father as he stood at the door of the Tabernacle with his companions, we find from Numbers xxvi. 11, that "notwithstanding, the children of Korah died not."

His confederates, Dathan and Abiram, refused to come up when Moses sent to call them, and they stood in the door of their tents with "their wives, and their sons, and their little children," and when the earth opened her mouth all were swallowed up, but Korah's sons were spared. They lived to fill the place which their father had despised, and their descendants became porters and singers in the house of God. We see by the headings of the psalms that many of them were specially for the sons of Korah, and as we study these songs in connection with the sad story of Numbers xvi. we find that a new force is added to many passages. Thus, in singing "God is our refuge and strength, a very present help in trouble; therefore will not we fear, though the earth be removed, and though the mountains be carried into the midst of the sea," their thoughts must have gone back to the terrible scene of judgment, when "the earth opened her mouth, and swallowed them up, and their houses, and all the men that appertained unto Korah, and all their goods," but still the sons of Korah were able to trust and not be afraid.

When in the eighty-fourth psalm they sang "A day in thy courts is better than a thousand. I had rather be a doorkeeper in the house of my God, than to dwell in the tents of wickedness," there seems to be a special reference to the time when Moses spake, saying, "Depart, I pray you, from the tents of these wicked men, and touch nothing of theirs, lest ye be consumed in all their sins," while we learn from 1 Chronicles ix. that the sons of Korah were actually appointed "keepers of the entry." Their father was not satisfied with his position, and had wished for other service, but they had learnt something of the blessedness of the man spoken of in Proverbs viii. 34, 35, "Blessed is the man that heareth me, watching daily at my gates, waiting at the posts of my doors. For whoso findeth me findeth life, and shall obtain favour [or acceptance] of the Lord."

The porters, if they entered into the meaning of the burnt-offering, would have special opportunities of learning this truth, as day by day they must have watched the preparation of that sacrifice which spoke of the acceptance of the offerer through the offering, and in the description of the temple in Ezekiel xl. 38, we read that they washed the burnt-offering by the posts of the gates. Blessed indeed is it thus to stand watching and waiting, and rejoicing in the assurance of our acceptance in the Beloved.

Korah was not satisfied with Levitical service, but coveted the priestly office that he might offer incense, and for this he perished at the door of the Tabernacle, the place where his sons afterwards ministered. The forty-fifth psalm, one of those which is "for the sons of Korah," seems the psalm of all others which is fragrant with incense as it speaks of Him whose "garments smell of myrrh, and aloes, and cassia," and thus, as in verse 16, "instead of thy fathers shall be thy children."

We have a beautiful picture of the work of the Levites, and especially of the porters, in 2 Chronicles xxiii. and 2 Kings xi., in connection with the King's Son that shall reign, and the "crowning day that's coming by-and-bye." Athaliah thought that she had destroyed all the seed royal, but one from among the slain was hidden in the house of the Lord, while "Athaliah did reign over the land." It seemed as though she had succeeded in her evil design, but at the right time the High Priest "gathered the Levites out of all the cities of Judah, and the chief of the fathers of Israel," and they were let into the secret. He "shewed them the king's son," and said to them, "Behold the king's son shall reign, as the Lord hath said of the sons of David." So is it now. At Calvary Satan thought he had made an end of the King's Son, but He arose from among the dead, and has been hidden from the eyes of men for nearly two thousand years. We know, however, that the god of this world will not always reign over the land. "The King's Son shall reign," and "He must reign, till He hath put all enemies under His feet." Meanwhile there is a secret band of followers, those called to the service of God, who have had a glimpse of Him. He could say, "The world seeth me no more; but ye see me." After they had had this sight, the Levites were stationed as "porters of the door," "at the king's house," and "at the gate of the foundation." Everything was changed for them from henceforth. Before, probably they grieved at the usurper's reign, but now they knew that it would soon cease, and they were on the alert for the rightful heir to be proclaimed. The priests and Levites were alone permitted to enter into the house of the Lord, and were gathered round the king, so that when he came out they came too. Jehoiada said to them, "Be ye with the king when he cometh in and when he goeth out." Does not this beautifully set before us the blessed hope that is ours? We are waiting to be summoned to take our place at His side before He comes to reign, and when we are gathered, "some from earth, from glory some," it will be ours henceforth to be for ever with the Lord. "Till He come," He has "commanded the porter to watch," that when He cometh, "the servants may open to Him immediately." "Blessed are those servants whom the Lord when He cometh shall find watching." As the Levites stood expecting the signal, they were provided with spears, bucklers, and shields, not new, untried weapons, but those "that had been king David's, which were in the house of God." The whole armour of God is given to us, that having done all we too may stand; and the shield and sword that are provided are those which were used by our Lord Himself in His encounters with the enemy.

At last "they brought out the king's son, and put upon him the crown . . . and made him king . . . and set the king upon the throne of the kingdom." He who is now the hidden One, who has only His little band of followers, will one day be crowned with "many crowns," and then will it be said, "The kingdoms of this world are become the kingdoms of our Lord and of His Christ: and He shall reign for ever and ever." (Rev. xi. 15.) But before the king could reign Athaliah had to be put to death. "And all the people of the land rejoiced: and the city was quiet, after that they had slain Athaliah with the sword." This is but a faint foreshadowing of the time when Satan will be bound, and "the Son of man shall send forth His angels, and they shall gather out of His kingdom all things that offend, and them which do iniquity." (Matt. xiii. 41.) But as we study this picture, and hear Him say, "Surely I come quickly," our hearts respond, "Even so, come, Lord Jesus."

In the ministry of the priests and Levites there was no room for human improvements. God gave the pattern for the tabernacle, for the temple, and for their service; but when they tried to alter God's plan, His judgment descended upon them. Perhaps David thought that the new cart upon which they placed the ark was an improvement on the old-fashioned method of carrying it on the shoulders of the priests; but he was only copying the Philistines, and had to go back to the old plan before it was finally brought into its place. Uzzah would not have fancied that there was a need for him to steady the ark, if it had been carried in God's way, and thus he would not have perished for his presumption.

The offering of incense and sacrifice seems to have been the highest aspect of the priests' ministry, which none but the sons of Aaron might perform. Mere earnestness and sincerity would not have been sufficient to warrant their approaching God in the holy place. There must be birth into the family of Aaron, and when those who were not amongst his sons tried to occupy the position of priests, and thus departed from God's pattern, quick judgment fell upon them. Jeroboam and Uzziah were both smitten while offering incense, and Saul's presumption in taking the place of a priest was the first of the acts of disobedience which cost him the kingdom. Instead of waiting for Samuel, he himself offered the burnt-offering, and, "Now," said Samuel, "thy kingdom shall not continue; the Lord hath sought him a man after his own heart, and the Lord hath commanded him to be captain over his people, because thou hast not kept that which the Lord commanded thee." We see therefore that it is no light thing to assume the position of a worshipper, for while all God's family are called to worship Him as priests in spirit and in truth, none but those who have been born again can do so.

The incense offered by the priests must have been a type of *Him* whose "name is as ointment poured forth," and surely the fact that *our prayers* are offered in His name accounts for their being compared to incense. In themselves there would be nothing to make them a sweet savour to God; it is only as offered through Him, perfumed with His name, and with the "much incense" of His merits, that they can rise as incense. There was a close connection between the offering of the morning and evening burnt-offering and the incense (see Ex. xxix. 38, 39; xxx. 7, 8); and David links the two together—"Let my prayer be set forth before thee as incense, and the lifting up of my hands as the evening sacrifice" (Ps. cxli. 2)—as though he recognized that his prayer was accepted because of the acceptableness of the spotless burnt-offering. It has been pointed out that the time of the evening sacrifice is on several occasions a time of crisis, and the moment for special answers to prayer. Thus, in I Kings xviii. 29, we find that when the priests of Baal called upon their god "until the time of the offering of the evening sacrifice, that there was neither voice, nor any to answer, nor any that regarded." But in verse 36 we read, "It came to pass, at the time of the offering of the evening sacrifice, that Elijah the prophet came near," and as he prayed the fire of the Lord fell. Ezra's prayer was offered at the time of the evening sacrifice (Ezra ix. 4, 5), and Daniel tells us that while he was speaking in prayer the man Gabriel, being caused to fly swiftly, touched him "about the time of the evening oblation." (Dan. ix. 21.) From Acts iii. 1; x. 2, 3, 30, we see that this special hour of prayer was the ninth hour, the very hour in which He, who was the Antitype of all burnt-offerings, yielded up the ghost, having "given Himself for us, an offering and a sacrifice to God for a sweet smelling savour." When He expired, the priest must have been standing at the golden altar, offering the incense, and as the veil was rent from the top to the bottom there was for the first time no barrier between the golden altar and the mercy-seat.

Communion also is likened to incense in Proverbs xxvii. 9, "Ointment and perfume rejoice the heart; so doth the sweetness of a man's friend by hearty counsel." When our hearts are in fellowship with Christ, refreshment is brought to Him. He says to the bride in the Song of Solomon, "How fair is thy love, my sister, my spouse, how much better is thy love than wine! and the smell of thine ointments than all spices!" but if *our love* is sweet to Him, it is only a love which He Himself has implanted in our hearts. The spices that grow in the garden are all His planting, and thus whether we take the incense to represent our prayer, our fellowship with Him, or our love, He must first fill our hands with incense ere we as priests approach the golden altar. The sweet savour is to be rising constantly to God. Not only at special times of prayer, but throughout *our whole lives* it should be true of us, "We are unto God a sweet savour of Christ."

Besides the incense it was the priests' duty to offer burnt offerings and to kindle meat offerings, and to do sacrifice continually, and thus at the brazen altar the different views of Christ's work were constantly prefigured. The altar was four-square, and while its four sides speak of the salvation which may be offered to all the world, whether dwellers in the North, South, East, or West, they also remind us of the four great offerings (the sin offering and the trespass offering being considered together), and thus point to the fourfold aspect of the work of Christ as foreshadowed in the offerings.

In the first chapter of John's epistle we seem to have this set before us in the same order as in the offerings, beginning, as in Leviticus i., with the Godward side, and ending with the provision for our sinfulness. In verses 1 to 3 we have the burnt offering aspect, the offering that was all upon God's altar, of which the priests might not partake, but which they could only look upon, and their hands handle. In verses 3 to 7 there is the thought of fellowship and joy. As in the meat offering and peace offering the priest partook of "the food of the offering," "the bread of his God" (Lev. iii. 16; xxi. 22), so we can say, "Truly our fellowship is with the Father and with His Son Jesus Christ," and in verses 7 to 10 we have God's provision for sin and sins, as typified by the sin offering and the trespass offering.

All these were offered by the priests, but in Leviticus xxi. we read that "no man that hath a blemish of the seed of Aaron the priest shall come nigh to offer the offerings of the Lord made by fire: he hath a blemish." Sin known and indulged must interfere with worship. There must be "holiness, without which no man shall see the Lord," and "they that worship Him must worship Him in spirit and in truth." While this passage in Leviticus speaks to us primarily of the holiness of God, it reminds us of a contrast between the old and the new dispensation. According to the Levitical law none with a blemish might draw near, but in the gospel He says, "Go out quickly into the streets and lanes of the city, and bring in hither the poor, and the maimed, and the halt, and the blind." Their blemishes did not disqualify them from coming into His house; on the contrary, they were the very things that caused them to be invited. So has it been with each one of us. We were full of blemishes, but the great Physician, who made the blind to see and the lame to walk, can and does heal us, so that we may with boldness draw near and "offer unto the Lord an offering in righteousness."

While the sacrifices in the first place typified Christ, Paul speaks of three other offerings of sweet smelling savour to God. We are to offer *ourselves* as "a living sacrifice, holy, acceptable unto God"; and this, like the burnt offering of old, is to be continuous. It was to be burning "all night unto the morning," and we are to be yielded to Him, not occasionally, but always, all through the dark night of His absence, "until the day break and the shadows flee away." Then there is "the sacrifice of *praise*" which we are to offer "to God continually, that is, the fruit of our lips, giving thanks to His name." And Paul speaks of the *gifts* which the Philippians had sent by Epaphroditus as "an odour of a sweet smell, a sacrifice acceptable, well-pleasing to God."

It is impossible to enumerate here all the varieties of service that the priests and Levites were called upon to perform, but the passages that follow speak for themselves, and illustrate the varied ministry to which we are called, in our twofold character of servants and worshippers.

May this study of His word lead us each one to more thorough devotedness to the person of our Lord, and more faithfulness in His service, as we realize afresh that if we belong to Him it is our privilege to take our share in the united testimony of the Church during the little while between the cross on Calvary and His coming again.

ALL MANNER OF SERVICE

Levites and Priests

To do the **service** of the tabernacle.— *Num.* iii. 7.

The Levites wait upon their **business.**— 2 *Chron.* xiii. 10.

The singers were over the **business** of the house of God.—*Neh.* xi. 22.

Ye **serve** the Lord Christ.—*Col.* iii. 24.

Not slothful in **business**; fervent in spirit; **serving** the Lord.—*Rom.* xii. 11.

The priests the sons of Aaron were **busied** in offering of burnt offerings and the fat until night.—*2 Chron.* xxxv. 14.

And thou shalt appoint Aaron and his sons, and they shall **wait** on their priest's office.—*Num.* iii. 10.

That they may minister unto me in the **priest's** office—*Exodus* xxx. 30.

And the **priest's** office shall be theirs for a perpetual statute.—*Exodus* xxix. 9.

Or ministry, let us **wait** on our ministering. —*Rom.* xii. 7.

An holy **priesthood,** to offer up spiritual sacrifices, acceptable to God by Jesus Christ . . . a royal **priesthood.**—1 *Peter* ii. 5, 9.

And hath made us kings and **priests** unto God and his Father.—*Rev.* i. 6.

Ministering unto Him

To stand before the Lord to **minister unto him.**—*Deut.* x. 8.

With good will doing service, as **to the Lord,** and not to men.—*Eph.* vi. 7.

Christ's servant. *—1 *Cor.* vii. 22.
   * R.V., Christ's bondservant.

Serving the Priests

Because their office was **to wait on the sons of Aaron** for the service of the house of the Lord, in the courts, and in the chambers, and in the purifying of all holy things, and the work of the service of the house of God. —1 *Chron.* xxiii. 28.

Wherefore their brethren the Levites did **help** them, till the work was ended, and until the other priests had sanctified themselves.— 2 *Chron.* xxix. 34.

For we preach not ourselves, but Christ Jesus the Lord ; and ourselves **your servants for Jesus' sake.**—*2 Cor.* iv. 5.

My **helpers** in Christ Jesus.—*Rom.* xvi. 3.

In His Name

For the Lord thy God hath chosen him out of all thy tribes, to stand to minister **in the name of the Lord,** him and his sons for ever.—*Deut.* xviii. 5.

To **bless in his name.**—*Deut.* x. 8.

And whatsoever ye do in word or deed, do all **in the name of the Lord Jesus.**—*Col.* iii. 17.

His name through faith in his name hath made this man strong.—*Acts* iii. 16.

Grant unto thy servants, that with all boldness they made speak thy word, by stretching forth thine hand to heal ; and that signs and wonders may be done by **the name** of thy holy child Jesus.—*Acts* iv. 29, 30.

Carrying and Setting Up the Tabernacle

And when the tabernacle setteth forward, the Levites shall take it down : and when the tabernacle is to be pitched, the Levites shall set it up.—*Num.* i. 51.

And the tabernacle was taken down ; and the sons of Gershon and the sons of Merari

And daily in the temple, and in every house, they ceased not to teach and preach Jesus Christ.—*Acts* v. 42.

Now there are diversities of gifts, but the same Spirit.   And there are differences of set forward, bearing the tabernacle. . . . And the Kohathites set forward, bearing the sanctuary : and the other did set up the tabernacle against they came.—*Num.* x. 17, 21.

administrations, but the same Lord. And there are diversities of operations, but it is the same God which worketh all in all. . . . But now are they many members, yet but one body. And the eye cannot say unto the hand, I have no need of thee : nor again the head to the feet, I have no need of you. 1 *Cor.* xii. 4-6, 20, 21.

Bearing the Ark

At that time the Lord separated the tribe of Levi, to **bear the ark** of the covenant of the Lord.—*Deut.* x. 8.

A chosen vessel unto me, to **bear** my name.—*Acts* ix. 15.

Always **bearing** about in the body the dying of the Lord Jesus, that the life also of Jesus might be made manifest in our body.—2 *Cor.* iv. 10.

They took knowledge of them, that they had been with Jesus.—*Acts* iv. 13.

The service of the sanctuary belonging unto them was that they should bear upon their **shoulders.**—*Num.* vii. 9.

Take **my yoke** upon you, and learn of me ; for I am meek and lowly in heart : and ye shall find rest unto your souls. For my yoke is easy, and my burden is light.—*Matt.* xi. 29, 30.

Keeping His Charge

And they shall **keep** his charge.—*Num.* iii. 7.

I have **kept** the faith.—2 *Tim.* iv. 7.

That good thing which was committed unto thee **keep** by the Holy Ghost which dwelleth in us.—2 *Tim.* i. 14.

Builders

After him **repaired** the Levites, Rehum the son of Bani. . . . And after him repaired the priests, the men of the plain.—*Neh.* iii. 17, 22.

They which **builded** on the walls, and they that bare burdens, with those that laded, every one with one of his hands wrought in the work, and with the other hand held a weapon. For the builders, every one had his sword girded by his side, and so builded. And he that sounded the trumpet was by me.—*Neh.* iv. 17, 18.

According to the grace of God which is given unto me, as a wise **masterbuilder,** I have laid the foundation, and another buildeth thereon. But let every man take heed how he **buildeth** thereupon. For other foundation can no man lay than that is laid, which is Jesus Christ. Now if any man build upon this foundation gold, silver, precious stones, wood, hay, stubble ; every man's work shall be made manifest : for the day shall declare it, because it shall be revealed by fire ; and the fire shall try every man's work of what sort it is.—1 *Cor.* iii. 10-13.

Warriors

This is it that belongeth unto the Levites : from twenty and five years old and upward they shall go in to wait upon the service of the tabernacle of the congregation.—*Num.* viii. 24.

R.V. marg., to war the warfare in the work.

That thou by them mightest **war a good warfare.**—1 *Tim.* i. 18.

Thou therefore endure hardness, as a good **soldier** of Jesus Christ.—2 *Tim.* ii. 3.

Knowing that I am set for the **defence** of the gospel.—*Phil.* i. 17.

And he said unto them, Thus saith the Lord God of Israel, Put every man his **sword** by his side, and go in and out from gate to gate throughout the camp, and slay every man his brother, and every man his companion, and every man his neighbour. And the children of Levi did according to the word of Moses.—*Exodus* xxxii. 27, 28.

And the **sword** of the Spirit, which is the word of God.—*Eph.* vi. 17.

Trumpeters

And the sons of Aaron, the priests, shall **blow with the trumpets**; and they shall be to you for an ordinance for ever throughout your generations. And if ye go to **war** in your land against the enemy that oppresseth you, then ye shall **blow an alarm** with the trumpets; and ye shall be remembered before the Lord your God, and ye shall be saved from your enemies. Also in the day of your gladness, and in your solemn days, and in the beginnings of your months, ye shall blow with the trumpets over your burnt offerings, and over the sacrifices of your peace offerings.— *Num.* x. 8–10.

For from you **sounded out** the word of the Lord.—1 *Thess.* i. 8.

For if the **trumpet** give an uncertain sound, who shall prepare himself to the battle? So likewise ye, except ye utter by the tongue words easy to be understood, how shall it be known what is spoken?—1 *Cor.* xiv. 8.

Singers

And they ministered before the dwelling place of the tabernacle of the congregation with **singing**.—1 *Chron.* vi. 32.

So the number of them, with their brethren that were instructed in **the songs of the Lord,** even all that were cunning, was two hundred fourscore and eight.—1 *Chron.* xxv. 7.

And Chenaniah, chief of the Levites, was for **song**: he instructed about the **song,** because he was skilful.—1 *Chron.* xv. 22.

Such as taught to **sing praise.**—2 *Chron.* xxiii. 13.

And David spake to the chief of the Levites to appoint their brethren to be the singers with instruments of musick, psalteries, and harps and cymbals, sounding, by lifting up the voice with **joy.**—1 *Chron.* xv. 16.

And to stand every morning to **thank** and praise the Lord, and likewise at even.— 1 *Chron.* xxiii. 30.

It came even to pass, as the trumpeters and singers were as **one,** to make **one** sound to be heard in praising and thanking the Lord.— 2 *Chron.* v. 13.

And the Levites and the priests praised the Lord **day by day,** singing with loud instru-

Speaking to yourselves in psalms and hymns and spiritual songs, **singing** and making melody in your heart to the Lord.—*Eph.* v. 19.

Let the word of Christ dwell in you richly in all wisdom; teaching and admonishing one another in psalms and hymns and spiritual songs, **singing** with grace in your hearts to the Lord.—*Col.* iii. 16.

Rejoice in the Lord alway: and again I say, **Rejoice.**—*Phil.* iv. 4.

In every thing **give thanks.**—1 *Thess.* v. 18.

That ye may with **one** mind and **one** mouth glorify God, even the Father of our Lord Jesus Christ.—*Rom.* xv. 6.

And they, continuing **daily** with one accord in the temple, and breaking bread from house

ments unto the Lord.—2 *Chron.* xxx. 21.

And they sang praises with **gladness,** and they bowed their heads and worshipped.— 2 *Chron.* xxix. 30.

to house, did eat their meat **with gladness** and singleness of heart, praising God, and having favour with all the people. And the Lord added to the church daily such as should be saved.—*Acts* ii. 46, 47.

Prophesying

Moreover David and the captains of the host separated to the service of the sons of Asaph, and of Heman, and of Jeduthun, who should prophesy with harps, with psalteries, and with cymbals : and the number of the workmen according to their service was : of the sons of Asaph . . . which **prophesied** according to the order of the king. Of Jeduthun : the sons of Jeduthun . . . who **prophesied** with a harp, to give thanks and to praise the Lord.—1 *Chron.* xxv. 1-3.

Follow after charity, and desire spiritual gifts, but rather that ye may **prophesy.**— 1 *Cor.* xiv. 1.

For to one is given by the Spirit the word of wisdom . . . to another **prophecy.**— 1 *Cor.* xii. 8, 10.

But he that **prophesieth** speaketh unto men to edification, and exhortation, and comfort.—1 *Cor.* xiv. 3.

Praying

Then the priests the Levites arose and blessed the people : and their voice was heard, and **their prayer came up** to his holy dwelling place, even unto heaven.— 2 *Chron.* xxx. 27.

And Mattaniah the son of Micha, the son of Zabdi, the son of Asaph, was the principal to begin the **thanksgiving** in **prayer.**— *Neh.* xi. 17.

(A Prayer of the Levites.—*Neh.* ix. 4-37.)

And this is the confidence that we have in him, that, if we ask any thing according to his will, **he heareth us :** and if we know that he hear us, whatsoever we ask, we know that we have the petitions that we desired of him.—1 *John* v. 14, 15.

Be careful for nothing ; but in every thing by **prayer** and supplication with **thanksgiving** let your requests be made known unto God.—*Phil.* iv. 6.

Confessing

And they did eat throughout the feast seven days, offering peace offerings, and making **confession** to the Lord God of their fathers. —2 *Chron.* xxx. 22.

If we **confess** our sins, he is faithful and just to forgive us our sins, and to cleanse us from all unrighteousness.—1 *John.* i. 9.

Messengers

For he is the **messenger** of the Lord of hosts.—*Mal.* ii. 7.

Now then we are **ambassadors** for Christ. —2 *Cor.* v. 20.

Teachers

And Hezekiah spake comfortably unto all the Levites that **taught the good knowledge** of the Lord.—2 *Chron.* xxx. 22.

And they shall **teach** my people the difference between the holy and profane, and cause them to discern between the unclean and the clean.—*Ezekiel* xliv. 23.

Now thanks be unto God, which always causeth us to triumph in Christ, and maketh manifest **the savour of his knowledge** by us in every place.—2 *Cor.* ii. 14.

Let him that is **taught** in the word **communicate** unto him that **teacheth** in all good things.—*Gal.* vi. 6.

But be thou an **example** of the believers, in word, in conversation, in charity, in spirit, in faith, in purity.—1 *Tim.* iv. 12.

And did **turn** many away from iniquity.—*Mal.* ii. 6.

Unto whom now I send thee, to open their eyes, and to **turn** them from darkness to light, and from the power of Satan unto God.—*Acts* xxvi. 17, 18.

Recorders

And he appointed certain of the Levites to minister before the ark of the Lord, and to **record** and to thank and praise the Lord God of Israel.—1 *Chron.* xvi. 4.

Who **bare record** of the word of God, and of the testimony of Jesus Christ, and of all things that he saw.—*Rev.* i. 2.

And when they were come, and had gathered the church together, they **rehearsed** all that God had done with them, and how he had opened the door of faith unto the Gentiles.—*Acts* xiv. 27.

Scribes

And of the Levites there were **scribes**.—2 *Chron.* xxxiv. 13.

Ye are **our epistle** written in our hearts, known and read of all men : forasmuch as ye are manifestly declared to be **the epistle of Christ** ministered by us, written not with ink, but with the Spirit of the living God ; not in tables of stone, but in fleshy tables of the heart.—2 *Cor.* iii. 2, 3.

Listeners to the Word

And the king went up into the house of the Lord, and all the men of Judah, and the inhabitants of Jerusalem, and the priests, and the Levites, and all the people, great and small : and he **read** in their ears all the words of the book of the covenant that was found in the house of the Lord.—2 *Chron.* xxxiv. 30.

He that is of God **heareth** God's words.—*John* viii. 47.

Wherefore, my beloved brethren, let every man be swift to **hear,** slow to speak, slow to wrath : for the wrath of man worketh not the righteousness of God. Wherefore lay apart all filthiness and superfluity of naughtiness, and **receive** with meekness the engrafted word, which is able to save your souls. But be ye doers of the word, and not **hearers** only, deceiving your own selves.—*James* i. 19-22.

Keepers of the Book

He shall write him a copy of this law in a book out of that which is before the priests the Levites.—*Deut.* xvii. 18.

And they taught in Judah, and had the **book of the law** of the Lord with them, and went about throughout all the cities of Judah, and taught the people.—2 *Chron.* xvii. 9.

And Moses wrote this law, and delivered it unto the priests the sons of Levi, which bare the ark of the covenant of the Lord, and unto all the elders of Israel.—*Deut.* xxxi. 9.

And hath committed unto us **the word** reconciliation.—2 *Cor.* v. 19.

But as we were allowed of God to be put in trust with **the gospel**, even so we speak.—1 *Thess.* ii. 4.

Let **the word of Christ** dwell in you richly in all wisdom.—*Col.* iii. 16.

Proclaimers of the Word

And Moses commanded them, saying, At the end of every seven years, in the solemnity of the year of release, in the feast of tabernacles, when all Israel is come to appear before the Lord thy God in the place which he shall choose, thou shalt **read** this law before all Israel in their hearing. Gather the people together, men, and women, and children, and thy stranger that is within thy gates, that they may hear, and that they may learn, and fear the Lord your God, and observe to do all the words of this law.—*Deut.* xxxi. 10–12.

Holding forth the word of life.—*Phil.* ii. 16.

Preach the word ; be instant in season, out of season ; reprove, rebuke, exhort with all longsuffering and doctrine.—*2 Tim.* iv. 2.

The Opening, or the Key

And the **opening** * thereof every morning pertained to them.—1 *Chron.* ix. 27.

* In the other two passages where this word is used (Judges iii. 25 and Isa. xxii. 22) it is translated "key."

Woe unto you, lawyers ! for ye have taken away **the key** of knowledge : ye entered not in yourselves, and them that were entering in ye hindered.—*Luke* xi. 52.

Compel them to come in, that my house may be filled.—*Luke* xiv. 23.

Setting a Seal

And because of all this we make a sure covenant, and write it ; and our princes, Levites, and priests, **seal** unto it.—*Neh.* ix. 38.

He that hath received his testimony hath set to his **seal** that God is true.—*John* iii. 33.

Porters

And Shallum the son of Kore, the son of Ebiasaph, the son of Korah, and his brethren, of the house of his father, the Korahites, were over the work of the service, **keepers of the gates** of the tabernacle : and their fathers, being over the host of the Lord, were **keepers of the entry.**—1 *Chron.* ix. 19.

All these which were chosen to be **porters** in the gates were two hundred and twelve.—1 *Chron.* ix. 22.

For the Son of man is as a man taking a far journey, who left his house, and gave authority to his servants, and to every man his work, and commanded **the porter** to watch. —*Mark* xiii. 34.

And ye yourselves like unto men that wait for their lord, when he will return from the wedding ; that when he cometh and knocketh, they may **open** unto him immediately. Blessed are those servants, whom the Lord when he cometh shall find watching . . . And if he shall come in the second watch, or come in the third watch, and find them so, blessed are those servants.—*Luke* xii. 36-38.

According to the glorious gospel of the blessed God, which was committed to my **trust.**—1 *Tim.* i. 11.

Blessed is the man that heareth me, watching daily at my gates, **waiting** at the posts of my doors.—*Prov.* viii. 34.

For these Levites, the four chief porters were in their set **office.** *—1 *Chron.* ix. 26.

* Margin, their trust.

And these are they that **waited** * with their children.—1 *Chron.* vi. 33.

* Margin, stood.

To **stand** before the Lord.—*Deut.* x. 8.

Having done all, to **stand.**—*Eph.* vi. 13.

And were over the **chambers*** and trea-
suries of the house of God.—1 *Chron.* ix. 26.

* Margin, storehouses.

Then said he unto them, Therefore every
scribe which is instructed unto the kingdom
of heaven is like unto a man that is an
householder, which bringeth forth out of his
treasure things new and old.—*Matt.* xiii. 52.

Overseers

And certain of them had the charge of the
ministering **vessels,** that they should bring
them in and out by tale. Some of them also
were appointed to oversee the vessels, and all
the instruments of the sanctuary.—1 *Chron.*
28, 29.

In a great house there are not only **vessels**
of gold and of silver, but also of wood and
of earth ; and some to honour, and some to
dishonour. If a man therefore purge himself
from these, he shall be a vessel unto honour,
sanctified, and meet for the master's use, and
prepared unto every good work.—2 *Tim.* ii.
20, 21.

And the men did the work faithfully : and
the **overseers** of them were Jahath and
Obadiah, the Levites, of the sons of Merari ;
and Zechariah and Meshullam, of the sons of
the Kohathites, to set it forward ; and other
of the Levites, all that could skill of instruments of musick. Also they were **over** the
bearers of burdens, and were **overseers** of
all that wrought the work in any manner of
service.—2 *Chron.* xxxiv. 12, 13.

And Shabbethai and Jozabad, of the chief
of the Levites, had the oversight of the outward business of the house of God.—*Neh.* xi.
16.

Obey them that have the rule **over** you,
and submit yourselves : for they watch for
your souls, as they that must give account,
that they may do it with joy, and not with
grief: for that is unprofitable for you.—*Heb.*
xiii. 17.

And we beseech you, brethren, to know
them which labour among you, and are **over
you in the Lord,** and admonish you ; and
to esteem them very highly in love for their
work's sake. And be at peace among yourselves.—1 *Thess.* v. 12, 13.

Having Charge of the Spices, &c.

And the fine flour, and the wine, and the
oil, and the frankincense, and the spices.—
1 *Chron.* ix. 29.

But the fruit of the Spirit is love, joy,
peace, longsuffering, gentleness, goodness,
faith, meekness, temperance : against such
there is no law.—*Gal.* v. 22, 23.

Pronouncing the Leper Clean or Unclean

Then he shall be brought unto Aaron the
priest, or unto one of his sons the priests.—
Lev. xiii. 2.

Whose soever sins ye remit, they are
remitted unto them ; and whose soever sins
ye retain, they are retained.—*John* xx. 23.

And such were some of you : but ye are
washed, but ye are sanctified, but ye are
justified in the name of the Lord Jesus, and
by the Spirit of our God.—1 *Cor.* vi. 11.

Cleansing the Temple

And the priests went into the inner part of
the house of the Lord, to **cleanse** it, and
brought out all the uncleanness that they
found in the temple of the Lord into the
court of the house of the Lord. And the
Levites took it, to carry it out abroad into
the brook Kidron.—2 *Chron.* xxix. 16.

And he set the porters at the gates of the

And what agreement hath the temple of
God with idols? for ye are **the temple** of the
living God ; as God hath said, I will dwell in
them, and walk in them ; and I will be their
God, and they shall be my people. Wherefore come out from among them, and be ye
separate, saith the Lord, and touch not the
unclean thing ; and I will receive you, and

house of the Lord, that none which was **unclean** in any thing should enter in.— *2 Chron.* xxiii. 19.

will be a Father unto you, and ye shall be my sons and daughters, saith the Lord Almighty.—*2 Cor.* vi. 16-18.

Offerers of Incense

They shall put **incense** before thee.—*Deut.* xxxiii. 10.

And they burn unto the Lord every morning and every evening burnt sacrifices and **sweet incense.**—*2 Chron.* xiii. 11.

For we are unto God a **sweet savour** of Christ. *2 Cor.* ii. 15.

Let my prayers be set forth before thee as **incense.**—*Ps.* cxli. 2.

Golden vials full of **odours,** which are the prayers of saints.—*Rev.* v. 8.

And there was given unto him much **incense,** that he should offer it with the prayers of all saints upon the golden altar which was before the throne. And the smoke of the incense, which came with the prayers of the saints, ascended up before God out of the angel's hand.—*Rev.* viii. 3, 4.

Thy name is as ointment poured forth, therefore do the virgins love thee.—*Song of Sol.* i. 3.

Verily, verily, I say unto you, Whatsoever ye shall ask the Father in **my name,** he will give it you.—*John* xvi. 23.

And some of the sons of the priests made the ointment of the spices.—*1 Chron.* ix. 30.

While the king sitteth at his table, my spikenard sendeth forth the smell thereof.—*Song of Sol.* i. 12.

How fair is thy love, my sister, my spouse! how much better is thy love than wine! and the smell of thine ointments than all spices! —*Song of Sol.* iv. 10.

There came unto him a woman having an alabaster box of very precious ointment, and poured it on his head.—*Matt.* xxvi. 7.

Offerers of Sacrifice

And it came to pass, **when God helped** the Levites that bare the ark of the covenant of the Lord, that they offered seven bullocks and seven rams.—*1 Chron.* xv. 26.

Neither shall the priests the Levites want a man before me to offer burnt-offerings, and to kindle meat-offerings, and to do sacrifice continually.—*Jer.* xxxiii. 18.

And whole burnt sacrifice upon thine altar. —*Deut.* xxxiii. 10.

That they may offer unto the Lord an **offering** in righteousness.—*Mal.* iii. 3.

Having therefore obtained **help of God,** I continue unto this day, witnessing both to small and great. . . . That Christ should **suffer,** and that he should be the first that should rise from the dead.—*Acts* xxvi. 22, 23.

For I determined not to know any thing among you, save Jesus Christ, and him crucified.—*1 Cor.* ii. 2.

To the praise of the glory of his grace, wherein he hath made us accepted in the beloved. In whom we have redemption through his blood, the forgiveness of sins, according to the riches of his grace.—*Eph.* i. 6, 7.

An holy priesthood, to offer up **spiritual sacrifices,** acceptable to God by Jesus Christ. —*1 Pet.* ii. 5.

I beseech you therefore, brethren, by the mercies of God, that ye present your bodies a living sacrifice, holy, acceptable unto God, which is your reasonable service.—*Rom.* xii. 1.

Preparing the Passover

And they killed the **passover,** and the priests sprinkled the blood from their hands, and the Levites flayed them . . . And they roasted the passover with fire according to the ordinance : but the other holy offerings sod they·in pots, and in caldrons, and in pans, and divided them speedily among all the people. And afterward they made ready for themselves, and for the priests.—2 *Chron.* xxxv. 11, 13, 14.

Purge out therefore the old leaven, that ye may be a new lump, as ye are unleavened. For even Christ our **passover** is sacrificed for us : therefore let us keep the feast, not with old leaven, neither with the leaven of malice and wickedness ; but with the unleavened bread of sincerity and truth.—1 *Cor.* v. 7, 8.

Distributing Portions

And Kore the son of Imnah the Levite, the porter toward the east, was over the free-will offerings of God, to **distribute** the oblations of the Lord, and the most holy things. And next him were Eden, and Miniamin, and Jeshua, and Shemaiah, Amariah, and Shecaniah, in the cities of the priests, in their set office, to give to their brethren by courses, as well to the great as to the small : beside their genealogy of males, from three years old and upward, even unto every one that entereth into the house of the Lord, his **daily portion** for their service in their charges according to their courses.—·2 *Chron.* xxxi. 14–16.

For they were counted **faithful,** and their office was to distribute unto their brethren.—*Neh.* xiii. 13.

And the Lord said, Who then is that faithful and wise **steward,** whom his lord shall make ruler over his household, to give them their **portion** of meat in due season ? Blessed is that servant, whom his lord when he cometh shall find so doing.—*Lev.* xii. 42, 43.

Let a man so account of us, as of the ministers of Christ, and stewards of the mysteries of God. Moreover it is required in stewards, that a man be found **faithful.**—1 *Cor.* iv. 1, 2.

Giving and Gathering

Thus speak unto the Levites, and say unto them, When ye take of the children of Israel the tithes which I have given you from them for your inheritance, then ye shall **offer** up an heave offering of it **for the Lord,** even a tenth part of the tithe.—*Num.* xviii. 26.

And the priest the son of Aaron shall be with the Levites, when the Levites take tithes ; and the Levites shall bring up the tithe of the tithes unto the house of our God, to the chambers, into **the treasure house.** —*Neh.* x. 38.

And he gathered together the priests and the Levites, and said to them, **Go out** unto the cities of Judah, and **gather** of all Israel money to repair the house of your God from year to year, and see that ye hasten the matter. . . . And they made a proclamation

Every man according as he purposeth in his heart, so let him give ; not grudgingly, or of necessity : for God loveth a cheerful giver.—2 *Cor.* ix. 7.

But I have all, and abound : I am full, having received of Epaphroditus the things which were sent from you, an odour of a sweet smell, a sacrifice **acceptable, well-pleasing** to God.—*Phil.* iv. 18.

Now concerning **the collection** for the saints, as I have given order to the churches of Galatia, even so do ye. Upon the first day of the week let every one of you lay by him in store, as God hath prospered him, that there be no gatherings when I come.—

through Judah and Jerusalem, to bring in to the Lord **the collection** that Moses the servant of God laid upon Israel in the wilderness. . . . Now it came to pass, that at what time the chest was brought unto the king's office by the hand of the Levites, and when they saw that there was much money, the king's scribe and the high priest's officer came and emptied the chest, and took it, and carried it to his place again. Thus they did day by day, and gathered money in abundance. And the king and Jehoiada gave it to such as did the work of the service of the house of the Lord, and hired masons and carpenters to repair the house of the Lord, and also such as wrought iron and brass to mend the house of the Lord. So the workmen wrought, and the work was perfected by them, and they set the house of God in his state, and strengthened it.—*2 Chron.* xxiv. 5, 9, 11–13.

1 *Cor.* xvi. 1, 2.

Chosen of the churches to travel with us with this grace, which is administered by us to the glory of the same Lord, and declaration of your ready mind : avoiding this, that no man should blame us in this abundance which is administered by us : . . . the **messengers** of the churches, and the glory of Christ. Wherefore shew ye to them, and before the churches, the proof of your love, and of our boasting on your behalf.—*2 Cor.* viii. 19, 20, 23, 24.

CAST OUT IN REJECTION

Have ye not **cast out** the priests of the Lord, the sons of Aaron, and the Levites.— *2 Chron.* xiii. 9.

Blessed are ye, when men shall hate you, and when they shall **separate** you from their company, and shall reproach you, and cast out your name as evil, for the Son of man's sake. Rejoice ye in that day, and leap for joy : for, behold, your reward is great in heaven : for in the like manner did their fathers unto the prophets.—*Luke* vi. 22, 23.

So they **cast him out** of the vineyard, and killed him.—*Luke* xx. 15.

And they **cast** him **out.** Jesus heard that they had cast him out.—*John* ix. 34, 35.

ENCOURAGEMENTS AND REWARDS

And he set the priests in their charges, and **encouraged** them to the service of the house of the Lord.—*2 Chron.* xxxv. 2.

And these are the singers, chief of the fathers of the Levites, who remaining in the chambers were **free.** *—1 Chron.* ix. 33.

* R.V., free from other service.

Take it of them, that they may be to do

Therefore, my beloved brethren, be ye stedfast, unmoveable, always abounding in the work of the Lord, forasmuch as ye know that your labour is not in vain in the Lord.— 1 *Cor.* xv. 58.

But now being made **free** from sin, and become servants to God, ye have your fruit unto holiness, and the end everlasting life.— —*Rom.* vi. 22.

If the Son therefore shall make you **free,** ye shall be **free** indeed.—*John* viii. 36.

But my God shall supply all your need

the service of the tabernacle of the congregation; and thou shalt give them unto the Levites, to every man **according to his service.** And Moses took the wagons and the oxen, and gave them unto the Levites.—*Num.* vii. 5, 6.

According to the commandment of the Lord they were numbered by the hand of Moses, every one **according to his service,** and according to his burden.—*Num.* iv. 49.

And ye shall eat it in every place, ye and your households: for it is [your reward for your service in the tabernacle of the congregation.—*Num.* xviii. 31.

according to his riches in glory by Christ Jesus.—*Phil.* iv. 19.

For God is not unrighteous to forget your work and labour of love, which ye have shewed toward his name.—*Heb.* vi. 10.

And every man shall receive his own **reward** according to his own labour.—1 *Cor.* iii. 8.

Suffering Loss

And the Levites that are gone away far from me, when Israel went astray, which went astray away from me after their idols; they shall even bear their iniquity. Yet they shall be ministers in my sanctuary, having charge at the gates of the house, and ministering **to the house:** they shall slay the burnt offering and the sacrifice **for the people,** and they shall stand before them to minister **unto them.** Because they ministered unto them before their idols, and caused the house of Israel to fall into iniquity; therefore have I lifted up mine hand against them, saith the Lord God, and they shall bear their iniquity. And they shall **not** come near **unto me,** to do the office of a priest unto me, nor to come near to any of my holy things, in the most holy place: but they shall bear their shame, and their abominations which they have committed.—*Ezek.* xliv. 10-13.

Receiving Reward

But I will make them keepers of the charge of the house, for all the service thereof, and for all that shall be done therein. But the priests the Levites, the sons of Zadok, that kept the charge of my sanctuary when the children of Israel went astray from me, they shall come near **to me** to minister **unto me,** and they shall stand **before me** to offer **unto me** the fat and the blood, saith the Lord God: they shall enter into my sanctuary, and they shall come near to my table, to minister **unto me,** and they shall keep my charge.—*Ezek.* xliv. 14-16.

Now if any man build upon this foundation gold, silver, precious stones, wood, hay, stubble; every man's work shall be made manifest: for the day shall declare it, because it shall be revealed by fire; and the fire shall try every man's work of what sort it is. If any man's work abide which he hath built thereupon, he shall receive a **reward.** If any man's work shall be burned, he shall **suffer loss:** but he himself shall be saved; yet so as by fire.—1 *Cor.* iii. 12-15.

PRAYERS

Bless, Lord, his **substance**.—*Deut.* xxxiii. 11.

And **accept** the work of his hands—*Deut.* xxxiii. 11.

Smite through the loins of them that rise against him, and of them that hate him, that they rise not again.—*Deut.* xxxiii. 11.

All these things shall be added unto you.—*Matt.* vi. 33.

How shall he not with him also freely give us **all** things?—*Rom.* viii. 32.

Wherefore we labour, that, whether present or absent, we may be **accepted** of him.—2 *Cor.* v. 9.

For he that in these things serveth Christ is **acceptable** to God, and approved of men.—*Rom.* xiv. 18.

Nay, in all these things we are more than **conquerors** through him that loved us.—*Rom.* viii. 37.

But thanks be to God, which giveth us the **victory** through our Lord Jesus Christ.—1 *Cor.* xv. 57.

PROMISES

He will **bless** the house of Aaron.—*Ps.* cxv. 12.

As the host of heaven cannot be numbered, neither the sand of the sea measured : so will **I multiply** the seed of David my servant, and the Levites that minister unto me.—*Jer.* xxxiii. 22.

Who hath **blessed** us with all spiritual blessings in heavenly places in Christ.—*Eph.* i. 3.

For it became him, for whom are all things, and by whom are all things, in bringing **many sons** unto glory, to make the captain of their salvation perfect through sufferings. —*Heb.* ii. 10.

Then had the churches rest throughout all Judæa and Galilee and Samaria, and were edified ; and walking in the fear of the Lord, and in the comfort of the Holy Ghost, were **multiplied.**—*Acts* ix. 31.

PRECEPTS

O house of Aaron, **trust** in the Lord : he is their help and their shield.—*Ps.* cxv. 10.

Let the house of Aaron now say, that his **mercy** endureth for ever.—*Ps.* cxviii. 3.

Bless the Lord, O house of Aaron : **bless** the Lord, O house of Levi.—*Ps.* cxxxv. 19, 20.

Be **careful for nothing** ; but in everything by prayer and supplication with thanksgiving let your requests be made known unto God. —*Phil.* iv. 6.

God, who is rich in **mercy**.—*Eph.* ii. 4.

According to his abundant **mercy** hath begotten us again unto a lively hope by the resurrection of Jesus Christ from the dead.— 1 *Peter* i. 3.

Blessed be God, even the Father of our Lord Jesus Christ, the Father of mercies, and the God of all comfort.—2 *Cor.* i. 3.

Worthy is the Lamb that was slain to receive power, and riches, and wisdom, and strength, and honour, and glory, and **blessing.** —*Rev.* v. 12.

THIS IS THE SUM

This is **the sum** of the tabernacle, even of the tabernacle of testimony, as it was counted, according to the commandment of Moses, for the service of the Levites, by the hand of Ithamar, son· to Aaron the priest.—*Exodus* xxxviii. 21.

Now of the things which we have spoken this is **the sum**: We have such an high priest, who is set on the right hand of the throne of the Majesty in the heavens; a minister of the sanctuary, and of the true tabernacle, which the Lord pitched, and not man.—*Heb.* viii. 1, 2.

A CONNECTING LINK

A great company of the **priests** were obedient to the faith.—*Acts* vi. 7.

And Joses, who by the apostles was surnamed Barnabas (which is, being interpreted, The son of consolation), **a Levite**, and of the country of Cyprus, having land, sold it, and brought the money, and laid it at the apostles' feet.—*Acts* iv. 36, 37.

IV

Future Rest and Service

IN studying the work of the porters we have already looked at one prophetic picture, and there are several other passages in connection with priestly and Levitical service which speak to us of future rest and service. They were not always to carry about the ark; the time came when, after many wanderings, it was brought into its place—first, into the tent in Jerusalem prepared by David, and finally into the temple of Solomon. "For David said, The Lord God of Israel hath given rest unto His people, that they may dwell in Jerusalem for ever: and also unto the Levites; they shall no more (R.V. have need to) carry the tabernacle, nor any vessels of it for the service thereof." (1 Chron. xxiii. 25, 26.) And Josiah "said unto the Levites that taught all Israel, which were holy unto the Lord, Put the holy ark in the house which Solomon the son of David king of Israel did build: it shall not be a burden upon your shoulders." Do not these pictures prefigure the time when the earthly testimony and wilderness days will be over, and the temple will be complete? The scene in 2 Chron. v. beautifully foreshadows this time. The materials had been made ready, but now the preparation is over, and the house is finished. Solomon has done what he speaks of in Prov. xxiv. 27, "Prepare thy work without, and make it fit for thyself in the field; and afterwards build thine house." Every stone was "made ready before it was brought thither: so that there was neither hammer, nor axe, nor any tool of iron, heard in the house while it was in building"; and the vessels and instruments for the house of the Lord "in the plain of Jordan did the king cast them in the clay ground." (2 Chron. iv. 17.) But in the fifth chapter the work is finished, and all that David had dedicated is brought in and placed among the treasures of the house of God. Solomon's temple, as has been so often pointed out, is but a picture of that other temple "built upon the foundation of the apostles and prophets, Jesus Christ Himself being the chief corner-stone; in whom all the building fitly framed together,

229

groweth unto an holy temple in the Lord." It, too, is being built of stones made ready before being brought thither. "The field is the world," and God Himself prepares His work without, makes it fit for Himself in the field, and afterwards builds His house. He, too, moulds His vessels in the clay ground in the plains of Jordan, but the time is coming when His house will be finished, and "He shall bring forth the headstone thereof with shoutings, crying, Grace, grace unto it." The picture in 2 Chron. v. is a faint foreshadowing of the day when this temple will be complete. Like that spoken of by David, "the house that is to be builded for the Lord must be exceeding magnifical, of fame and glory throughout all countries." As Paul wrote to the believers at Ephesus, he probably thought also of that other temple at Ephesus, where they feared that through Paul's teaching, "the temple of the great goddess Diana should be despised, and her magnificence should be destroyed, whom all Asia and the world worshippeth." As we stand in the room devoted to the ruins of the temple of Diana in the British Museum, we see that this has indeed come to pass; but the temple of which the despised Ephesian believers formed a part has stood against all the assaults of the enemy, and is to be the admiration, not of all Asia and the world, but of the whole universe.

In the beautiful picture in Chronicles the priests and Levites take a prominent part, and as they stand arrayed in white linen, with harps in their hands, making one sound in thanking and praising the Lord, they remind us of the glorious company described in the fifth chapter of Revelation, "having every one of them harps, and golden vials full of odours, which are the prayers of saints. And they sang a new song, saying, Thou art worthy to take the book, and to open the seals thereof: for Thou wast slain and hast redeemed us to God by Thy blood out of every kindred, and tongue, and people, and nation; and hast made us unto our God kings and priests: and we shall reign on the earth."

The priests and Levites in Chronicles stood at the east end of the altar, and in this we have prefigured our standing place to all eternity. The east end of the altar was the place of the ashes (Lev. i. 16), and the ashes spoke of accepted sacrifice. In the twentieth psalm David prays, "The Lord hear thee in the day of trouble . . . remember all thy offerings, and accept" —or, as we read in the margin, "turn to ashes"—"thy burnt sacrifice." God showed His acceptance of the offering by sending the fire, and the ashes proved that the fire had said, "It is enough." (Prov. xxx. 16.) The fire did its work on Calvary. God was satisfied, and we take our stand now and throughout eternity on this glorious fact as we sing, "Unto Him that loved us, and washed us from our sins in His own blood, and hath made us kings and priests unto God and His Father; to Him be glory and dominion for ever and ever. Amen."

FUTURE REST AND SERVICE

No More Burdens

For David said, The Lord God of Israel hath given **rest** unto his people, that they may dwell in Jerusalem for ever: and also unto the Levites; they shall no more* carry the tabernacle, nor any vessels of it for the service thereof.—1 *Chron*. xxiii. 25, 26.

* R.V., have need to.

And said unto the Levites that taught all Israel, which were holy unto the Lord, Put the holy ark in the house which Solomon the son of David king of Israel did build; it shall not be a burden upon your shoulders: serve now the Lord your God, and his people Israel.—2 *Chron*. xxxv. 3.

And these are they whom David set over the service of song in the house of the Lord, after that the ark had rest.—1 *Chron*. vi. 31.

There remaineth therefore a **rest** to the people of God.—*Heb*. iv. 9.

Him that overcometh will I make a pillar in the temple of my God, and he shall go **no more out.**—*Rev*. iii. 12.

Therefore are they before the throne of God, and serve him day and night in his temple: and he that sitteth on the throne shall dwell among them. They shall hunger no more, neither thirst any more; neither shall the sun light on them, nor any heat.—*Rev*. vii. 15, 16.

Yea, saith the Spirit, that they may rest from their labours; and their works do follow them.—*Rev*. xiv. 13.

Day and Night Service

And these are the singers, chief of the fathers of the Levites, who remaining in the chambers were free: for they were employed in that work **day and night.**—1 *Chron*. ix. 33.

Therefore are they before the throne of God, and serve him **day and night** in his temple.—*Rev*. vii. 15.

White Robes

And it shall come to pass, that when they enter in at the gates of the inner court, they shall be clothed with **linen** garments. — *Ezekiel* xliv. 17.

Let us be glad and rejoice, and give honour to him: for the marriage of the Lamb is come, and his wife hath made herself ready. And to her was granted that she should be arrayed in **fine linen,** clean and white: for the fine linen is the righteousness of saints. —*Rev*. xix. 7, 8.

The Temple Completed and Filled

Thus all the work that Solomon made for the house of the Lord was **finished**: and Solomon brought in all the things that David his father had dedicated; and the silver, and the gold, and all the instruments, put he among the treasures of the house of God. . . .

That he might present it to himself a glorious church, not having spot, or wrinkle, or any such thing; but that it should be holy and without blemish.—*Eph*. v. 27

When he shall come to be glorified in his saints, and to be admired in all them that believe (because our testimony among you was believed) in that day.—2 *Thess*. i. 10.

And it came to pass, when the priests were come out of the holy place : (for all the **priests** that were present were sanctified, and did not then wait by course : also the Levites which were the singers, all of them of Asaph, of Heman, of Jeduthun, with their sons and their brethren, being arrayed in **white linen,** having cymbals and psalteries and **harps,** stood at the east end of the altar, and with them an hundred and twenty priests sounding with trumpets.)

It came even to pass, as the trumpeters and singers were as one, to make **one sound** to be heard in praising and thanking the Lord ; and when they lifted up their voice with the trumpets and cymbals and instruments of music, and praised the Lord, saying, For he is good ; for his mercy endureth for ever :

Then the house was filled with a cloud, even the house of the Lord ; so that the priests could not stand to minister by reason of the cloud : for the glory of the Lord had filled the house of God.—*2 Chron.* v. 1, 11–14.

And when he had taken the book, the four beasts and four and twenty elders fell down before the Lamb, having every one of them **harps,** and golden vials full of odours, which are the prayers of saints.—*Rev.* v. 8.

And they sung **a new song**, saying, Thou art worthy to take the book, and to open the seals thereof : for thou wast slain, and hast redeemed us to God by thy blood out of every kindred, and tongue, and people, and nation ; and hast made us unto our God kings and **priests** : and we shall reign on the earth.—*Rev.* v. 9, 10.

And the temple was filled with smoke from the glory of God, and from his power ; and no man was able to enter into the temple.—*Rev.* xv. 8.

THROUGH Thy precious body broken
Inside the veil.
Oh ! what words to sinners spoken—
Inside the veil.
Precious as the blood that bought us ;
Perfect as the love that sought us ;
Holy, as the Lamb that brought us
Inside the veil.

Lamb of God, through Thee we enter,
Inside the veil.
Cleansed by Thee we boldly venture
Inside the veil.
Not a stain : a new creation ;
Ours is such a full salvatior ;
Low we bow in adoration
Inside the veil.

Soon Thy saints shall all be gathered
Inside the veil.
All at home—no more be scattered—
Inside the veil.
Nought from Thee our hearts shall sever:
We shall see Thee, grieve Thee never :
" Praise the Lamb !" shall sound for ever
Inside the veil.